POLITICAL PHILOSOPHY NOW

*Chief Editor of the Series*:
Howard Williams, University of Wales, Aberystwyth

*Associate Editors*:
Wolfgang Kersting, University of Kiel, Germany
Steven B. Smith, Yale University, USA
Peter Nicholson, University of York, England
Renato Cristi, Wilfrid Laurier University, Waterloo, Canada

**Political Philosophy Now** is a series which deals with authors, topics and periods in political philosophy from the perspective of their relevance to current debates. The series presents a spread of subjects and points of view from various traditions which include European and New World debates in political philosophy.

For other titles in this series, please see the University of Wales Press website: *www.wales.ac.uk/press*

POLITICAL PHILOSOPHY NOW

# Rorty's Politics of Redescription

Gideon Calder

UNIVERSITY OF WALES PRESS • CARDIFF • 2007

© Gideon Calder, 2007

British Library Cataloguing-in-Publication Data
A catalogue record for this book is available from the British Library.

ISBN 978-0-7083-1959-8 (paperback)
ISBN 978-0-7083-1960-4 (hardback)

All rights reserved. No part of this book may be reproduced, stored in a retrieval system, or transmitted, in any form or by any means, electronic, mechanical, photocopying, recording or otherwise, without clearance from the University of Wales Press, 10 Columbus Walk, Brigantine Place, Cardiff, CF10 4UP.
*www.wales.ac.uk/press*

The right of Gideon Calder to be identified as author of this work has been asserted by him in accordance with sections 77 and 78 of the Copyright, Designs and Patents Act 1988.

Printed in Great Britain by Antony Rowe Ltd, Wiltshire

For my mother

# Contents

| | |
|---|---|
| Preface | viii |
| Acknowledgements | xi |
| Abbreviations | xii |
| Introduction | 1 |
| **1 Rorty's Project: Redescribing Pragmatism** | **11** |
| 1.1 Redescribing pragmatism, pragmatizing redescription | 12 |
| 1.2 Objectivity as intersubjectivity? | 52 |
| **2 Redescription, Truth and Progress** | **63** |
| 2.1 Expanding logical space: poetry and progress | 66 |
| 2.2 Self-redescription | 84 |
| **3 Liberal Ironism** | **103** |
| 3.1 Expanding moral space: liberalism, ironism and solidarity | 104 |
| 3.2 Three versions of universalism | 129 |
| 3.3 *Achieving our Country*'s difficult turn | 143 |
| **4 Applications: History and Moral Practice** | **148** |
| 4.1 History and redescription | 148 |
| 4.2 Relationality and moral space | 164 |
| Conclusions | 175 |
| Notes | 184 |
| References | 212 |
| Index | 229 |

# Preface

> One always has more to say in disagreement than in agreement.[1]

Richard Rorty is among the most cited, influential and notorious of recent philosophers. His work has gained an audience that transcends not just traditional academic boundaries, but also – true to the democratic spirit of the American Pragmatist tradition to which it is allied – the boundaries of academia itself. He writes, always readably, about issues from Plato's cave to the lure of rare wild orchids, all the time drawing out implications resonating far beyond the specialized philosophical trades in which he himself was trained. He has recently – again – been listed among the 100 most influential 'global public intellectuals'.[2] But Rorty's work tends to be received with hesitance, a held nose, or indeed outright hostility amongst those most at home with its own vocabulary: contemporary practitioners of philosophy. The result, until relatively recently, is that its challenges have tended to be batted off or swerved around, rather than met 'head on'.

This book seeks to take Rorty seriously as a social, political and moral philosopher – but also to relate these aspects of his work to his wider assault on the core metaphysical and epistemological assumptions of modern philosophy. Like a previous, rather briefer and by nature less critical book of mine,[3] it takes as its central theme his case for 'redescription' of our cultural and intellectual parameters as a substitute for any mode of 'critique' based on 'objectivist' ideas of truth, reality or social progress. For Rorty, 'redescription' is a postmetaphysical process: it involves no claims about the ultimate nature of reality, or of human nature, but instead works simply according to the persuasive force of the narratives constructed. It is offered as a kind of all-purpose model for social progress across otherwise divergent spheres: in politics, in morals, in science, in the arts. My view is that interpreting Rorty's work through this lens provides a way of linking up his different writings in terms of a core underlying theme.

This is not, of course a 'neutral' interpretative exercise, somehow free of its own agenda. Like others, I find that Rorty's writing intrigues and incites, stirs and seduces, pesters and provokes, all in roughly equal measure. But I may as well be blunt: I disagree, to some extent or other, with most of his substantive claims. On the other hand, in the thirteen years that I have been reading it, I have never ceased to find it illuminating, thought-provoking and a joy to spend time with. Still, there are certain problems in finding an appropriate idiom through which to respond. Given Rorty's notoriety as a debunker of key tenets and operative metaphors of the Western philosophical tradition, and his general conclusion that Philosophy (with a capital P) is no longer a viable enterprise, should one approach his work *Philosophically*, or on its own terms?[4] By doing the former, and criticizing it according to the very standards it has sought to deny, you invite the charge that you have missed its point: that you are, as it were, criticizing a hamster for not being the lizard that it was never pretending to be in the first place. By doing the latter, you find that a strictly immanent critique will be hampered by the particular, often idiosyncratic parameters of Rorty's own depiction of the issues at stake. Attempting a dialectical approach, I have deployed both of these lines of argument while hoping that they might issue in a third: a perspective from which both the strengths and shortcomings of Rorty's project might be seen as pointing beyond its own presentation of the issues. Thus – if this isn't to over-egg the metaphors – Rorty's characterization of the choice between hamsterhood or lizardhood, while rich and suggestive in many ways, does not exhaust the possibilities on offer.

Labelling is not everything, but it is important. Rorty's is, I think, the most sustained, inventive and resourceful among contemporary attempts to expose the contingency of Philosophical concerns – and in particular, to try to neutralize them by showing how they take place in a self-sustaining bubble of a certain philosophical tradition's own making. At the same time, as we shall see, it makes free use of resources provided by the very tradition it asks us to ignore, and furtively holds hands with positions with which it would not want to be seen consorting. This makes it difficult to squeeze Rorty's thinking into some ready-to-hand categorical box while preserving its distinctiveness; he himself, as we shall see shortly, has labelled his work in terms of a wide array of '-isms'. So through the book, as a default option, I stick with the description of his project which he himself has mostly favoured: as pragmatist.

Another point worth mentioning is that except where there is a particular reason to do otherwise, I have treated Rorty's thinking synoptically rather than trying to outline its trajectory from the early

1960s to the present. Viewing him as a social and political thinker, certain works – *Consequences of Pragmatism*, and especially *Contingency, Irony, and Solidarity* and *Achieving our Country* – demand more attention than others. But despite changes in terminology, and the odd retraction of a previous position, Rorty's work strikes me as integrated to a degree which is very rare among philosophers whose work has spanned so many decades, and so many areas. It is clustered around certain constant themes. For this reason, it is essential to devote substantial space in any account of his social and political thinking to the views about metaphysics and epistemology which, to a large degree, set for them their particular, distinctive tone.

Gideon Calder<br>
Cardiff

# Acknowledgements

I would like to thank Duncan Campbell for suggesting this project; Sarah Lewis and Elin Lewis at UWP for stewarding it with such good humour, and an anonymous reader for their very helpful feedback; my colleagues at Cardiff and now Newport – especially Christopher Norris (supervisor of the Ph.D. work from which much of the book stems), Carol Jones, David Morgans and Steve Smith – for their insights and companionship; students in my classes since 1995 for helping me think straight; Richard Rorty for his generosity throughout my research; the Grangetown/Canton/Roath Half 'n' Halves for their Monday-night rekindling of total football; Arabella Smith, as always, for things far too many to mention; and Jenni Calder, to whom, with love and gratitude, this book is dedicated.

Parts of some chapters have appeared elsewhere in earlier versions. Elements of chapter 2, section 1, were first sketched out in 'Savour it or spit it out: Rorty's "metaphor" metaphor', *Philosophical Writings*, 2 (1996). Some points of chapter 3 surface in 'Liberalism without universalism?', in Bob Brecher, Jo Halliday and Klara Kolinská (eds), *Nationalism and Racism in the Liberal Order* (Aldershot: Ashgate, 1998), and others, along with parts of 4.2, in 'Soft universalisms: beyond Young and Rorty on difference', *Critical Research in Social and Political Philosophy (CRISPP)*, 9/1 (2006). Section 4.1 is adapted from 'Pragmatism, Postmodernism and the Possibility of an Ethical Relation to the Past', *Theoria*, 106 (2005). I am grateful to all concerned – editors and publishers – for their kind permission to reprint revised versions of the material in question.

# Abbreviations

A number of abbreviated references to texts by Richard Rorty are given in what follows.

AB  (with Derek Nystrom and Kent Puckett) *Against Bosses, Against Oligarchies: A Conversation with Richard Rorty* (Charlottesville, VA: Prickly Pear Pamphlets, 1998).
AC  *Achieving our Country: Leftist Thought in Twentieth-Century America* (Cambridge, MA: Harvard University Press, 1998).
BUL 'Being that can be understood is language', *London Review of Books* (16 March 2000): 23–5.
CIS *Contingency, Irony, and Solidarity* (Cambridge: Cambridge University Press, 1989).
CP  *Consequences of Pragmatism* (Minneapolis: University of Minnesota Press, 1982).
DP  (with Simon Critchley et al.) *Deconstruction and Pragmatism* (London: Routledge, 1996)
EHO *Essays on Heidegger and Others: Philosophical Papers*, vol. 2 (Cambridge: Cambridge University Press, 1991).
FP  'Feminism and pragmatism', *Radical Philosophy*, 59 (1991): 3–14.
FR  (with Gianni Vattimo) *The Future of Religion*, ed. Santiago Zabala (New York: Columbia University Press, 2005)
HE  *Hoffnung statt Erkenntniss: Eine Einfürung in die Pragmatische Philosophie* (Vienna: Passagen Verlag, 1994).
HNN 'The higher nominalism in a nutshell: a reply to Henry Staten', *Critical Inquiry*, 12 (1986): 462–6.
JLL 'Justice as a larger loyalty', in Matthew Festenstein and Simon Thompson (eds), *Richard Rorty: Critical Dialogues* (Cambridge: Polity Press, 2001), 223–7.
LT  (ed.), *The Linguistic Turn: Essays in Philosophical Method*, 2nd edn (Chicago: University of Chicago Press, 1992; orig. 1967).
ORT *Objectivity, Relativism, and Truth: Philosophical Papers*, vol. 1 (Cambridge: Cambridge University Press, 1991).

# ABBREVIATIONS

PCL  'Pragmatism, categories, and language', *Philosophical Review*, 70 (1961): 197–223.
PMN  *Philosophy and the Mirror of Nature* (Oxford: Blackwell, 1980; orig. 1979).
PSH  *Philosophy and Social Hope* (Harmondsworth: Penguin, 1999).
RC  *Rorty and his Critics*, ed. Robert B. Brandom (Oxford: Blackwell, 2000).
RP  *Rorty and Pragmatism: The Philosopher Replies to his Critics* (exchanges between Rorty and seven others), ed. Herman J. Saatkamp, Jr. (Nashville, TN: Vanderbilt University Press, 1995).
TP  *Truth and Progress: Philosphical Papers*, vol. 3 (Cambridge: Cambridge University Press, 1998).
UT  'Universality and truth', in Robert B. Brandom (ed.), *Rorty and his Critics* (Oxford: Blackwell, 2000), pp. 1–31.

# Introduction

Encountering Rorty as a social and political philosopher, one has to grapple with a mixed-up set of labels applied to his thinking, both by himself and others. This includes 'isms' – 'pragmatist', 'postmodernist', 'liberal ironist', 'anti-foundationalist' – and other kinds of adjectives: 'progressive', 'free-wheeling', 'anti-authoritarian', 'complacent', 'subversive', or (a personal favourite) 'unbuttoned'. Each has been applied with equal vigour; each has its element of authenticity. But none, in the end, seems fully to pin down the particular shape of Rorty's social thinking. This is because it is distinctive not so much for the content of its normative claims, but for the way in which they are made – and the philosophical (or anti-Philosophical) assumptions on which those claims are based. Hence this book's emphasis on 'redescription' as a key distinctive element of Rorty's contribution to contemporary social thought. His work seeks to redescribe the Western philosophical tradition, to show how many of its key concerns have been futile or misconceived. It also recommends redescription as a means by which we might both escape the clutches of that tradition, and achieve social progress in a wider sense: in particular, by recognizing the contingency of the core contentions on which even our most cherished values and social practices depend.

As already said in the preface, this book will take Rorty as, primarily, a pragmatist. This tradition, embodied especially in the work of William James and John Dewey, has sought to reorientate philosophy as a discipline geared not towards the pursuit for its own sake of axioms or deep truths, but towards helping us deal practically with the world around us in better ways. The prime weapon used by pragmatists against the Philosophical tradition which perceives its discipline as a natural kind, concerned with a timeless agenda of other capitalized concerns (like the fundamental, eternal nature of Truth, Justice, Goodness, Objectivity and Subjectivity) is to historicize those concerns. The staple tactic of this approach is to show that such concerns arise, and are 'cashed out' (in James's phrase), on the basis of contingent socio-historical priorities and habits of thinking.[1] Hence the momentous impact of Rorty's work in a professionalized discipline which has all too commonly viewed its own agenda as being radically severed from, and most likely placed above, the wider world with which its practitioners – and their agenda – have nonetheless always been entangled. That this conception of things is most typical amongst those philosophers in the predominantly Anglo-American analytic tradition has often enough been remarked upon. Acknowledged less often, and more grudgingly, has been Rorty's pre-eminent and constructive role in exposing the fragility of any aspiration to escape from history – even the history of one's own discipline – in addressing matters of ultimate philosophical import. Ian Hacking has suggested that, 'no matter how loosely we construe membership in an analytic and primarily anglophone philosophical tradition, Rorty was the first member to apply the technique of historicist undoing to that tradition'.[2]

Applying this technique, and drawing out its implications, has led Rorty to conclude that there really is nothing about 'traditional' philosophical questions and concerns which cannot be exposed as precisely that: an upshot of the *traditions* of thinking and social practice from which they happen to have emerged, rather than of independently substantive, and so pressing, considerations. Undergraduate-level political philosophy modules, for example, often begin with Plato's *Republic* – and with good reason, given its richness and range as a resource of ideas, and its influence on the framing of questions in the Western tradition. But it would be a familiar kind of error, for Rorty, to presume from the influence of Plato's own agenda on political philosophy that he somehow hit upon the essence of eternal questions that confront us in some inevitable way. Neither in the apparatus of philosophical criticism nor in its subject matter is there anything which *necessarily* presents itself as an issue or a problem. With both sides thus historicized, there is no sense in which philosophy can be regarded as answering 'eternal' questions in a way that somehow reaches deeper than the rest of culture. Hence his conclusion that it is best not to 'see philosophy as criticizing anything':

> When people refer to philosophy as 'critical', they seem to say, 'Scientists or politicians use the vocabulary of some other philosopher; they shouldn't use that vocabulary, they should use mine!' When people say that philosophy criticizes science, or other areas of culture, all it comes down to is that it's criticizing the residues of past philosophies, as they appear in cultural practice.[3]

Hence, 'we do not need philosophy for social criticism'; rather, we need descriptions of social conditions which might lead to future beneficial change, not least with regard to our thinking about philosophy and its erstwhile privileged role.[4] We are stuck with the vocabularies of our predecessors until we redescribe them in order to make them better for achieving our particular social goals. Philosophy does not 'reveal' or 'reflect' or 'show' or 'prove'; it simply redescribes the terms of some given debate in order to fulfil some contingent purpose. It can best be seen as 'the reinterpretation of our predecessors' reinterpretation of their predecessors' reinterpretation'.[5] Conceived in these terms, it is a *literary* genre, delimited 'not by form or matter, but by tradition'.[6] If the tradition provides its starting context, its future will be dictated only by the imagination, which is limitless. Redescription is a matter of imaginatively making new descriptions 'hang together' with existing ones. Whereas 'metaphysicians' will ask whether some new description really has captured the nature of our subject matter, pragmatists will prefer to ask whether new descriptions can be 'woven together with previous vocabularies in a helpful way'.[7]

## The horizontal and the vertical

I see 'redescription', conceived in these terms, as the central motif of Rorty's thinking primarily because it captures the import of a metaphor which he uses only occasionally, but which in turn captures a definitive, arguably *the* definitive, theme of his work. The metaphor contrasts 'vertical' and 'horizontal' inquiry. Vertical claims are those which posit some relation (for instance, 'representation') between an idea or a piece of language and an entity assumed to exist on a different ontological level: God, perhaps, or 'the way the world really is'. To put it another way, vertical thinking presumes that there are shallower and deeper levels of whatever is under investigation: the self, culture, economic structures – and that access to the deeper levels (the underlying 'core' of the self; the underlying 'structure' of language) will help us explain the way such phenomena appear to the naked eye. Horizontal claims make no such reference to a different ontological level; they refer only to other, preceding ideas or sentences. Indeed, with a suitably 'horizontalized' conception of things, we will realize that there is no descriptive access – and no practical use in seeking to refer – to a separate ontological level from that bequeathed to us by the horizons of previous descriptions and redescriptions. We move only among descriptions, which are 'deep' or 'shallow' only according to the stress we have come to put on them, not because of the purchase they provide on a reality beyond themselves. As we will see in the chapters which follow, the import of this claim resonates throughout Rorty's writings. We are invited to accept redescription as a more than adequate substitute for the Philosophical concern with Truth conceived as something *apart* from our descriptions for appropriately pragmatic reasons. It pays to do so.

Hence the title of this book, and its prime concerns: the ways in which Rorty sees 'redescription' as a replacement for what Philosophers have tended to see themselves as doing, the philosophical claims which lie behind this move, and their wider social and political implications. I use 'politics' to describe all this for two main reasons. One is that pragmatists in general, in viewing all theory as normative, have tended to commend their own position in ethical-political terms. The recommendation might go something like this: it is a waste of our time to worry about Philosophical questions of the traditional kind, because they distract us from the more important task of making life better here, now, and in the future. Rorty's own version of this claim is best articulated in *CP*, where he describes pragmatism as being typified by 'the doctrine that there are no constraints on inquiry save conversational ones – not wholesale constraints derived from the nature of the objects, or of the mind, or of language, but only those retail constraints provided by the remarks of our fellow-inquirers'.[8] In substituting horizontal 'conversation' for vertical inquiry, Rorty declares the virtues of conversation to be '*simply* moral', rather than based on metaphysical or epistemological back-up. Similarly, the 'cash values' (to return to the Jamesian metaphor) of that conversation's outcomes are to be gauged in terms of their utility in furthering human, rather than objective, or other-worldly, aims. Hence philosophy is useless in social criticism, where 'loyalty' to one's conversational partners and willingness to listen become the appropriate intellectual attitudes.[9]

The other reason is that, because of its removal of other (cognitive, or metaphysical) explanations for the way in which different descriptions do, in fact, get adopted and put to social use, Rorty's thinking makes intellectual progress inherently political. This is partly because the description which wins out, and so becomes 'objective', will be that which has been most successful in asserting itself in the wider public arena. It is also because the claim that Philosophy can have no special contributory role in this process is itself a political one. It is a decision about what does and does not count as a valid contribution to the forging of a community's future horizons of practice. Philosophy does not so count. Thus, while Rorty's thinking is, in key respects, rather lacking in a substantive conception of the social and political, its *import* is socio-political insofar as it is in these arenas that its appeal, and real effects, will primarily lie.[10]

## The approach of this book

In what follows I have no particular corner to defend in terms of the analytical-philosophical agenda. What I do want to argue, throughout, is that the rejection of philosophy as a viable tool of social criticism is itself a political move, and one which is far from neutral in terms of its impact on the possibility of the sort of progressive social change which Rorty himself would advocate. As we will see in Chapter 1, Rorty presents the distinction between 'more and less useful descriptions' as a replacement for the Platonist/Enlightenment distinction between appearance and reality.[11] He characterizes as bankrupt the Enlightenment 'demand to unmask completely, to make all things new, to start from nowhere, to substitute new true consciousness from old false consciousness'.[12] While I do not set out here to defend any particular model or account of the heritage of the Enlightenment, I would insist that in its more radical variants it has held rather subtler and more dialectical aims than the desire to 'start from nowhere'.

Indeed, I find in Rorty's claim that we might costlessly shed the entirety of metaphysical baggage an aim of precisely this order. Jürgen Habermas has described Rorty's work as the programme of 'a disappointed metaphysician'.[13] Certainly, every time Rorty rejects a picture or a dualism which has 'held philosophy captive', his conception of the alternatives available remains conspicuously in thrall to residual aspects of the picture rejected. Since that picture tends to be Platonist or Cartesian rather than appealing to those alternative lines of philosophical descent which have been resolutely this-worldly and historically minded in their conceptions of the nature and scope of critique, it seems to me that Rorty's victory over the Philosophical tradition is achieved in a rather hollow way. To be specific: it largely ignores the detail of those alternative post-Enlightenment strands – Marxist, phenomenological, or otherwise – which have said similar things about the dangers of reification and idealization *without* thereby throwing out the baby of emancipatory critique along with the bathwater of the assumptions from which those dangers have derived.

This is a line I pursue throughout this book, interspersing exegesis of the Rorty canon with weavings in of alternative resources which, I argue, either deal better with certain of Rorty's own prime concerns or show those concerns to be misplaced. Two main points should be made about the trajectory of what follows. One is that I treat Rorty's work as broadly continuous – despite periodic changes in key elements of its vocabulary – from 1960 to the present day. This is partly for reasons of space: the goal of deep comparison between his early and late writings was jettisoned early on in the face both of the sheer quantity of his output, and its constancy in terms of the themes and claims I here address. It is also because, *malgré* Rorty's own consistent nominalism, I think that, whatever terms he may be using at a given point (and his chosen descriptors are always rich, suggestive and provocatively loose), he is always talking about pretty much the same things. The other point I should make at this stage is that I do not, for similar reasons of space and coherence, explore the proliferating interconnections between Rorty's own redescriptions and the positions of the cast of philosophical heroes and villains who make regular appearances in his work. Some – Quine and Davidson, Lyotard and Habermas, and the earlier, first-generation pragmatists – are dealt with more than others, such as Nietzsche, Heidegger, Derrida and Putnam, versions of whom punctuate the Rortian narrative. An upshot of this is that I do not spend much time contesting Rorty's often rather questionable use of his philosophical heroes for his own, often rather discrepant, ends.[14] By and large, my approach has been to take his own usages at face value and to explore their coherence and implications.

There are two main points of focus in those explorations. One concerns the relation between subjectivity and objectivity, or self and world – and the relation of both to language or discourse. The other concerns the viability of ethical-political universalism. My core objection to Rorty's project is that it denies the scope for adequate thinking about either of these issues. In what might be a summary of his views on the first of them, he writes that 'it is useless to think that objects will constrain us to believe the truth about them, if only they are approached with an unclouded mental eye, or a rigorous method, or a perspicuous language'.[15] My response is that it is not 'useless' to see our practices as already involving a prior recognition of the existence of an independent reality, including objects and others, and that, if this is the case, we are *already* substantially 'constrained' whether we choose so to view ourselves or not. In other words, 'vertical' considerations inevitably intrude on the horizontal. The latter kinds of process cannot take place in some pure, hermetically sealed environment: it is hard even to conceive of a 'conversation' that is not 'about' the world beyond itself. As to the universalism issue, my hunch is that without a fuller account of human nature or being than Rorty will sanction, his own avowedly liberal and cosmopolitan hopes will prove both incoherent and unrealizable. These are big claims. I hope in what follows to show that, reading Rorty critically, we find a (perhaps unlikely) dialectical foil through which they can be justified.

## Chapter outline

The four main chapters of this book might be viewed as responses to a series of questions: (1) Why does Rorty see the Western tradition in philosophy as something to be 'overcome' or 'circumvented', rather than persevered with? (2) What is 'redescription', and how for Rorty does this operate as a replacement for 'vertical' philosophizing of the kind he would rather we left behind? (3) How does Rorty seek to develop 'liberal ironism' as an anti-foundationalist alternative to the liberalism he regards as the most precious legacy of the modern philosophical tradition? (4) How might we apply the core themes of Rorty's thinking in areas where he himself does not necessarily take it – but which nonetheless shed light on its strengths and weaknesses?

Chapter 1 seeks to set out Rorty's overall 'framework' in terms of two salient, binding themes. The first is 'deconstructive': his critique and rejection of the stakes of the metaphysical tradition, which provides the basis for an appeal to pragmatism and to ethnocentrism as strategies by which we might neutralize that tradition's core concerns. The second concerns his 'constructive' forging of a pragmatism which (in distinction to that of his mentor John Dewey) switches its central motif of 'coping' from an ideas-based or experience-based notion to a linguistic one. I look at how Rorty's rejection of the traditional (Cartesian, Lockean) picture of the relation between subject and object, leads to an alternative picture of the relationship between human objectives and the world, and consider (in 1.2) the conceptions of truth and objectivity which Rorty presents as alternatives to their traditional variants. In the process, I explore Rorty's neo-pragmatism in the light of criticisms of Dewey's version by the first-generation Frankfurt School thinkers, most notably Horkheimer and Adorno. I consider the extent to which Rorty is guilty of charges of 'linguistic idealism', and of an implicit social conservatism in his denial of the scope for appeals either to reality or to transcendent criteria in the critique of existing ideas, norms or practices.

Chapter 2 goes deeper into the 'constructive' side of Rorty's philosophy. It explores his accounts of progress, in two main senses: the progression of societies' understandings of themselves, through science, and the process of 'self-creation' through which individuals forge their own distinctive identities. Both are prime examples of the notion of progress happening through 'expanding' (rather than deepening, or discovering) the existing parameters of theory and practice. For Rorty this process is achieved through inventive redescription: and primarily, through the appeal to the pragmatic utility of an alternative picture to that which is currently adhered to. In 2.1 I explore Rorty's account of the way metaphors work, when adopted as useful, to change the ways in which we understand, and interact with, our natural and social environments – and gauge the extent to which this offers a convincing account of intellectual and social progress. I then go on, in 2.2, to focus on his account of self-creation – a combination of a 'non-reductive physicalist' account of the self with a Nietzschean valorization of the importance of describing one's life on one's own terms, according to one's own dictates. I argue that this is perhaps the least persuasive aspect of Rorty's thinking: that his picture is torn between a deflationary, Darwinian, naturalistic view of the self and a Romantic emphasis on the importance of the forging of a truly 'individual' existence. In the end, it is argued, this move founders on the lack of a convincing account of the relation between agency, language and reality.

Rorty's forays into moral, political and social philosophy find their first concerted articulation in his 1989 work *Contingency, Irony, and Solidarity*. Here he seeks to defend the institutions and principles of a mainstream liberal politics, while arguing that there can be no substantive 'philosophical' basis with which to bolster such practices. He also defends a split between the public sphere (where his ideal citizens would affirm their commitment to liberal principles) and the private sphere (where they would engage in creative self-redescription, aware that even their most cherished beliefs are contingent). Finally, he argues for a conception of human solidarity based not on the appeal to a common human nature, but instead on the achievement of an 'expansion of moral space' to include those 'strangers' who were once regarded as a 'they', but can potentially be part of a sense of 'we'.

Chapter 3 explores these central claims of Rorty's political philosophy, as expressed in *CIS* and elaborated on in subsequent work. Section 3.1 explores Rorty's claim to offer an alternative to the 'universalism' of classical liberalism as a model for moral solidarity, and considers Rorty's political thinking in the context of debates between liberals and communitarians in recent Anglophone political philosophy, looking particularly at Rorty's deployment of Rawls as a thinker who has escaped the traditional assumption that frameworks for social justice require metaphysical back-up. In both 3.1 and 3.2 I compare his critique of universalism with that of post-structuralist thinkers, particularly Jean-François Lyotard, suggesting that both are less far distanced from classical liberalism than they are presented as being. 3.2 makes a case for an alternative understanding of universalism which avoids the pitfalls typical of the models most familiar from mainstream liberalism. And in 3.3 I explore Rorty's Harvard lectures of 1997, *Achieving our Country*, often taken as a rebuff to accusations of political complacency levelled at Rorty from the political Left. Significantly, he attempts there to put some space between his own project and the more or less postmodernist orthodoxies recently dominant in cultural studies and literature departments across the US (and, for that matter, the UK). While he offers a powerful case for a return to a politically engaged academy, making concrete, constructive suggestions for progressive reform, I argue that this mission sits rather uncomfortably with the 'gist' of much of Rorty's other writing. In particular, his own emphasis on the ontological centrality narrative and resdescription itself offers a reinforcement of the shibboleths of cultural studies. The alternative to a 'spectatorial', purely cultural politics which Rorty seeks would, it is suggested, better be founded on an alternative theoretical rubric.

The fourth chapter moves from exploring Rorty's work 'immanently', on its own terms, to looking at ways in which it might 'cash out' in terms of particular issues of current political import. Section 4.1 looks at how Rorty's pragmatism might shed light on our understanding of history and historiography – and in particular, on the ethical dimensions of our relation to the past. My concern here is that, for all his prioritization of historical context, Rorty offers us a rather 'thin' view of history, in which it is reduced to the contours of an 'eternal present', always redescribable according to currently dominant concerns. In other words, the 'thickening' of description leads to the 'thinning out' of historicity. I then return to questions about political and moral practice, focusing on the inter-relations between subject, language and world. Here, I argue, Rorty's work has been both profoundly suggestive and also rather limited. On the side of subjectivity, it would benefit from a form of analysis about which Rorty himself is rather dismissive – namely phenomenology, of which I take Merleau-Ponty's understandings of bodily agency as a prominent example. As regards the nature of 'reality', it is argued that contemporary critical realism provides a way of escaping the Cartesian picture by which the conditions of subjectivity are radically disengaged from the world, without (as Rorty's thinking risks) 'thinning out' the world so that it plays no significant part in our processes of 'self-creation'.

Those conclusions expose philosophical commitments of my own which are, even when near to Rorty's, differently pitched. Sometimes they are quite radically discrepant. The critical realism, and the qualified universalism, defended in the book are hardly consonant with the themes of Rorty's work which do most to make it distinctive. The book as a whole offers an account of that work which both tries to do justice to its importance, and its distinctiveness, while recognizing its limits. In the conclusion, I offer a kind of overall summing up of both its contributions and its shortcomings. Those shortcomings are not exclusive to Rorty. I argue that they are symptomatic, in different ways, of problems inherent in classical liberal political philosophy, and in many currently influential attempts to escape that tradition. Rorty is fairly described as a kind of 'liberal postmodernist'. It is significant that in the end, for all the idiosyncrasies of his work, it tends at crucial points to rehearse quite standard difficulties encountered by far less subtle or inventive exponents of those two, quite separate, strands of thinking.

# 1 • Rorty's Project: Redescribing Pragmatism

> The point is always the same – to perform the social function which Dewey called 'breaking the crust of convention', preventing man from deluding himself with the notion that he knows himself, or anything else, except under optional descriptions.[1]

> Habermas . . . is not content to let the narratives which hold our culture together do their stuff. He is scratching where it does not itch.[2]

The gist of Rorty's project has been to stop us scratching in places where only philosophical habit has made us think that there are itches. His remedy for itching consists not in applying further philosophical dressing, but in switching our attention elsewhere. The operative hunch is that, given time, a change in the optional descriptions that guide inquiry will divert our attention from pseudo-problems and make us realize that this change of priorities is metaphysically costless. Thus we can be rescued from the stubborn hunch that the mind, or knowledge, or the world, throw up questions that have 'a sort of supernatural ability to adhere to people who try to throw them away'.[3]

If philosophy has spent most of the time since Descartes, and especially since Kant, refining aspects of its own agenda, and discarding certain questions as no longer viable, then Rorty, from one angle, is simply following up on this practice, and extending its trajectory. But he extends it beyond the existing pattern. Previous philosophical revolts (for instance Kant's, Husserl's or the early Wittgenstein's) have involved the introduction of a new methodology which seeks to replace some given incumbent, and thereby replace mere 'opinion' with 'knowledge', more rigorously conceived. They have all, Rorty writes in 1967, failed – and for the same reason. 'The revolutionaries were found to have presupposed, both in their criticisms of their predecessors and in their directions for the future, the truth of certain substantive and controversial philosophical theses . . . Every philosophical rebel has tried to be presuppositionless, but none has succeeded.'[4] The appeal to rigour has relied upon an appeal to some spurious form of base-level methodological neutrality. Rorty's work makes no claim to be presuppositionless. As a pragmatism, it is marked by the agenda simply to help us find 'better ways of coping' with the world and with each other. It rejects as misconceived not just neutrality, but methodology itself.

Against some interpretations, I see it as being broadly continuous since the late 1950s in terms of its inner dynamic. That dynamic is therapeutic, in the sense that Wittgenstein invokes:

> It is not our aim to refine or complete the system of rules for the use of our words in unheard-of ways . . . The real discovery is the one that makes me capable of doing philosophy when I want to. The one that gives philosophy peace, so that it is no longer tormented by questions which bring itself in question.[5]

As we shall see, the clearing away of 'pseudo'-problems (of itches not worth scratching) in Rorty's own project bears a distinctly positivistic inflection.[6] It is a redescription of the terms of the debate, according to which optional descriptions can take the place of philosophical necessities without loss, or the leaving of some niggling remainder.

In the first part of this chapter I consider what I see as the two main thematics of Rortian therapy. The first – a critique and rejection of the stakes of the metaphysical tradition – provides the basis for an appeal to pragmatism and to ethnocentrism as neutralizing that tradition's core concerns. The second fills out that conception of pragmatism by switching its trademark epistemic conception of 'coping' from an experiential to a linguistic register. I then explore more closely, in 1.2, the conceptions of truth and objectivity which for him are left once the rubble of the tradition has been cleared away. I argue that some of the rubble, if by this we understand certain 'traditional' metaphysical problems, sticks more stubbornly than Rorty likes to make out.

## 1.1. Redescribing pragmatism, pragmatizing redescription

Very often, Rorty makes his case by contrast-effects. A typical suggestion might be this: 'Look at things this way, as most people have tended to, most of the time – but on the other hand, notice the untold benefits of looking at things *this* way instead.' Much of the force of his debunkings has depended on invoking a lingering idea on the part of professional philosophers that their discipline is one 'that will (any day now) produce noncontroversial results concerning matters of ultimate concern' – a discipline which supposedly 'discovers', 'reveals', 'represents' or 'reflects' underlying realities about human beings and their relation to the world and each other.[7] As Rorty maps it out in *Philosophy and the Mirror of Nature*, the story of (most of) modern philosophy is the story of the consolidation of this unfortunate self-image. It stems from a prioritizaton of the faculty of *vision* in conceiving of the human subject's relation to itself and to the world. From this stems the assumption that, to be adequate, ideas or statements must somehow reflect or *represent* the world in consciousness or in language.

Hence the book's opening claim: 'The picture which holds traditional philosophy together is that of the mind as a great mirror, containing various representations – some accurate, some not – and capable of being studied by pure, nonempirical methods.'[8] We can, I think, derive from Rorty's case in PMN that the entrenchment of this notion has taken the form of a three-stage process. The first stage is Descartes's radical separation of mind and world – and, with it, the forthright inauguration of the 'mind as mirror' metaphor. A second is owed in part to Locke: the claim that a 'theory of knowledge' will be based on an adequate grasp of 'mental processes'. The third comes with Kant's transformation of philosophy from 'queen of the sciences' to a *foundational* discipline: something underlying, rather than overseeing, other areas of enquiry by asking a benchmark question installed as basic to their success: how is knowledge possible?[9] In combination, these three moments serve to cement the idea that philosophy needs to show how knowledge is possible in order for us to have an adequate explanation of how we cope with the world. Rorty's chief point is to demonstrate that the need for such a foundation and the assumption that there is a specifically *philosophical* (as opposed to scientific, or moral) problem of knowledge are fundamental misconceptions. Philosophy swerved towards them as the result of Descartes's inaugural metaphor. As a result, it has spent much of the past 400 years providing useless solutions to illusory problems. These problems coincide with the 'representationalist' problematic.

It is crucial, then, to Rorty's case that Descartes divides mind and world in a way which is *unprecedented*. The basis of its novelty is this: that while notions of disembodied spirit abound throughout cultural history, and very notably in Plato's Greece, Descartes's originality lies in his positing of a strict divide between an 'inner life' of consciousness and events in the external world. In doing so he extends 'thought' – the mark of consciousness – to cover everything from doubting to imagining to feeling. The term 'idea' becomes a term for the contents of the human mind. On this basis, Locke is able to use 'idea' in a way which has no Greek equivalent at all. Hence its definition in the *Essay Concerning Human Understanding*: 'Whatever the mind perceives in itself, or is the intermediate object of perception, thought, or understanding.'[10] Hence also Locke's contention that it is *ideas*, rather than the world, which are the object of thinking – or, put the other way around, that objects are known through the ideas in the mind which represent them. Given that 'every man being conscious himself that he thinks, and that which his mind is applied to whilst thinking being the *ideas* that are there', the problem for Locke is: 'how did he come by them?'[11] This is what Quine has called 'the idea idea': specifically, the claim that there is something internal to consciousness which determines the meaning of linguistic utterance – but more generally, the claim that ideas are a perceptual 'given', demanding an explanation of their structure and provenance.[12] Thus, while Locke and Descartes differ over their provenance (that is, over whether they are innate or derived from sense-experience), they combine to present ideas as that which is *immediate* to thinking. Now

> there had been no term, even of philosophical art, in the Greek and medieval traditions coextensive with the Descartes-Locke use of 'idea'. Nor had there been the conception of the human mind as an inner space in which both pains and clear and distinct ideas passed in review before a single Inner Eye. There were, to be sure, the notions of taking tacit thought, forming relations in *foro interno*, and the like. The novelty was the notion of a single inner space in which bodily and perceptual sensations, . . . mathematical truths, moral rules, the idea of God, moods of depression, and all the rest of what we now call 'mental' were objects of quasi observation.[13]

And objects, thus, of reflections of the mind conceived as mirror. Without such a notion, 'the notion of knowledge as accuracy of representation would not have suggested itself'.[14] With it, a conception is engendered of the mind's eye as infallible, to the extent that what it sees clearly (in terms of 'clear and distinct ideas', in Descartes's phrase) is thereby made real. The knowing subject thus becomes, in Iris Young's Rorty-esque phrasing, 'a gazer, an observer who stands above, outside of, the object of knowledge': it is conceived as that which sees without direct involvement with that which is seen.[15]

It should be noticed here that Rorty's critique of the Cartesian subject is not so much a transformation as a consolidation of the tendency of much of twentieth-century thinking on such questions. Young's depiction follows what have become quite standard lines of rejection. The Cartesian ego attains its status as a universal subject of pure reason precisely by way of a clean divorce from its own body and thus from any position in space, time or history, and any relation to its own 'sensuous continuity with flowing, living things'.[16] A recurring motif in this book is the question whether granting the force of this critique has the implications which Rorty – and others whom might broadly be designated 'postmodernists' – will assume. And a second question is whether Rorty does indeed succeed in shedding the baggage of Cartesian dualism and all that it implies. At crucial points, as we shall see, the divorce seems less than final.

The particularity of Rorty's case is that it is made in terms immanent to a tradition – Anglo-American analytical philosophy – which he sees as having taken rather longer than its European counterpart to shed the Cartesian–Lockean–Kantian self-image. With the adoption of the 'mirror' metaphor, a set of what seemed definitively *philosophical* quandaries were set in train. Their remnants still linger in so far as questions of knowledge, truth and reason are taken as being in need of definitively *philosophical* definition. When so conceived, these questions cannot admit of final answers. For if seeking knowledge is the seeking of adequate reflections (representations) of a mind-independent world, the problem arises of how we can *know* with any certainty that the world is adequately represented in our knowledge. We are condemned to internal circularity: representations can be checked for accuracy only by reference to other representations. The mind is cut adrift in a self-referential bubble of a non-extended consciousness opposed to the realm of extended physical bodies, or 'that which is not consciousness'.[17]

Descartes's own distinction between ideas and physical reality rests, of course, on the role of doubt.[18] Ideas – whether pains, beliefs, fantasies or whatever – are such that the subject cannot doubt that she has them, whereas doubt is possible about everything physical. 'Indubitability', along with immediacy, thus becomes the mark of the mental.[19] Knowledge of the physical world is mediated by ideas. It is a matter of reflection. Hence the problem looms of how to ascribe the same sort of certainty to our beliefs about the external world. Thus, in Descartes's wake, the need for certainty has led to an increasingly empiricist emphasis on finding evidential knowledge about the world. Though departing from Descartes's rationalism, such thinking has still founded itself on the mind-as-mirror metaphor. Hence 'science, rather than living, became philosophy's subject, and epistemology its center'.[20] Conceived as a potential resolution to the *philosophical* problem of how to guarantee the accuracy of our representations, though, putatively scientific accounts cannot – for all the success of natural science at providing useful descriptions of the world – allow us to escape the problem.

They cannot do so because they will end up invoking what Wilfrid Sellars called 'the Myth of the Given'. This emerges in the assumption that the Eye of the Mind 'gets some things firsthand', and then proceeds to infer (through scientific procedures) to other things entailed by these 'ground floor entities'.[21] Thus, some ('really real') entities are somehow naturally suited to be immediately present to consciousness, to be knowable directly, and others not. Thus, on this picture, introspection carries with it privileged epistemic access to mental entities which must be intrinsically more knowable than anything physical could be knowable to anyone.[22] This is locked into the binary opposition between the necessary (or firsthand) and the contingent (or secondhand), which duly confers two different sorts of ontological status on these separate sorts of mental events. This in turn makes space for the definitively empiricist claim that sense-experience (being our access to the 'given') provides the bedrock for empirical knowledge.

Rorty takes all such definitions to have been exposed as fake by Quine's groundbreaking rejection in 'Two Dogmas of Empiricism' of the tenability of any firm distinction between the necessary and the contingent, or the foundations of our knowledge and the knowledge we then happen to garner on their basis.[23] Quine's contention was that nothing about our empirical observation of people making claims could reveal a firm distinction between necessary (or analytic) truths and contingent (synthetic) truths. This was taken to threaten the livelihood even of those philosophical approaches – like logical positivism, or Carnap-style logical empiricism – which sought to set aside metaphysical questions concerning the nature of the mind in favour of an approach geared entirely towards the empirical verifiability of statements (rather than ideas) as the gauge of true relations to the world. Positivism's aim in this linguistic variant was to show how any meaningful sentence could be reduced, logically, to statements purely about sense-experience. If demonstrable, this approach would enable us to resolve all theoretical disagreements of whatever magnitude by reference to the neutral bedrock of observational experience. It would also reveal the meaninglessness of metaphysical speculation, consisting as it does of propositions which are neither empirically verifiable nor analytically true (in Kant's sense: true by virtue of the meanings of the terms involved, or because the predicate is 'contained in' the subject, or because their denial is self-contradictory). In sum, positivist empiricism claimed that all knowledge is reducible to atomic propositions that correspond to discrete perceptions, or 'sense data'.

Quine's claim was that there is no available distinction between statements which are logically (or linguistically) true and those which are made true or false by experience. This is because *no* individual statement is confirmed or refuted individually, or atomistically, by some correspondingly atomized experience. Rather, the process is *holistic*: we assess the veracity of statements by reference to a 'corporate body' of other such statements. Since these will include the so-called 'foundational' statements on the basis of which the rest of observation is supposed to proceed, it follows that, given the arrival of a new guiding principle by which to formulate knowledge, it is incorporated into what Quine calls the 'man-made fabric' of 'the totality of our so-called knowledge or beliefs'. This fabric 'impinges on experience only along the edges', reacting to it as a whole, rather than in terms of individual sentence–experience relations. Quine was thus rejecting any sharp distinction between the form and content of language. As he famously put it elsewhere, 'The lore of our fathers is a fabric of sentences ... It is a pale grey lore, black with fact, white with conventions. But I have found no substantial reason for concluding that there are any quite black threads in it, or any white ones.'[24]

And if we are unable to examine the content of knowledge in clean separation from its form, Quine concludes, we must admit that epistemology should be 'naturalized'. This is to say that it should be remodelled as the study of the actual processes by which human beings attain knowledge, rather than by way of a consideration of the formal conditions of possibility for our attaining true knowledge in the first place. We already know things: the trick is not to set this knowledge aside in the quest for a systematic account of the conditions of epistemic success, but to explain, naturalistically, how we do in fact acquire beliefs. The logical positivist hope that philosophy might proceed 'from speculation to science' by way of the renunciation of metaphysical, meaningless (because unverifiable) statements is thus scuppered by the impossibility of examining statements in isolation in the first place, or treating them in purely formal terms.[25] The attempt to posit verifiability as the criterion by which adequate and inadequate representations of the world might be distinguished seems to be no more helpful than the attempt to find a way of relating ideas, unmediated, to the world.

What *will* allow us to escape the aporias of representationalism, argues Rorty, is the relinquishing of the image which gives rise to them in the first place, and of philosophy's self-conception as something distinct from, and prior to, science. We must set aside as a surplus philosophical confection the idea of the mind as a special area of study, located in inner space, containing elements or processes that make knowledge possible.[26] We must set aside, too, the idea that language, as necessary mediator of our ideas, might provide a substitute for the mind in this respect. In so doing, we can also relinquish the idea that the aim of knowing is a highly polished and so accurate mental or linguistic mirror – a formal representation of the content of the world. And by doing *this*, we can set aside epistemology and metaphysics as possible disciplines. That is to say, we can set aside the idea of a knowing subject which must, to ensure objectivity, refer to objects in the right way, by checking its subjective representations – ideas, or statements – against the objective world. Dissolve the subject–object relation so conceived, and you duly dissolve the problem of knowledge, and the problem of the fundamental nature of reality. Both of these are products of the Cartesian problem of 'getting in touch with the world', a problem entrenched, but further warped, by Kant's distinction between the phenomenal world of appearances (of 'common sense', as Rorty puts it, comprising people, cows, stars, storms, etc.) and 'the-world as-possibly-unknown' – the noumenal world of the thing-in-itself.[27] This latter claim founders on the rock of Sellars's denial that we can distinquish between what is empirically *given* to consciousness and what consciousness adds to this, by virtue of its form, in the creation of knowledge.

And so will be resolved a string of problems which arise precisely from the assumption that some aspects of existence are given, or 'found', and others made, or constructed by the human subject (or language, or anything else). These problems cluster around the issue of objectivity, and its relation to subjectivity. On the Cartesian model, epistemology dominates ontology – a key feature of what Dewey, Rorty's favoured representative of the pragmatist tradition, called the 'spectator theory of knowledge'. It requires a strict dualism between a spectating subject and the known object of representation. According to Dewey, this leads to outright subjectivism:

> When objects are isolated from the experience through which they are reached and in which they function, experience itself becomes reduced to the mere process of experiencing, and experience is therefore treated as if it were also complete in itself. . . . Since the seventeenth century this conception of experience as the equivalent of subjective private experience set over against nature, which consists wholly of objects, has wrought havoc in philosophy.[28]

Rorty takes the impetus of Dewey's thinking here to coincide with that of Quine. By presenting human beings in naturalistic terms – as 'just one more species doing its best' to cope with its environment as the chance product of evolution – such perspectives enable us to circumvent the whole raft of problems which the subject–object distinction brings in its train.[29] If there is 'no ontological break between human and non-human reality', then we are diverted from explanations of how to find conditions of the very possibility of our having adequate representational knowledge of the world, to explanations of the way we actually do interact with the world, and how we might do so better. In the process, our approach is temporalized. It graduates into what Rorty calls 'historicism': 'the doctrine that there is no relation of "closeness of fit" between language and the world: no image of the world projected by language is more or less representative of the way the world really is than any other'.[30] Rather than 'copying' reality, language is a tool which enables us to cope with it.

Thus predisposed, we can view truth in terms not of representation, but of expediency, adopting James's description of 'the true' as 'only the expedient in our way of thinking'.[31] To put this in Quinean terms, if we can't find an available fit between atomized statements and observed reality, nor between our entire fabric of beliefs and the whole of the empirical data which might verify them, then there must be non-empirical, but also non-logical, principles according to which we succeed in coping with the world. These principles will be pragmatic: they will be warranted in so far as they *work*. Pragmatism – most particularly in the work of Dewey and James – stakes the meaning and truth of our beliefs in terms of their practical effects for human beings, naturalistically conceived.[32] The main ingredients of Rorty's account in *PMN* – Descartes as villain of the modern philosophical piece, an assault on both idealism and realism, and the call for a non-representationalist account of knowledge – are prefigured in the arguments of the first-generation pragmatists, as well as co-figured in the findings of later analytic philosophers working within the Philosophical tradition and trying to iron out problems in its own construction.

What marks Rorty's case apart is that it pursues the logic of these analyses beyond the scientific naturalism which tends to emerge from their original castings, towards what can be called a 'linguistic historicism'. This amounts, using Rorty's own words, to 'the doctrine that there are no constraints on inquiry save conversational ones – no wholesale constraints derived from the nature of the objects, or of the mind, or of language, but only those retail constraints provided by the remarks of our fellow-inquirers'.[33] It seems to me that the traces of positivism remain in Rorty's linguistic historicism. Indeed, the case can be made that Rorty's own thinking represents a sort of uneasy confluence of certain aspects of positivism with the 'historicism' which Rorty, on the back of Dewey and Quine, takes to render positivism, at least of the standard variety, untenable.

*Redescribing pragmatism*

Suspicions early in the work of Charles Sanders Peirce (the other principal figure in pragmatism's first generation) towards 'the spirit of Cartesianism' bear marked similarities to Rorty's own emphases. In dispatching the idea that our perception of the world contains 'images' (or representations), Peirce characterizes that spirit in terms of the claims that philosophy 'must begin with universal doubt', and that the 'ultimate test of certainty is to be found in the individual consciousness'.[34] Rejecting these claims, Peirce argues, first, that the idea that philosophy might begin with universal doubt is a strict impossibility; that it is 'as useless a preliminary as going to the North Pole would be in order to get to Constantinople by coming down regularly on a meridian'.[35] Doubt for its own sake, without reasons for so doing, is for Peirce simply a piece of empty methodological theatre. For without a specific *reason* for our specific doubt (say, 'my body might not exist'), one would not know how to proceed from it. And we won't have such a reason until we actually do envisage some concrete difficulty with proceeding according to our assumed belief that our body does in fact exist. Rorty would doubtless be quite happy with this.

But a contrast emerges when considering Peirce's objection to the second claim. For Peirce, the problem with the formal assertion that 'whatever I am clearly convinced of, is true' is that it precisely negates the very need for a test of certainty in knowledge. If I *were* convinced, that would be the end of the story. But, Peirce writes, 'thus to make single individuals absolute judges of truth is most pernicious'. On this basis philosophy could move way ahead of the physical sciences in terms of the certainties it is fit to dispense – without ever putting its theories 'on probation until an agreement is reached' about its status.[36] Peirce insists that we can speak securely of knowledge, truth and reality only post-hoc, once agreement has been reached in the community of inquirers. His 'spirit of experimentalism' insists that philosophy ought to 'imitate the successful sciences in its methods, so far as to proceed only from tangible premises which can be subjected to careful scrutiny', rather than appealing to the shaky abstractions of monologic metaphysical inquiry. Thus, in prospective enquiry, clarity in our thoughts about some object of knowledge will derive from considering what conceivable practical effects it might give rise to.

This faith in science is a recurring theme amongst the earlier pragmatists. The same spirit of experimentation can be found in Dewey's claim that experience should not be hypostatized, Descartes-style, as a veil between us and the world – that 'rather, it penetrates into [the world], reaching down into its depths, and in such a way that its grasp is capable of expansion'.[37] For Dewey and Peirce, science represented precisely the practice through which our experience of the world was best immersed in it, rather than isolated from its objects. Thus natural science gave privileged access to the real world apart from metaphysical distractions, precisely by removing the 'veil' through which the 'idea idea' insists that our access to the natural world must be mediated. So rather than, as with Rorty's version of Kant, philosophy seeking to undergird the sciences, philosophy on this basis is instructed to be more *like* the sciences in proceeding towards agreement based on observation.

Dewey shared the hope that this might issue in an improved philosophical method, and shared a sense, too, that this method would derive from a closer approximation to the humbler, more humdrum, experimental engagement of the professional scientist. The key for him was to displace the assumption that an especially philosophical account of truth – superior to that of science – is needed in order to gauge whether truth is duly realized in such ordinary investigative activity. On the contrary: 'as to truth, philosophy has no pre-eminent status'.[38]

As Donald Davidson notes, Dewey's conclusions here were twofold: 'that access to truth could not be a special prerogative of philosophy, and that truth must have essential connections with human interests'.[39] The first claim issues in a pluralistic conception of the ways in which truth emerges through experience, along with an insistence that it is through the techniques of science that we will gauge their worth. Thus, while 'truth is a collection of truths', in combination 'these constituent truths are in the keeping of the best available methods of inquiry and testing as to matters-of-fact; methods which are, when collected under a single name, science'.[40] The second claim, about truth's essential link to human interests, brings truth 'down to earth' in another respect: by recasting philosophy's role as a constructive exploration of the problem of how to relate truth to human desires and intentions. Note that, at this stage, this relativity is not taken as an outright denial that the problem of truth has anything to do with correspondence to reality.[41] Nor, *a fortiori*, is it taken as an indication that there is nothing that philosophy can say about the question of truth. Rather, it is to focus on the ways in which experimental science embodies 'the best available methods of inquiry'.

As the philosophers of the early Frankfurt School noted, this attention to science in place of metaphysics placed pragmatism in close proximity to positivism.[42] The drive of logical positivism was to replace the strictly meaningless claims of metaphysics with exclusive attention to the 'facts' given immediately in observation. The spirit of early pragmatism is perhaps best explained in terms of James's view, already mentioned, of truth's inseparability from 'what it would be better for us to believe' – and that hence, 'the truth is the name of whatever proves itself to be good in the way of belief'.[43] This may not sound like positivism, if by the latter we understand the more formal attitude that we must confine ourselves to what is positively given by strict procedures of verification. Rather than centring on empirical testing, James couches the pragmatic attitude as follows (not one of his most elegant passages): 'Consider what effects that might conceivably have practical bearing you conceive the object of your conception to have. Then your conception of those effects is the WHOLE of your conception of the object.'[44] The emphasis on practical – rather than just passive – observation may seem a departure from the positivistic ethos.

But James himself goes on to make the equation with positivism in describing the advantages of the doctrine just described:

It will serve to show that almost every proposition of ontological metaphysics is either meaningless gibberish – one word being defined by other words, and they by still others, without any real conception ever being reached – or else is downright absurd; so that all such rubbish being swept away, what will remain of philosophy will be a series of problems capable of investigation by the observational methods of the true sciences – the truth about which can be reached without those interminable misunderstandings and disputes which have made the highest of the positive sciences a mere amusement for idle intellects, a sort of chess – idle pleasure its purpose, and reading out of a book its method.[45]

And indeed the practical aspect is phrased, in James, in terms which 'cash out' in positivistic terms:

'Grant an idea or belief to be true', [pragmatism] says, 'what difference will its being true make in any one's actual life? How will the truth be realized? What experiences will be different from those which would obtain if the belief were false? What, in short, is the truth's cash value in experiential terms?' The moment pragmatism asks this question, it sees the answer: *True ideas are those that we can assimilate, validate, corroborate and verify. False ideas are those that we can not.* That is the practical difference it makes to us to have true ideas; that, therefore, is the meaning of truth, for it is all that truth is known-as.[46]

An ambiguity emerges in these formulations. James might seem to be dealing in two separate theories, spliced together as if rather more isomorphic than they really are. One is a direct precursor of logical positivism, making an idea's 'cash value' dependent upon its validation in terms of predictive import. On these terms, the role of consciousness would appear to be that of purely passive register of empirical data. The other is perhaps the more familiar pragmatist variant: that the meaning and truth of a proposition depend on the future consequences that result from believing in it – quite independent of whether the proposition itself is isolably true or false.[47] In the latter case, it seems as if *anything* one might happen to believe in would be rendered meaningful and truthful as long as believing in it had consequences which were (in whatever indeterminate sense) 'good'.

The implications of this seem intrinsically conservative. For in either sense of truth – predictive, or in terms of its consequential benefits – it seems to collapse rather too readily into a reinforcement of in-place conventional belief. It will do this either by uncritical acceptance of the evidence given to consciousness, without admitting the possibility that appearances may be deceptive, or by relativizing truth to standards of 'benefit' or 'utility' which themselves are not up for critical interrogation. Thus Max Horkheimer, in considering the ramifications of Goethe's line 'What is fruitful is alone true' and its articulation in early twentieth-century pragmatism, regards the pragmatist theory as emblematic of the stultifying tendencies inherent in staking truth entirely in terms of its confirmation or verification through 'beneficial' consequences:

> The pragmatist theory of truth in its exclusive form, without any contradictory metaphysics to complement it, corresponds to limitless trust in the existing world. If the goodness of every idea is given time and opportunity to come to light, if the success of the truth – even after struggle and resistance – is in the long run certain, if the idea of a dangerous, explosive truth cannot come into the field of vision, then the present social structure is consecrated and – to the extent that it warns of harm – capable of unlimited development.[48]

The problem here is thus that truth conceived in terms of 'what pays' may prove to be endlessly self-confirming, growing ever more solid and reassuring in its veracity, precisely because it works to close off the very possibility of a genuine challenge to existing social practices. Despite its apparent rooting in the 'here and now', in everyday 'reality' conceived without recourse to metaphysics, pragmatism may thus not be able to attend to social and historical particularity. Ideas will be verified according to their functional utility, but this can only be confirmed in terms of predominantly given attitudes and interests – and so make the present totality in effect the ultimate ground of truth.[49] Thus, for Horkheimer as for Adorno, the installation of an idea as a 'brute fact' on the basis of experience will bring thinking to a halt while material reality remains in process.[50] And hence – in both positivism and pragmatism – successful reports of past experience are installed as 'laws' which dictate the terms in which we might interpret future experience.

Given that social structures themselves may not develop melioristically, pragmatism runs the risk of affirming received belief at the expense of a disjunction from material reality. It risks positing a false consensuality: 'The epistemological doctrine that truth promotes life, or rather that all thought that "pays" must also be true, contains a harmonistic illusion if this theory of cognition does not belong to a whole in which the tendencies toward a better, life-promoting situation really find expression.'[51] And, one might add: it closes off the very possibility of recognizing any such 'macro' constraints or tendencies, since its model of truth is one in which the isolated idea is tested for veracity against given purposes and interests, and the sole criterion of truth is (Horkheimer again) 'the satisfaction of the subject'.[52] The possibility of 'dangerous, explosive truth' is thus neutralized in advance, since (by definition) it will not fit with those given interests: 'nothing at all may remain outside, for the mere idea of outsidedness is the very source of fear'.[53] Thus, 'the fathers of pragmatism made the satisfaction of the subject the criterion of truth'.[54]

Now it may be premature to raise these objections at this point, since they may not apply to Rorty's own version of pragmatism, precisely because it has reorientated the classical model in crucial respects.[55] First, though, the continuities as Rorty sees them. What he retains from the pragmatist tradition – and what puts him in direct opposition to the logic of Horkheimer's case – is the sense that there is *no available distinction* between 'appearance' and 'reality', so that it is not the case that workable descriptions might be discrepant in respect of some deeper or separate reality. Present in Kant's distinction between the noumenal and phenomenal, this distinction is taken to be characteristic of inherited metaphysics since Plato. It is in the simile of the cave, in *The Republic*, that the idea of a deeper reality beyond the everyday world of mediated experience is given its classic articulation.[56] Here, the socially constructed world of everyday experience is directly contrasted with the world of the eternal 'Forms' to which right philosophical reasoning will direct us. Rorty sees a string of kindred distinctions as formative to the modern tradition inaugurated by Descartes: between the apparent and the real, the made and the found, the absolute and the relative. According to the prejudices of this tradition, the second term in each case will be prefaced by a 'merely'; the presumption being that the true exists beyond the ordinary horizons of practice.

It is worth noting at this point that Rorty thus lumps together metaphysical conceptions which are otherwise most often regarded as being opposed. For Plato, the reality 'beyond' appearances, i.e. the Forms, is ideal in the metaphysical sense: they are ideal objects or patterns, invisible, intangible and only apprehensible by the mind after due preparation and training. They exist eternally, working behind the scenes to change the phenomenal, readily visible world. Thus while 'opinion' (*doxa*) is based on appearances, and so subject to flux and only pragmatic justification, 'knowledge' (*episteme*) is that which, by-passing sense perception, makes direct mental contact with the Forms. The Forms are more real than the fleeting exemplifications of them we find in the particular objects of everyday experience. Thus, the truly real is immaterial. Plato regards materialism as the diametrical opposite of this approach; the claim that the physical represents the final extent of what exists. Thus conceived, the view finds a clear – and forthrightly reductive – articulation in the insistence that consciousness and human being are entirely explicable in physicalistic terms. This view, characteristic of the ancient atomism of Democritus, finds its epitome in the opening pages of Hobbes's *Leviathan*: 'all that exists is matter in motion', the human body being described in purely mechanical terms, and its relation to the world conceived on the model of relations of strict cause and effect.[57]

But Plato's conception of materialism as necessarily reductive is, of course, shaped by his concern to preserve the reality of the Forms. For there is also, from Aristotle down to Marx and beyond, a tradition as unrelated to Hobbes's account as it is to Plato's.[58] This is not the point at which to give a full account of this tradition, although it is one to which I return in Chapter 4. Suffice to say, for now, that while it conceives reality as material, it does not conceive materialism as a commitment to the denial of consciousness as a distinct entity by cleanly reducing it to the body conceived in purely physicalist terms. Marx's position professedly 'distinguishes itself both from idealism and materialism' by conceiving conscious activity as both definitively human and as being in unity with our embodiment as natural beings.[59] In so doing, it also avoids the strict Cartesian dualism of mind and body by conceiving them in dialectical relation. And on these terms – the basis of Horkheimer's objection to the pragmatist view of truth – the nature of reality is perceived as being transitive, rooted in historically specific and social forms, even while there are intransitive aspects (such as the dialectical relation of mind and body) to our subjective relation to that reality. Thus the appeal to a 'reality' beyond 'appearances' need not be the appeal – as with appeals to eternal Forms – to an unchanging, intangible realm in a state of dualistic severance from the world of the 'everyday'.

Indeed certain aspects of the earlier pragmatism lend themselves to this picture. Its anti-Platonism, anti-Cartesianism and its emphasis on human activity, rather than the Forms, as controlling the patterns of reality – together with the residual realism of Peirce, if not James[60] – might suggest a bringing 'down to earth' of philosophy in some ways symmetrical to that invoked by Aristotle and Marx in response to the idealisms of their predecessors. But if Rorty is right, and pragmatism's definitive legacy is the relinquishing of the appearance–reality distinction, then, indeed, ideology critique in the Frankfurt School mode will be a casualty. Concomitant with the relinquishing, says Rorty, will be an insistence that it makes no difference that there is no available distinction between what is 'made' (in the process of our contingent social practices) and what is 'found', in the sense of a reality existing antecedently to the workings of those practices. This might be rephrased as a distinction between what is 'inside' and 'outside' of current convention. Rorty insists that this distinction depends on a Platonic diremption between the malleable, changing phenomenal world and the static, eternal world of the Forms. Thus Horkheimer, by rejecting the claim that in-place conventional belief somehow constitutes the totality of reality, must be contrasting two ontological orders, the very identification of which can only be identified with the aid of Platonic–Cartesian–Kantian tools.

And this, for Rorty, is a dispensable theoretical conceit. He takes the upshot of James and Dewey's reorientation of the philosophic method to consist in pressing the anti-Platonist question: 'Does our purported theoretical difference make any difference to practice?'[61] This counts as irrelevant any fine-tuned philosophical dispute which does (or will) not make a difference to our practical engagement with the world. For Rorty the 'appearance–reality' distinction here slips out of possible utility, since it rests upon a strictly 'theological' hunch that there must be something beyond the muddling along of human beings which we might treat as an index of our progress in a given sphere. This hunch registers itself in Horkheimer's qualms about 'limitless trust in the existing world'; the assumption therein being that there is utility to be had in trust in a world *beyond* the horizons of practice. Whether in terms of religion or of ideology critique, this ascribes an intrinsic and primary nature to the world revealable only by that kind of vision which might penetrate the veil of appearances. *Pace* the programme of the Enlightenment, characterized by Adorno and Horkheimer as 'the disenchantment of the world; the dissolution of myths and the substitution of knowledge for fancy', there is no such veil to be penetrated.[62]

Still, Rorty's pragmatism is explicitly on the side of the Enlightenment's disenchantment and dedeification of the world. This works, I think, in two steps. One is by showing that the core concerns of the philosophical tradition can be sidestepped, or 'circumvented', rather than somehow worked through to a resolution. One circumvents by seeing supposedly necessary problems as the products of contingent vocabularies of inquiry. Thus the later Wittgenstein, for Rorty, works 'satirically' to demonstrate how we might painlessly stop talking about Philosophical problems (Philosophy, when capitalized, signifying the pursuit of the True – necessary – nature of reality or knowledge or human being) without having to out-Philosophize the Philosophers:

> he just shows, by examples, how hopeless the traditional problems are – how they are based on a terminology which is as if designed expressly for the purpose of making solution impossible, how the questions which generate the traditional problems cannot be posed except in this terminology, how pathetic it is to think that the old gaps will be filled by constructing new gimmicks.[63]

On this basis, we can resist the 'entire cultural tradition which made Truth – successful crossing of the void which divides men from the world – a central virtue'. And by so resisting, we will, as a second step, disenchant the world since the 'enchantment' of the world is the product of its being situated, mysteriously, behind the veil of ideas. Rorty couches this in terms of 'de-divinization', in the sense that in the appearance–reality distinction the latter part, whether theologically or materialistically conceived, figures as a divinized quasi-person possessing a separate, intrinsically *privileged* language which, with due application, we might learn how to speak:

> once upon a time we felt a need to worship something which lay beyond the visible world. Beginning in the seventeenth century we tried to substitute a love of truth for a love of God, treating the world described by science as a quasi divinity. Beginning at the end of the eighteenth century we tried to substitute [through Romanticism] a love of ourselves for a love of scientific truth, a worship of our own deep spiritual or poetic nature, treated as one more quasi divinity . . . [We should] try to get to the point where we no longer worship *anything*, where we treat *everything* – our language, our conscience, our community – as a product of time and chance.[64]

So pragmatism is both anti-theological therapy and – given that belief in the appearance–reality distinction makes reality akin to God – anti-Philosophical therapy. We are thus freed from anxieties and itches caused by the need to find a conception of truth adequate to doing justice to the reality side of the distinction – a conception of truth which means more than simply 'that which best enables us to cope with our environment':

To take the traditional idea of Truth seriously, you have to do more than agree that some beliefs are true and some false, and call 'true' those which fit best with your and other's previous beliefs . . . To respect Truth and Reality in the proper way, it is not enough to come in when it rains, and to shun bears. To acquire the right sort of respect, it helps if you can manage to become an epistemological sceptic – manage to worry about whether human language is capable of representing the way Reality is in itself, whether we are calling Reality by the names it prefers. To worry in this way, you need to take seriously the question whether our descriptions of reality may not be all too human, all too influenced by our hopes and fears. It helps to anguish about whether Reality (and therefore Truth itself) may not stand aloof, beyond the reach of the sentences in which we formulate our beliefs. You must be prepared to distinguish, at least in principle, between beliefs which embody Truth and beliefs which are merely good to steer by.[65]

Given that we cannot make such a distinction, Rorty restates James's and Dewey's equation of truth with human interest, and with what works – and *exhaustively* so. There is no remainder; such would depend on something which 'stood aloof', to which the pragmatically useful might be compared.

Considering these three passages, though, a contradiction emerges. Notice that Rorty's conception of de-divinization involves a transition *from* a belief that there is something beyond the visible world which somehow explains the way it appears to us, *to* the adoption of an attitude that every aspect of this world is 'a product of time and chance'.[66] But the transition, so conceived, involves a sleight of hand. For the claim that the world is 'a product of time and chance' is precisely a claim about the provenance of the visible world. If the materialistic picture of a world in process is, for all that, reliant upon Plato's founding distinction between appearance and reality (because it seeks a basic explanation for the way in which the phenomenal world appears to us) then so, surely, is the claim that every aspect of the phenomenal world is the product of contingency rather than necessity. At this stage Rorty must insist, pragmatist-style, that it suits our interests better to view things in these terms. But this sort of claim implies the sub-claim that those worldviews which do not rest on such a vision of contingency must work less well than those which do. And it is not clear that this is the case. Does it suit scientists better to view the pursuit of truth as the pursuit of something to steer by? Does it suit Muslims to view Islam in those terms? It seems unlikely, on the face of it. But then even if it did, the problem remains that proving the utility of the pragmatist view of truth – and the setting aside of the appearance–reality distinction – must have recourse to a form of anthropological claim which does not figure in Rorty's account. In fact, he makes his case purely in philosophical terms. In contradistinction to the spirit of his valorization of Wittgenstein and Dewey, he has made his case neither by pure satirization (for he argues for an alternative conception of truth) nor by open experimentation (for he has not provided for empirical testing of his view against other, predominant, alternatives).

This isn't to say that anything about Rorty's approach must *require* any such (positivistic) comparison. But it is to say that, if 'practices of justification' are 'just practices', and if we should explain 'rationality and epistemic authority by reference to what society lets us say', and treat truth as 'conformity to the norms of the day', Rorty runs into a fairly straightforward problem of self-referential inconsistency.[67] For the articulation of this position seems to require a standpoint from beyond the orbit or framework of given practices: a place from which to diagnose their relativity to place and time (a 'skyhook', to use Rorty's favoured metaphor).

We can add to this another point. Rorty's case against representationalism is couched in terms of a rejection of the oculocentrism of the Platonic–Cartesian–Kantian tradition: its reliance upon a founding metaphor of 'vision' in characterizing the subject's relation to a (more or less dimly conceived) world. And yet Rorty's justification for pragmatism is that it 'works' (for instance) to 'try *looking* at things this way', or to *see* the problems encountered by *x* mode of inquiry as products of the contingent definition of *x*. As we will 'see' throughout what follows, these are the regular terms in which we are invited to proceed. Perhaps it is pedantry to point out Rorty's own reliance on a supplementary metaphor of vision in so presenting things. But perhaps not. Characterizing philosophy, the Vienna Circle philosopher of mathematics and language Friedrich Waismann once wrote that 'if I were asked to express in one single word what is its most essential feature I would unhesitatingly say: vision'. He goes on: 'what is decisive is a new way of seeing and, what goes with it, the will to transform the whole intellectual scene'.[68] This is, of course, precisely the sort of self-image which Rorty would urge us to set aside. Still, it characterizes precisely what he himself aims to accomplish in arguing that we set that image aside: to replace it with another one. To say that this objection must rely itself on the assumption of oculocentrism is only to argue that so, then, must Rorty's own case. Its suasive power arises precisely from its utility as a mode of seeing.

If nothing else, these circularities suggests that Rorty requires another move to flesh out his account of pragmatism, beyond an appeal to 'practices of justification' and the call for a switch in guiding metaphors.[69] He has, I think, two such moves, key to the reconfiguring of pragmatism mentioned earlier. One is to endorse a specific sense of *ethnocentrism*. His own views will be 'true' – if true they are – solely in the sense that they prove 'good to steer by'. 'True' in this sense – as we will see in more detail in 1.2 – is merely a compliment we pay to beliefs which achieve some desired effect. Now the effects desired will indeed vary between cultures and communities of inquiry. But the *term* true, as 'an expression of commendation', 'means the same in all cultures', just like 'me' and 'bad' do. It is not, then, that 'truth' is relative to something else (like the in-place conventions of a given community). This would imply a positive theory of truth, which is precisely what Rorty does not want to offer. The 'ethnocentric' view, by (claimed) contrast, is that 'there is nothing to be said about either truth or rationality apart from descriptions of the familiar procedures of justification which a given society – *ours* – uses in one or other area of inquiry'.[70]

Thus the way in which truth happens to cash out will depend on those procedures, but this does not entail that truth itself is actually relative. Even the articulation of this position is, then, dependent upon already shared understandings and norms. But this is not a worry: it need not claim transcendental authority in order to prove good to steer by. It need not rest upon a definition of truth only available from some transcendent perspective. Indeed the problem of relativism itself arises only on the basis that there might be a distinction between the way things 'really' are and the way in which they (subjectively or communally) 'appear' to us. (That this view of 'truth' itself involves a distinction between the necessary and the contingent is a theme to which I return in 1.2.) Rorty sees pragmatism as issuing in a healthy corrective to this framing of the issues. Since pragmatists do not believe there is a way things really are,

> they want to replace the appearance–reality distinction by that between descriptions of the world and of ourselves which are less useful and those which are more useful. When the question 'useful for what?' is pressed, they have nothing to say except 'useful to create a better future'. When they are

asked, 'Better by what criterion?', they have no detailed answer, any more than the first mammals could specify in what respects they were better than the dying dinosaurs. Pragmatists can only say something as vague as: Better in the sense of containing more of what we consider good and less of what we consider bad.[71]

What's 'good to steer by' will depend on these historically contingent, ethnocentric considerations.

This leads us to the second move. This divests Rorty's case of any appeal to experience or observation – an appeal typical, as we have seen, in first-generation pragmatism – in demonstrating the cash value of his approach. As I see it, this move takes the form of a claim about the ontological primacy of language, something we have yet specifically to address here. It is raised by Rorty's use of the word 'descriptions' in the above passage. This, he thinks, replaces the 'ideas' of the Cartesian tradition as the currency of knowledge, while collapsing the dichotomy between subject and object on which the Cartesian picture depended. As will be seen in what follows, I am not convinced that Rorty achieves this move satisfactorily. Rorty leaves us in a more idealistic place than he admits. He relies upon a smuggled-in, latter-day wedge between language and object. This separates the workings of description and redescription from entanglements with the world and posits them as operative in another sphere, unconstrained by a reality which, since 'the world does not speak', has no effect on the tenability of those descriptions.[72]

So while Rorty regards doubts about whether the world 'really' exists as the product of the representationalist problematic (how might we be sure that our representations are adequate to the externally existing world?), he adopts what Bob Jessop has called an 'empty realism'. This position requires that we

> affirm that there is a real world external to thought but [that] the entities in that world are inaccessible abstractions; indeed they lack determination until discursively constituted into so many beings. The same entity can become different beings according to the particular discursive context in and through which it is constructed . . . [D]iscursive articulation is the primary ontological level of the constitution of the real.[73]

One might call this position a form of *discourse foundationalism*. Against the claim that either self or world provides constraints on our descriptions of either, language itself is presented not as *mediating*

# RORTY'S PROJECT: REDESCRIBING PRAGMATISM

between subject and object, but as *constitutive* of both subject and object. I explore the implications of empty realism further below. Meanwhile it is worth addressing the nature of Rortian pragmatism's 'linguistic turn'.

*Pragmatizing redescription: horizontal over vertical*

In *PMN*, as we have seen, Rorty rejects the idea that there 'could be such a thing as "foundations of *all* knowledge" (*all* knowledge – in every field, past present, and future) or a "theory of representation" (*all* representation, in familiar vocabularies and those not yet dreamed of)'. Such an idea depends on the assumption that there is some sort of a priori constraint which 'imposes limits on the possible results of empirical enquiry'.[74] Facing up to the absence of such constraints leads Rorty to propose *redescription* as an alternative to 'philosophical' enquiry. Redescription – or the recontextualization, reinterpretation or reimagining of given attitudes, practices or ways of looking at problems – is distinguished by the renunciation of the aim of finding adequate representations. Instead, its aim is to help us *cope* better with the world.

A metaphor invoked intermittently, but illuminatingly, by Rorty in presenting this distinction is that between *vertical* and *horizontal* relations. Its original setting out comes in the 1961 essay 'Pragmatism, categories, and language', in terms of a contrast between philosophical approaches. In a 'vertical' search, one seeks 'something determinate underlying the indeterminate – something of which the indeterminate is an epiphenomenon'.[75] The 'horizontal' counterpoint is to insist that any such determinate thing will itself be indeterminate. (Rorty, as we have seen, goes on, via Quine, to employ this strategy in his rejection of the appearance–reality distinction.) On the horizontal approach, there is no groundless ground beyond the contingent interplay of descriptions, nothing by reference to which we might secure the ontological status of a given claim. But in vertical searches, one proceeds – whether 'up' or 'down' – to enter into a sort of regress. One discovers that one is moving on an endless ladder as soon as one has to replace one apparently determinate, rock-bottom factor with another, still deeper one as soon as each becomes exposed as unfounded. Horizontally, we need seek nothing which is somehow different in *kind* (being necessary rather than contingent) from that encountered in our previous step; in fact, on the horizontal plane, there is no room for distinct 'kinds' of any sort. It will be different only in *degree*, a matter of sideways steps. This is because, on a horizontal understanding, there is nothing to be 'found' at the bottom of the ladder which explains the basis on which the other steps have been 'made'. The horizontal regress is thus benign:

> The relation between step *n* and step *n-1* is thus not like the relation between creator and created, but like that between a mystifying book and a brilliant commentary on it; the book was there already, even though perhaps nobody could make much of it until the commentary came along. Nor would there be anything surprising in somebody writing a commentary on the commentary, and so on ad infinitum. Movement along a horizontal regress lacks the sort of jolts we feel whenever we are forced to a new level in a vertical regress (the sort of jolt felt by the child when the question 'Who made God?' first occurs to him) and it also lacks the sense of utter futility which grips us when we realize that we can always be forced to move on from any level of a vertical regress.[76]

Since the horizontal process does not involve the destination of some purely determinate end-point (like God), it regresses harmlessly from one step to the next, since each determination is indeterminate. While it might render the original datum *more* determinate, it cannot (because of its own indetermination) render it *perfectly* determinate.

It is not just idle comparison-mongering to note the parallel between Rorty's account here and that arising from Saussure's structuralist account of language (which as far as I know, Rorty had yet to encounter).[77] For Saussure, linguistic signs derive meaning from their place within language understood as a system of differences. While this system is necessary for language to generate meaning as it does, the relation between signifer (or sound-image) and signified (the concept it carries) is arbitrary, or relative to the semiotic conventions on which meaning depends. The upshot of Saussure's account is a picture in which the relations between signs, deriving their meaning from their place in the overall system of meanings, operate unconstrained by referential relations between signifier and object. Thus language is a system of differences without positive terms: without a vertical 'linking of a name and a thing'.[78] There is, to be sure, a sort of vertical element in Saussure's account: namely, the relation between signifier and signified. The relation between signifier (for example, 'tree') and signified (the concept of a tree) is for Saussure stable and unitary, even though signifiers are arbitrary.[79] Within a language, while 'tree' links up with the concept of a tree on a purely arbitrary basis (any other signifier might have done the job just as well), once the link is forged it is secure. But as post-structuralists duly pointed out, if language really is a system of differences, then the relations between signifiers will not be as stable as Saussure imagined. Chains of meaning (as in the standard example of looking up a word in a dictionary) are, then, never finally circumscribable within the boundaries of a system. If we accept that there are no positive terms to resolve the issue, then one is simply referred from signifier to signifier in an endless process – a process with neither prescribable rules nor any guarantee that the signified of a signifier will remain intact during its transition from one context to the next. This strikes me as a prime example of the horizontal process which Rorty describes above: a process which in principle cannot find resolution by reference to some 'transcendental signified' by which to constrain the eternal slippage – or horizontal regress – from one signification to the next.

And just as Saussure claims that ideas do not exist independently of words, but rather as the correlates of signifiers, so Rorty, in differentiating himself from the first-generation pragmatists, affirms that 'language is not a device for representing reality, but rather a reality in which we live and move'.[80] Because 'the specification of a referent is always going to be in some vocabulary', one is really, in comparing the linguistically 'constructed' with the world 'beyond', 'comparing two descriptions of a thing rather than a description with the thing-in-itself'.[81] Thus questions of 'truth' become treatable only in terms of comparisons of bits of discourse in the light of their utility. In this light, Rorty draws a distinction between two philosophical approaches, one (roughly) Kantian and the other (roughly) Hegelian:

> The first tradition thinks of truth as a vertical relationship between representations and what is represented. The second thinks of truth horizontally – as the culminating reinterpretation of our predecessors' reinterpretation of their predecessors' reinterpretation . . . This tradition does not ask how representations are related to nonrepresentations, but how representations can be seen as hanging together . . . [I]t is the difference between regarding truth, goodness and beauty as eternal objects which we try to locate and reveal, and regarding them as artifacts whose fundamental design we often have to alter.[82]

So Rorty's 'linguistic historicism', following the second alternative, makes the horizontal axis the only one available – and makes the vertical axis fundamentally Platonic in its origin and maintenance. Important to notice here is that Rorty includes among the purveyors of the first, vertically oriented approach the founders of philosophy's linguistic turn – most conspicuously, the logical positivists.[83] For although, in a 'purifying move', they switched from ideas to sentences in their focus on thought–world relations, they still saw the central philosophical issues as 'a series of questions about the relations between words and the world'.[84] Because, with Quine (and indeed Saussure), we can see that individual words or sentences do not atomistically pick out, picture, or in any way lock on to some particular aspect of the world, as if in a relation of direct correspondence, it follows that there are no distinctions of *kind* to be had, whether ontologically or epistemologically. We can replace traditional distinctions of this order with distinctions in degree of complexity, or unfamiliarity.

Thus progress in knowledge – whether scientific, or moral, or whatever – consists in integrating more and more data into Quine's fabric, or web, of belief, and in the process rendering it coherent and useful. It is, again, not a matter of (vertically) penetrating appearance until one comes upon reality. The workings of knowledge, through language, simply do not allow us so to proceed to the pinning down of that final determinate piece of the chain. To have such an aim would be equivalent to wanting to stop history: like 'aiming at being at the end of biological evolution – at being not merely the latest heir of all the ages but the creature in which all the ages were destined to culminate'.[85] No word, statement or idea can assume this role.

The vertical relation is thus symptomatic, for Rorty, of every dualistic portrayal of a more essential, fundamental, or 'real' level of reality beyond that involved in our ordinary practices as users of language. What Rorty means here is perhaps best explained by way of his frequent invocation of another metaphor: what Donald Davidson calls the 'scheme–content distinction'. Davidson presents this as the 'third dogma of empiricism', supplementary to Quine's two.[86] Quine having shown that different languages may involve different ways of distinguishing between analytic and synthetic statements, the assumption then emerges that operative notions of truth must be relative to the language we speak. This seems to take us to an outright relativism, in which the content of experience is given form by the system of categories to which we make appeal, and one such scheme, while perfectly adequate in itself, becomes strictly untranslatable into any other. Thus 'reality itself becomes relative to a scheme: what counts as real in one system may not in another'.[87] But talking in this way assumes, for Davidson, precisely that there is some strict dualism between (linguistic) scheme and (empirical) content in the first place – and that the first, taking the form of a language, might impose strictly internal (scheme-relative) conditions on valid interpretations of the latter, in a way beyond the grasp of speakers of different languages.

Davidson argues that this picture of radical incommensurability between languages comes unstuck once we consider that it only makes sense to talk about alternative conceptual schemes (to have 'clarity and bite' in our 'declarations of difference') if there is some way of our knowing that, and how, other such schemes do in fact differ from our own. The very idea of a conceptual scheme must itself depend on a level of shared understanding. This is a precondition for our recognizing even that speakers of radically different languages are speaking *a language*. Thus even 'to make meaningful disagreement possible ... depends on a foundation – *some* foundation – in agreement'.[88] In so far as we can, in however piecemeal and fudgy a way, communicate across languages we really have no intelligible basis on which to argue that those languages must be different in some fundamental way. So 'charity', in the form of a principle of willingness to assume that others whom we think we understand must also make sense of their experience in ways similar to our own, 'is forced upon us'. 'Whether we like it or not, if we want to understand others, we must count them right on most matters'.[89] If each language-speaker's practical knowledge were not, for the most part, accurate, their world would fall apart. On these terms the claim that there is some uninterpreted reality, given meaning by the imposition of different schemes, is shown to be a side-effect of Sellars's 'myth of the given'. We always already are in touch with the world, are understanding each other, without reference to some or other organizing scheme to make sense of these activities.

Rorty sees Davidson's argument as grist to the pragmatist mill for a single, multi-purpose reason. He takes the scheme–content distinction as a useful marker for that whole string of dualisms introduced by the spectator theory of knowledge. It stands for any positing of a metaphysical break: between 'subject and object';[90] between 'consciousness and the given';[91] 'the formal and the material, the logical and the psychological, the non-natural and the natural';[92] between 'appearance and reality', 'mind and body', 'language and fact', 'essence and accident';[93] between 'beliefs and the way things are';[94] between 'empirical conditions of actuality' and 'transcendental conditions of possibility'.[95] All of these, it seems, are represented under a common rubric: the distinction between 'determinate realities and a set of words or concepts which may or may not be 'adequate' to them'.[96]

Thus, through Davidson, we can see the scheme–content distinction as the common denominator of all those problems – representation, scepticism and so on – which arise from the Cartesian bifurcation between that which organizes knowledge, and that which is organized. Without it, according to Rorty, we are left only with the horizontal problem of trying to figure out how different descriptions might 'hang together', rather than prove adequate to a content from which they are radically discrepant. While other disciplines will look at particular clusters of descriptions, philosophy simply looks across different such genres, from a relatively wide angle. It does not, of course penetrate *deeper* than any other sphere of inquiry, since depth is a vertical metaphor. Without such metaphors, we can take up Sellars's invitation to see 'philosophy' as 'an attempt to see how things, in the broadest possible sense of the term, hang together, in the broadest possible sense of the term'.[97]

Rorty sees Quine, Sellars and Davidson as contributing to pragmatism's switch from experience to descriptions as the reference-point of knowledge. This leads to a holism best captured in a quote from Quine: 'it makes no sense to say what the objects of a theory are, beyond saying how to interpret or reinterpret that theory in another'.[98] On this horizontal conception, the question of privileged representations (or transcendental signifieds, or necessary truths) simply drops out of a picture of understanding in which we no longer confront the world with some given linguistic or conceptual scheme, but simply confront other such schemes.

Thus, 'justification is not a matter of a special relation between ideas (or words) and objects, but of conversation, of social practice'.[99] Relinquishing the picture of knowledge as accuracy of representation leads us to the conclusion 'that we understand knowledge when we understand the social justification of belief'.[100] Differences in certainty no longer correspond to differences in the object we purport to have knowledge of, and rationality is not exemplified in some adequate grasp by knowledge of its object. Rather, it consists in coming up with a description which others find convincing: 'our certainty will be a matter of conversations between persons, rather than a matter of interaction with nonhuman reality'.[101] Convincingness will not derive from some putative revelation of the underlying forces which work to make a given description successful. It will lie, instead, in the description of surface regularities.[102] The course of such conversation will be accordingly untethered by any pre-existing set of constraints. As inquiry it takes the form of 'muddling through, rather than conforming to canons of rationality – coping with people and things rather than corresponding to reality by discovering essences'.[103] Rather than light-minded chat, Rorty sees conversation 'as standing for the whole human enterprise – culture, if you like'.[104]

What is crucial, then, is that description and redescription proceed according to an open-ended practice unconstrained by some supposed 'way the world is' which might interrupt it, thwart it, or change its direction. This is how pragmatism, after the linguistic turn, conceives of the philosophical enterprise:

> To see keeping a conversation going as a sufficient aim of philosophy, to see wisdom as consisting in the ability to sustain a conversation, is to see human beings as generators of new descriptions rather than beings one hopes to be able to describe accurately.[105]

Without mirrors, without dualisms and without privileged representations, description is what is left over. For while 'language is incurably vague', it is 'perfectly real and utterly inescapable'.[106] What *is* escapable is the book that language is somehow radically separate from the rest of the reality in which we – naturalistically, holistically – negotiate our way. When this goes, so does the notion that anything might be 'vertically' privileged in the sense of being an 'unwobbling pivot . . . that [will] stay fixed forever and serve as a guiding star' during the course of conversation.[107]

That the linguistification of pragmatism leaves its pragmatism intact is borne out in Rorty's ultimate appeal to James's criterion of expediency in inviting us to adopt this picture. For the Philosophical tradition 'has outlived its usefulness'.[108] Vertical regresses have taken us nowhere; we are simply not in a position to resolve them. And, as we realize when we take 'seriously the notion that we only know the world and ourselves *under a description* – and that we just *happened on* that description – nature didn't tell us to apply it', it would be better not to try.[109] In an appropriately historicist account, 'there is no description either of nature or of experience that is more or less accurate or concrete than some rival (unless "more accurate" and "more concrete" are construed pragmatically, as "more useful for the following purposes . . .")'.¹¹⁰ Those purposes, says Rorty, will always be unviciously ethnocentric.

*Is Rorty a linguistic idealist?*

This prolonged exposition of the key ingredients of Rorty's thinking has been a necessary preamble to a critical response to it. My main point in the present section is to argue that Rorty's account of the relation between language and object does not in fact transcend or bypass the various distinctions he takes to be definitive of the Philosophical tradition. In fact, it restates them in a different key, and returns us to the characteristic circularities induced by the 'idea idea'. It is, in brief, a form of linguistic idealism.

Rorty takes it as a consequence of avoiding the scheme–content distinction that we are 'in touch with' reality in *all* areas of culture – ethics as well as physics, literary criticism as well as biology – in a sense of 'in touch with' which does not mean 'representing reasonably accurately' but simply 'caused by and causing'.¹¹¹ Central to this re-orientation is that we conceive of language not as a medium which somehow maps the world around us, but as a set of tools which we use in coping with that world. Sentences are simply 'strings of marks and noises used by human beings in development and pursuit of social practices'.¹¹² Our awareness of the world is enabled by and saturated in language: rather than the mind having some kind of 'direct access' to the 'reality' it perceives, all our awareness is under a description. Thus though language is not, in Rorty's terms, a 'medium' as such, all our dealings with the world are mediated, in the sense that we negotiate our way in the world by bestowing meaning upon it. Meaning itself is a property of sentences. Sentences in turn are meaningful by virtue of their place within wider vocabularies. Descriptions are functions of social needs. So 'nature' and 'reality' themselves are strictly beyond the scope of our description, and not, in themselves, productive to pursue. As we recognize that there is no social benefit to be had from such pursuit, the value of such questions as 'But what *is* reality, really?' will gradually, costlessly, fade away until we wonder why we ever got itchy about them in the first place. As one commentator has helpfully put it: it is not that Rorty is saying that 'there is no such thing as the outside world', but rather that 'the question "Does this description of the outside world accurately correspond to what it describes?" is one which we may want to stop asking'.¹¹³ Truth is not a relation between reality and something else. It is a compliment we pay to descriptions of the world which deliver fruitful side-effects in terms of our current stock of social priorities.

It is important that Rorty seeks to avoid the charge – levelled often enough at over-enthusiastic pursuers of a 'linguistic turn' – that the relativity of knowledge to description means that objects become artefacts of language. He denies that he is proffering the sort of linguistic idealism which would have it that there were no objects before language came along, or that the world is simply the way we say it is, a *product* or *effect* of our descriptions.[114] In the textbook example of a wholesale subjective idealism, Berkeley famously concluded: *esse* is *percipi* or *percipere*; 'to exist is to be perceived, or to perceive'.[115] Linguistic idealism might be stated as the belief that 'to exist is to be described'. And the kneejerk reaction to it tends to mirror a certain typical response to Berkeley: isn't it a wild extravagance to say that language itself *creates* the external, material world, or that, indeed, it *is* the only reality of which we can rightfully speak? Rorty's defence against the charge of linguistic idealism rests on the basic case that any such position must rest on the scheme–content distinction. That is to say, it must assume that there could be some kind of relationship of 'fit' or 'representation' between our language, on the one hand, and the world it describes on the other.

To avoid that unhelpful picture, Rorty suggests that we would be better to distinguish between what it takes for the world to be *causally* independent of us, and what it takes for it to be *representationally* independent. Many features of the objective world exist before we describe them in the ways we do. Once we've identified that there's a world, or described something as a dinosaur, it is clear that certain of its attributes – the depth of the oceans, or a dinosaur's skin colour, or its sex life – are causally independent of it having been described in any particular way. But one's descriptions do not somehow pick out, or represent, prior-existing properties: before we describe the dinosaur as a dinosaur, or whatever else, 'there is no sense to the claim that it is "out there" having properties'. For such a claim leads the claimer inexorably into the arms of the process description through which the identification of what is 'causally independent' will inevitably take place: '*What* is out there? The thing-in-itself? The world? Tell us more. Describe it in more detail. Once you have done so, but only then, are we in a position to tell you which of its features are causally independent of having been so described and which are not.'[116] So there is nothing describable about dinosaurs independently of our descriptions of them. To assume that there is is to fall back into the tired-out distinctions between appearance and reality, or content and scheme, which have provided an unbridgeable gap between our descriptions and the 'way the world is'.

It is certainly questionable, though, that Rorty escapes the clutches of those distinctions. Indeed, I would argue that he fails to evade linguistic idealism in a (more or less) Berkeleyan sense. To show why, it is worth returning to Rorty's objections in *PMN* to the reduction of metaphysics to epistemology. This, says Rorty, confines us to a whole raft of circularity problems which emerge once we try to find a way in which our ideas are adequate to the world. Berkeley's insistence that we 'cannot stand outside our own skins', that ideas can resemble only other ideas, rather than externally existing objects, would be a case in point. For this is generated solely from the initial presumption that we must start with a privileged inward gaze in order to guarantee the existence of external objects. Berkeley claims to show that we cannot succeed in so doing, and thus seeks to avoid altogether questions about the relation between experience and an independent reality.

But note that the tenor of Berkeley's case bears strong similarities to Rorty's own. Rorty insists that the problem of scepticism is the product of the appearance–reality distinction: no distinction, no problem about how we might prove that our knowledge pertains to some externally existing reality. This is precisely the tack which Berkeley takes in his *Three Dialogues between Hylas and Philonous*, where he relentlessly employs the 'ideas relate only to ideas' argument through Philonous, who declares at one point: 'You are therefore forced by your principles to deny the reality of sensible things, since you made it to consist in an absolute existence exterior to the mind. That is to say, you are a downright sceptic.'[117] For Berkeley, we are stuck within a sort of prison-house of ideas.[118] Now Rorty, of course, replaces this appeal to experience with an appeal to language. On these lines, as we have seen, the linguistic equivalent of what is, after all, the most comprehensive of idealisms would insist that there is no way of describing a pre-human world except by reference to descriptions in language. Thus, descriptions relate only to descriptions. And because there is no such thing as pre-linguistic consciousness, there can be no such thing as consciousness of non-described (or non-linguistic) objects.

And this, it seems, is *precisely* what Rorty argues. Remember that 'empty realism', in Jessop's formulation, requires that entities in the real world remain inaccessible abstractions until under a description. Thus, 'we can say nothing meaningful about the nature of entities apart from the fact that they exist'.[119] This fits Rorty's line clearly enough, as exemplified in his claim that 'causation is not under a decription, but explanation is'. Since explanation plays by culturally created rules, our understanding is triggered, but not thereafter affected or constrained, by the existence of 'brute physical resistance'.[120] But what, in fact, is the 'difference that makes a difference' between this and the Berkeleyan position? Berkeley, after all, does not argue that rocks do not actually *exist* – only that the condition of their actual existence is that ideas of a certain shape, colour and so on occur in someone's mind. They do not exist independently of our experience. Berkeley thus straightforwardly reduces ontology to epistemology, in a manner Rorty should (by his own lights) be duly critical of. It is because we only have recourse to ideas that we cannot in fact demonstrate the existence of things independently of those ideas.

Now Rorty claims to depart decisively from this line of argument by collapsing the gap between ideas – or descriptions – and the world with which everything is related in causal relations. Thus the world cannot be reduced to language, precisely because language is not 'interposed, like a cushion, between us and the world', and so fit to soak up all ontological significance. But consider the argument which Rorty uses against the claim that the world has determinacy apart from our descriptions. Its standard form is this: 'The world does not speak. Only we do. The world can, once we have programmed ourselves with a language, cause us to hold beliefs. But it cannot propose a language for us to speak. Only other human beings can do that.'[121] The world 'well lost' for Rorty is thus an anthropocentrically considered world: the world as interlocutor.

But any notion that the world need be an interlocutor in order to have determinate aspects rests entirely on the assumption that language is the source of determinacy. It thus rests precisely on the Berkeleyan case that all that we can be conscious of through ideas is other ideas. But this begs the question: whoever did think that the world *has ideas*? Or that it *speaks*? Or that 'a vocabulary is somehow already out there in the world' – the words which nature itself speaks?[122] Denying such notions does not exactly induce an arresting judder, even amongst the 'commonsense realists' whom Rorty takes most of us to be.[123]

Significantly, a similar device has been used by Nelson Goodman in support of his own, more explicitly Berkeleyan case. Famously, Goodman argues that not just constellations, but stars themselves are constructed through human labelling. Goodman suggests that the answer to the question 'What makes the stars "stars"?' is 'a particular version of things'. And the answer to the question 'What then makes a particular version right?' will itself be version-dependent.[124] We can, then, say that 'every right version is a world'.[125] As he puts it, the idea that descriptions might mirror the world suggests that 'before describing the world in English we ought to determine whether it is written in English, and that we ought to examine very carefully how the world is spelled'.[126] But again: all the realist needs, at base level, in order to disrupt the idealist case is to insist that the world exists independently of how we happen to describe it – not that the world must be 'like a language' for this claim to be sustainable. Rorty's own case seems to hinge on the claim that for any sort of realism to be conceivable, the world must *tell us* what to think. But in so arguing he has *already granted* the linguistic idealist thesis that language is the fundamental nature of reality. He has adopted discourse foundationalism – or, perhaps more accurately, linguistic monism.[127] He has made a metaphysical claim. From this, it follows that 'merely' causing us to have beliefs is no form of determinate causation at all.

Similarly, again, Rorty uses a Berkeleyan appeal to our actual experience as language users in order to 'demonstrate' a possible means of escape from the idealist circle. Take his example of describing dinosaurs. Dinosaurs exist, as Berkeley would happily agree. But for Rorty they do not exist 'out there', in a world beyond description, *until we have described them*. This rings slightly hollow, considering that Rorty has already denied doubting that 'most things in the universe are causally independent of us'. But that they exist prior to our description of them is presented as a neutral, empty form of existence – a special sort of existence applying only to the undescribed. As soon as dinosaurs are identified as having existed, they become part of the meaningful universe. Thus our very description of their having existed pre-discursively brings them from an empty vertical relation into a full horizontal relation. But again, it is tricky to discern any important distinction between this and the Berkeleyan position, which (appeals to God notwithstanding) seems horizontal in much the same way. Both reduce to what – if we have licence to call it so in Rorty's case – amounts to an *epistemological* manoeuvre. There is nowhere we can go to show that we know dinosaurs *not* as an idea/under a description. Certainly, Rorty would have to agree that the world *as we make sense of it through language* is thus an effect of our – or previous – descriptions. For a condition of our being able to make sense of it is its describability (we do not know the world except under descriptions). Ontology, or its equivalent, is meaningless apart from epistemology, or its equivalent. Matter is collapsed into discourse with no *practical* remainder, no excess.

And of course this mirrors, at a distance, the pernicious collapse of ontology into epistemology which Rorty regards as stemming from the unhealthy influence of the 'idea idea'. Remember that Rorty's objection there was to the claim that ideas were 'immediate', an epistemological starting point somehow given in experience. Berkeley's *tour de force*, on these terms, was to secure idea–world relationships at a stroke, by reducing the world to our perception of it. This is not to deny the world's existence, of course: just to explain our grasp of its existence by way of an inflation of the idea to the extent that it was the underlying guarantor of the existence of reality. The terms in Rorty's account have changed, but the upshot is much the same. Its effect is to render it impossible – as with Berkeley's solution to the problem of how to bridge idea and world – for our descriptions to be *in*adequate to their object. This is because they themselves bring into being the only meaningful sense in which we can know the object in the first place. There can be no ontological discrepancy. Thus the appearance–reality distinction is not *dissolved*, but *resolved*, as in Berkeley, by a reduction of reality into its appearance. Rorty cannot sustain the object which is under a description in separation from its decription. 'We are not', as he himself puts it, 'talking about the same thing if we say different things about it.'[128] Object, as it were, is dissolved into subject, and subject – in turn – into language or descriptive 'vocabulary'.[129]

Unless it isn't. It might be the case that Rorty's shadowy dualism between the world under causation and the free, decisionistic realm of description is not just shadowy, but a *genuine* dualism. A sort of reversal, in fact, of Kant's distinction of the phenomenal, determined world, and the noumenal world, beyond the reach of science, which allows for human agency. This would entail, of course, that his own description of the necessity of causality is itself not an optional, but a privileged description, revealing something that is 'really' the case about causation.

We will have to ignore, here, Rorty's claim, when discussing dinosaurs, that independent causality is *itself* a product of description. We might concentrate instead on those passages where he says things like: the claim that reality exists independently of human beings is trivial, but true; on the other hand, the claim that reality might be described in terms which have nothing to do with human beings is incoherent.[130] On these terms Rorty might indeed be invoking some sort of distinction between a world of appearances and a determinate reality beyond those appearances, to which our descriptions can never adhere. Thus in one evasion of the charge of linguistic idealism Rorty presents the pragmatist as rejoining that

> her position has nothing in common with idealism save the acknowledgement that inquiry does not consist in confrontation between beliefs and objects, but rather in the quest for a coherent set of beliefs... For she believes, as strongly as does any realist, that there are objects which are *causally* independent of human beliefs and desires'.[131]

We might read Rorty as *trying* to collapse the ontological into the epistemological, but actually failing, since his empty realism is rather less empty than he wants to admit.

To pursue this point, consider his objection to those 'textualist' thinkers, such as Derrida and Foucault, whose position entails what for him is a regrettable antihumanism: 'the substitution of inhuman intertextuality for human influence', after which 'language is a phenomenon which cannot be subsumed under the concept "man"'.[132] Perhaps here we see the covert reintroduction of a distinction between subject and object in order to preserve human agency in the form of *being a language-user*. This would explain how he can speak so readily of language being a 'tool', as 'marks and noises used to achieve purposes'. For this to be the case, it must surely come between subjectivity and objectivity, must be able to be picked up and used by one side of this divide in 'coping with' the other. (As we'll see in 2.2, this hidden dimension resurfaces, and causes complications, in Rorty's account of selfhood, which depends on the claim that we remodel ourselves by using language.) Perhaps, in sum, there are two levels: a lower-order level at which everything is mechanistically determined, and a higher level – the level of human privilege – at which our access to this lower level is always under a description.

But in this case, Rorty's story falls into another problem: put roughly, the existential gap. Perhaps like Sartre, in emphasiszing the 'nausea' encountered by the radically free subject in discovering a causally determined world beyond the unconstrained, free realm in which we choose our own values and orientations, Rorty is pointing to a fundamental gap which cannot be reconciled.[133] In Rortian terms, there is a world of 'real' causality which nonetheless, from the point of view of the language user, can be described equally well in mutually incompatible ways: as 'nothing but texts', just as accurately as 'nothing but matter in motion'.[134] Perhaps this world — the world of the determinate — is utterly resistant to, or beyond, any description we might give of it, such that they all simply rebound off its surface. Perhaps this is what he means when he claims that 'the world does not speak': the world of discourse, or conversation, swings free of the lower-level world of determinate causation. Hence, our projects are constrained only by that which our community allows, not by any responsibility to the world of causality beyond our description.

There is something, indeed, in this alternative account of Rorty's (if one might so call it) 'metaphysics'. For his appeal to causality does seem to run clean against the grain of Rorty's preference for the horizontal over the vertical (by positing a determinate world 'beneath' the indeterminacy of description), and seems, in his idealistic moments, to disappear almost as soon as it is invoked. His claim that there is a *definite* 'causal relation between the brute physical resistance or pressure and us', that causal forces 'print little replicas on our retinas' which we, unconstrainedly, then decide how to describe, does seem to posit two separate orders, the determinate and the indeterminate. But in this case, the existential gap intrudes to complicate the picture in a way avoided by the cosier, idealist picture given earlier. For Rorty has to explain how we can be free to unconstrainedly describe and re-describe our causally determined lower order environment while still being in hock to that causal determination as it impinges on us. Put differently, how can our radically free descriptions have any effect on an order of 'brute' reality already sufficiently determined by antecedent causes (the causes which 'print little replicas on our retinas')?[135]

In fact, though, I find it hard to see how Rorty, even while (some of the time, at least) maintaining something like this position, might actually *sustain* it with any degree of plausibility. In the end, the base-level determinate causality to which he refers in order to avoid the charge of linguistic idealism drops out of the picture in favour of an alternative claim: that the printing of little replicas on our retinas holds no determinate function at all. For as soon as Rorty claims, as he does, that 'the same causal relationships could be explained in many different ways, as many as there are ways of describing the things related', it becomes very difficult to see how those same causal relationships could not simply be redecribed as something different: 'non-causal relationships', for want of a more imaginative alternative. *Why* need we understand them as causal relationships, when the object of our understanding is always under an optional description, and when *nothing* is found rather than discursively made? And how might we understand the appeal to neutral, empty, base-level causality *except* as a claim about the language (as Rorty will call it) which nature itself speaks? Is this not how they would prefer to be described? Why need it hold, be such as can be relied upon, be the very replacement for the scheme–content distinction in making sense of our linguistic interaction with our environment, *unless* it is a 'real' aspect of a reality with which we are in touch? Why is it that 'the blank has no choice' about being at the receiving end of 'unmediated causal forces'? Those causal forces themselves are under a description. If they are not infinitely redescribable, and so changeable, then there is, somewhere down there, and at least in this minimal, empty aspect, a 'way the world is'.

## *'Identity-thinking' at a distance?*

The question, then, is how much of a residue Rorty's merging of the ontological into the epistemological (or into discourse) leaves behind in the way of a real world beyond the indeterminate play of discourse. If it is indeed nothing, then he is a linguistic idealist. If it is something, he is a sort of dualist. But in either case, he remains at most an *empty* realist, precisely for the reason that he cannot account for there being effects of the determinate world on our descriptions of it. Nor for our descriptions of the world having the effect on it – in creating dinosaurs as objects of our understanding – which he requires. Whether he rehearses Berkeleyan idealism, or a Cartesian–Sartrean dualism, he cannot in either case maintain *both* his appeal to 'brute causality' *and* his appeal to our capacity endlessly to redescribe that causality in terms unaffected by it. Either the ontological is simply merged into the epistemological, or the gap between them is so great that it is difficult to conceive of how it might be bridged – with or without a scheme–content distinction. To respond that this objection itself simply assumes the *appearance–reality* distinction would just highlight all the more Rorty's apparent inability to escape the terms he claims it has bequeathed – and more importantly, to provide a self-consistent remedy for the itches which those claims have induced.

Now it seems to me that we come full circle, here, back to the terms of the debate between Horkheimer and Adorno and the first-generation pragmatists. The charge as stated was that pragmatism reduces truth, and reality, to what is functionally useful in the interests of a given socio-historical configuration of interests. Rorty would claim to have evaded this charge by scrapping the scheme–content distinction, and along with it the idea that 'reality' might be reduced to anything vertically severed from it. If, in 'our' horizontal interactions with 'reality', either ourselves or it get changed in the process, this is not the result of a prioritization of one over the other, but *simply* of causal interaction.

We have seen, though, that Rorty, in order to sustain the claim that subjects are not simply determined by their enmeshedness with this world of blind cause and effect, must invoke access to a privileged realm of freedom. This is the freedom which derives from being a language user. Since language is a neutral tool, without a nature until it is used for a particular purpose, language users can describe and redescribe themselves and the world around them *unconstrainedly*. This is the Sartrean aspect of Rorty's thinking. For Sartre, we are utterly unconstrained by an objective world set absurdly, threateningly over against us. This is because consciousness is nothingness, and so out of the clutches of the determinate world. For Rorty, 'nobody was conscious of being conscious before we started talking about "consciousness"'; it is our descriptions which bestow both the human condition, and that of the world.[136] Thus it is our descriptions which take us into the realm of untrammelled contingency: the world which we can – social institutions allowing – 'make' with ultimate freedom, unconstrained by the 'found' world which lacks any 'intentional stubbornness' by which to put up resistance.[137]

Now the force of Adorno's objections to the hypostatizations of pragmatism and positivism is carried through in his wider critique of 'identity thinking'. He takes this to be inherent in idealism's assumption that the idea might be fully adequate or sufficient in its apprehension of the object, such that the object becomes reduced to, or identified with, the subject's knowledge of it. For Adorno there is always some objective, material remainder beyond thought. Idealism relies on exploitation of the fact that, on its own terms, the nonidentical can be defined only as a concept.[138] Hence the force of Berkeley's insistence that an idea can only be related to another idea. On this basis, subjectivity becomes constitutive of objectivity. Adorno's response is that even affirming subjectivity involves an appeal to objectivity: 'Every statement to the effect that subjectivity "is", no matter what or how, includes an objectivity' – if nothing else, the claim that the subject itself exists.[139] Subjectivity *needs* objectivity in order to realize itself. The priority of the subject as itself the absolute legitimizer of objectivity would require that we radically separate subject and object, *à la* Descartes, such that we the subject can be thought of as defining what the object 'is' from a place uncontaminated by its own relation to objectivity. Only on these terms could subjectivity be the *cause* of objectivity, generating it out of nothing, from a point of origin. Matter, in turn, would become a blank upon which the die of consciousness stamps its nature. In so stamping, it consumes it whole.

But this, for Adorno, is idealism's prime conceit: making immediate to consciousness that which is, in fact, never fully subsumable. It tries, but 'fails to absorb entity, which is what objectivity is in essence'.[140] The attempt involves the denial of the fact that 'the object can exist without the subject in a way that the subject can never exist without an object'.[141] If the absorption succeeded, then the need for critical thinking, for a subtler understanding of the object, would be removed, and thinking would (I suppose) be horizontalized: relating only to itself. Carrie Hull gives a helpful summing up of Adorno's argument:

> there will always be something we don't know, but the limit between subject and object, ideas and matter, is not absolute. Neither will it ever disappear . . . We cannot obtain absolute knowledge, nor can we say there will be some things that we will never know anything more about. Room for transformation lies in the awareness that concepts are less than their objects.[142]

It is this room for transformation which positivism denies, by seeking to reduce ontology to what can be proved, and so known, and to render what is beyond verification strictly meaningless. Positivism proceeds on the assumption that the individual sentence can pick out, isolate and absorb the correspondent aspect of objective reality. Rorty, of course, does not. After Quine, the description of reality becomes a horizontal, rather than referential, process. And yet Adorno's objection will apply just as forcefully in the reconceived pragmatist case. Rorty says it would be best to 'think of objectivity as a matter of ability to achieve agreement on whether a particular set of desiderata has or has not been satisfied', and to 'redefine "reality" as what the winners of the game talk about'.[143] Thus the process of horizontal reinterpretation, reassessment and redescription is not endless, as with the 'strong' post-structuralist claim that chains of meaning are in a state of endless referral and slippage. The process is brought to a halt, and constrained, by practice. It is what is asserted, taken up, used and so becomes sedimented and 'normal' which wins out. Thus, as he notes in 1961:

> For Peirce there is potentially a sign behind every sign, and for Wittgenstein there is potentially a language game behind every language game; but both consider these regresses harmless on the pragmatic ground that practice does not require the actualization of these potentialities.[144]

It is assertion, rather than validity, which dictates the terms. In proving useful for a purpose, a description *becomes* right – becomes fully adequate to an object which, true to empty realism, has no 'entity' (in Adorno's terms) in essence. Given that the contestation of descriptions takes place not by (vertical) reference to reality, but only by (horizontal) relation to other descriptions, truth thus becomes reduced to a convention. Redescription becomes what we might call a political process. But Rorty's politics of redescription, as we will see in Chapter 3, is restricted in advance to precisely the sort of stasis, and lack of space for transformation, which Adorno regards as being the most dangerous feature of identity thinking. (This is largely because, since he lacks an adequate conception of politics on which the process of redescription might proceed, that process becomes confined to an affirmation of the status quo.)

So Rorty's position is 'identity thinking at a distance' not because it relies upon the given immediacy of the object to consciousness, but because it relies upon the retroactive absorption of the object by descriptions imposed in contingent practice. He is led to this position, I think, by his *strict* exclusion of the vertical. If dinosaur bones are reduced to our description of them, then the dinosaurs that (he admits) existed can only be *our* dinosaurs, the product of our needs and interests. Put differently: the object becomes coextensive with our concept of it.

In rejecting the appearance–reality distinction, Rorty talks as if both sides are equally unhelpful, and misconceived – dependent on a fake dualism between scheme and content. As I read him, however, he does not dispose of the distinction, but rather lops off one half. This is the case with the range of dualisms he regards as perishing along with the scheme–content distinction. 'Reality' is removed and we are left with (discursively constructed) 'appearance'; 'finding' is removed and we are left with 'making'; 'object' is removed and we are left with language-using subject.[145] In each case, the second term becomes determinate. This is particularly pointed in the case of the relation between decriptions and the world. As Frank Farrell points out, when Rorty has removed the half of the positivist picture which requires that the world provides us with an empirical given, he retains the other half: that we then 'add schemes of linguistic ordering that process the data so as to yield correct predictions about future experiences'.[146] Conceiving 'prediction' in terms of 'enabling us to cope', the second half survives intact. So, as Farrell puts it: 'We have the construction of ways of talking that help us to manage but nothing is given to such ways of talking, from the direction of the world, that constrains how they are to develop.' Thus: 'the world . . . falls into insignificance in favour of the vocabularies themselves'.[147]

On this basis, I would argue that Rorty's position can be understood as historicist (or historicized) positivism. Recall that he defines historicism as 'the doctrine that there is no relation of "closeness of fit" between language and the world: no image of the world projected by language is more or less representative of the way the world really is than any other'.[148] Given his retention of positivism's 'linguistic ordering', we end up with a linguistic ordering of a world which language does not represent. In practice, as I hope to have shown, this leads to a sort of identity thinking at a distance: the distance being temporal, and defined by the amount of time it takes a given practice to cement a given description. In such a scenario 'language' and 'perspectives' and 'contexts' and 'socialization' do indeed, as Rorty says, 'go all the way down'.[149]

### 1.2. Objectivity as intersubjectivity?

If Rorty's positions seem slippery on the *relation* between language and object, it may be that they are firmed up in his consideration of what, specifically, 'objectivity' might mean after the demise of the appearance–reality distinction. The key here, again, is to see the *traditional*, Philosophical appeal to 'objectivity' as equivalent to the appeal to the word of God, or some imagined interlocutor called Nature, which demands that we see it in a certain way before we can set our relations to it aright. It is to install as privileged a voice from outside the horizons of current practice which somehow knows what truth is in advance.

Against those 'realists' who wish to ground solidarity in objectivity, those, with Rorty, who wish to reduce

> objectivity to solidarity – call them 'pragmatists' – do not require either a metaphysics or an epistemology. They view truth as, in William James's phrase, what is good for *us* to believe . . . For pragmatists, the desire for objectivity is not the desire to escape the limitations of one's community, but simply the desire for as much intersubjective agreement as possible, the desire to extend the reference of 'us' as far as we can . . . If we could be moved solely by the desire for solidarity, setting aside the desire for objectivity altogether, then we should think of human progress as making it possible for human beings to do more interesting things and be more interesting people, not as heading towards a place which has somehow been prepared for us in advance.[150]

'Objectivity', then, becomes coextensive with agreement within a given community. Without loss, we can understand our practices as being constrained by, or reliant upon, intersubjectivity rather than a reality beyond discourse. Thus objectivity is 'a matter of ability to achieve agreement on whether a particular set of desiderata has or has not been satisfied'.[151] We can thus have 'knowledge – objective knowledge – without representation, realism, or correspondence'.[152] It is horizontalized, in the specific sense of being made relative to the horizons of the community of describers in which a given truth-claim is made. On these terms, a 'subjective' contribution to the conversation is one which 'bring[s] in considerations which the others think beside the point'.[153]

In *PMN*, Rorty seems happy enough to affirm that 'truth' (which does not feature in the book's extensive index) is strictly relative to conversation (which has a long string of entries). He advises there that we 'settle back into the "relativism" which assumes that the only useful notions of "true" and "real" and "good" are extrapolations from . . . practices and beliefs'.[154] Since then, he has sought to separate out 'true' from 'real' and 'good' in this respect. While the latter two are still *simply* extrapolable from the current state of their intersubjective use, 'truth', by the time of the introduction to *CP*, is not. What he does, instead, is to distinguish truth from justification – or distinguish between truth, in a purely formal sense, and the capacity that certain sentences will have to cash out profitably in a given interpretive community. It is a somewhat tortuous extrication on Rorty's own pragmatist terms, but one he feels compelled to make by the accusation that defining truth as simply relative to an audience goes clean against the very sense of the term. The beliefs of different cultures may conflict. Truth, however couched, cannot be something which conflicts with itself. As he puts it himself: '"true for me but not for you" and "true in my culture but not in yours" are weird, pointless locutions. So is "true then, but not now".' This is because truth is an 'absolute notion': it is pointlessly paradoxical to relativize it to purposes or situations.[155] So in taking on board James's criterion of truth as what is 'good in the way of belief' – and hence justified – we cannot simply be *conflating* truth with justification. Rather, we are saying that justification is the only available *criterion* of truth, and that justification will cash out differently in different contexts. What this means is that truth itself has no cash value when taken apart from practices of justification: that while '"true" is an absolute term, its conditions of application will always be relative'.[156] Hence, unlike justification, we do not know truth when we see it.

One difference between truth and justification, then, is that while the second is *recognizable* and can be aimed at, the first is *unrecognizable*, and cannot be: 'we can never know for sure that a given belief is true, but we can be sure that nobody is presently able to summon up any residual objections to it, that everybody agrees it ought to be held'.[157] Thus while 'justification is relative to time and place, and truth is not', we 'are bound to treat our present views on nature and morals as true, for we know no better'; truth becomes, in practice, 'what ought to be believed'.[158] This is because while 'truth is ahistorical, . . . that is not because truths are made true by ahistorical entities'.[159] It cannot be 'out there – cannot exist independently of the human mind – because sentences cannot so exist, or be out there'; 'only descriptions of the world can be true or false'.[160] So while sentences, as truth-bearers, cannot be said to 'change in their truth-values as time goes by', there is nonetheless 'no quasi-object called Truth, which stays the same for all eternity'.[161] In fact, only someone unfortunately besotted with the scheme–content distinction could assume that true means something different in different societies, since 'only such a person could imagine that there was anything to pick out to which one might make "true" relative'.[162] Given that truth is not the same as justification, then, it is not relative.

This is because truth, being purely formal, has no property which *could* be relative. In calling a sentence 'true' we are not in fact saying that it 'possesses' something substantive, 'truth', which it might not have had. Rather, this is just another way of asserting the sentence. Rorty here endorses Davidson's 'disquotational' view of truth, itself proceeding from Tarski's purely semantic definition. It is neatly summarized by Putnam, using Tarksi's own oft-cited example: '"Snow is white" is true if and only if snow is white, and this is so not because *Snow is white* corresponds to snow being white, whatever that might mean, but because *saying* "'Snow is white' is true" is just saying "Snow is white" in a different way.'[163] This view, says Rorty, helps us 'realize that *the very absoluteness of truth is a good reason for thinking "true" indefinable and for thinking that no theory of the nature of truth is possible*. It is only the relative about which there is nothing to say.'[164] The question of truth is not, then, a substantial one when inspecting a sentence for signs of warranted assertibility. Then, there is nothing to say. The *substantial* question is whether it pays its way by the standards of those with whom we aim to cement our solidarity.

On this basis, Rorty thinks he can justify making the following claim:

> Pragmatists need not deny that true sentences are always true . . . [and] should agree with everybody else that 'Slavery is absolutely wrong' has always been true – even in periods when this sentence would have sounded crazy to everybody concerned, even the slaves . . . All that pragmatists need is the claim that this sentence is not *made* true by something other than the beliefs which we would use to support it.[165]

Truth, duly extricated from convention, can be preserved for the sake of semantic necessity – but not as anything with critical purchase on our current practices, even were we, if asked, to recognize 'Slavery is wrong' as being true. (Quite *how* we recognize this is a question to which I shortly return.)

Does the extrication work? This seems questionable, and for much the same reasons as Rorty's appeals to brute causality seem, on inspection, to be dissolved within the logic of his own linguistic idealism. For what Rorty has to do to preserve a sense of truth is to reduce its vertical dimension – the idea that it might, substantially, stand apart from our practices – into the general sweep of the horizontal. If he is an empty realist, he also subscribes to a self-professedly *empty* view of truth. It has no explanatory power, and exerts no influence on our practices, precisely because it is not available as a goal towards which conversation might be directed. This is why:

> when the secret police come, when the torturers violate the innocent, there is nothing to be said to them of the form 'There is something within you which you are betraying. Though you embody the practices of a totalitarian society which will endure forever, there is something beyond those practices which condemns you.'[166]

It is also why Rorty endorses Sartre's remark:

> Tomorrow, after my death, certain people may decide to establish fascism, and the others may be cowardly or miserable enough to let them get away with it. At that moment, fascism will be the truth of man, and so much the worse for us. In reality, things will be much as man has decided they are.[167]

Fascism *will be the truth of man*: not formally, but concretely. Because we would rather it wasn't, we should shore up our current practices, keep the spirit of free contribution to the conversation alive, and recognize the intrinsic link between democracy and the sort of cooperative inquiry most likely to lead to agreement. All of this will serve to cement an objectivity alternative to fascism.[168] We can preserve 'temporal, contingent, fragile' truthfulness (understood as 'keeping power honest') only by preserving that other fragile prize, 'the freedom to be honest with each other and not be punished for it'.[169] This will, presumably, help stop fascism becoming the truth of man by keeping our justificatory practices (the only criterion by which we can gauge truth) unfascistic. This in turn, presumably, would make *pragmatism* the 'truth of man', in so far as we are licensed to use such a term. In Rorty's sense, though, the 'truth' of this (in a strictly disquotational sense) seems not to be a difference that makes a difference when compared to the 'objectivity' which is constituted by objectivity.

Or maybe it does make a difference. Simon Thompson has argued that the claim about slavery's absolute wrongness can be made consistent, and non-redundant, by amplifying Rorty's distinction between justification and truth, 'so that the belief that is currently best qualified isn't necessarily true, and, contrariwise, there may be no warrant at present for asserting what is in fact a true belief':

> If we restrict our attention to the present time and place, then there is no difference between truth and justification that makes a difference in practice. That is, I can only defend the truth of my proposition by showing

that it is well justified, that I have a warrant for asserting it. But truth isn't *reducible* or *definable by reference* to particular procedures of justification. This becomes clear once we compare other standpoints to our own. If we look back to periods in the past, governed by standards of justification different to our own, then we can say that certain propositions made then [e.g. 'the world is flat' in fourth century BC Athens] were justified but were not true (and others [e.g. 'slavery is evil' in fourth century BC Athens] were true but not justified). Similarly, if we look forward to a future governed by other and better standards of justification, then we can say that certain propositions that we now believe with good reason to be justified will turn out not to have been true.[170]

Thompson presents Rorty's case as a plea for fallibilism: we might always, by our present lights, be wrong. Rather than the disquotational sense, in which 'that's true' is a sort of empty compliment, Thompson presses the *cautionary* use of true which Rorty has also gleaned from Davidson. Rather than flattering, this works negatively, 'in such expressions as "fully justified, but perhaps not true"'.[171] Pressing this home means that we we can 'characterize truth simply in terms of its similarities to and differences from justification'. Thus 'what we mean by "true" is *something which is the case, whether or not it is currently believed, albeit with good reason, to be so*'.[172]

There are, I think, several problems with this defence – more convincing though it is, in many ways, than Rorty's own statement of the issues. One is fairly straightforward. Why *is* 'slavery is wrong' true, for pragmatists? Thompson (following Rorty) seems just to pick a currently, intersubjectively, fairly uncontroversial sentence and hold it up as a belief which isn't just expedient or warranted, but is *really* true. *Really* true means, on his terms, true *not* merely by dint of what present procedures of justification happen to allow. Similarly, why is 'the world is flat' false? Presumably this must at some stage have been *proved*, finally, beyond all reasonable fallibilistic doubt. Otherwise it would be reducible back into those present standards of judgement which would render it merely justified. The question then is: how do we know? Given (for Rorty) our own ethnocentric predicament, what is it that arrives at some given point and bestows upon us the gift of this absolute knowledge? Even as Thompson glosses Rorty's account, it is not at all clear why or how or when we could know the truth when we saw it, or how, when 'looking back', we *know* that certain propositions made in ancient Athens were justified but not true. After all, truth is 'unrecognizable'. The sheer longevity of accepted practices of justification does not, presumably, afford the sort of vision that might enable us to 'see' what was invisible in ancient Greece. Thompson's position (which must crucially depart from Rorty's own, or at least amplify only selected aspects of it) does not seem to be able to explain how, even after hundreds of years of thinking that the world is spherical, we know that it isn't flat.

The second snag is this. Truth for Rorty does not refer, is not substantial, has no explanatory power and is indefinable. And yet Thompson's interpretation has it that the truth is borne out through experience. At least, that seems the obvious interpretation of the claim that what is justified now may well 'turn out not to have been true'. Doubtless this is right, and important. But he cannot, here, presumably, mean 'true in virtue of a world independent of our descriptions', since for Rorty there *is* no world independent of our descriptions. It cannot be true in any sense that would require the ascription of a *prior* veracity, such that truth is a destination that 'has somehow been prepared for us in advance'. So it will be true in the only available sense in which truth can be substantiated or cashed out: by the consonance of a sentence with the current tenor of justified warrantability.

Now given that such standards are affirmedly ethnocentric – what is 'good for us to believe', what those with whom we feel a sense of solidarity might be able intersubjectively to agree on, and so forth – at what stage do we get the sort of agreement which would secure the status of a sentence as 'eternally true'? Perhaps when our sense of solidarity is global? This cannot be right. Given that the horizontal is always a matter of degree – and that this is precisely why Rorty has to extricate truth, since truth cannot consistently be defined in terms of degrees – there seems no access to the sort of final comprehensiveness of perspective which might award 'truth' to a given candidate sentence.

What I'm getting at here is that it is precisely the point of Rorty's formulation of truth that it is absolute, has no utility, does not arise from the 'way the world is' and is unrecognizable. These attributes do not (unsurprisingly) neatly apply to the various examples so far given. That the sentence 'slavery is wrong' has had utility in changing social practices must, for Rorty, have *nothing* to do with the absolute rightness which he confers upon it. Similarly, the utility of 'the world is spherical' must have only a *purely* incidental relation to the fact that it names a property of the world as it is independent of our description of it (which, of course, for Rorty it doesn't).

But there is a deeper point here. For as Thompson presents it, fallibilism consists in the willingness to accept that 'since better standards of justification may come along in the future, our presently well-justified propositions may turn out not to be true'.[173] The trouble is, fallibilism itself must imply a strong objectivism to the extent that we might always be wrong about the way things 'really' are. It is the 'coming along' which confuses here. If it suggests a contingency and unpredictability about changes of vocabulary, then that seems consistent enough with Rorty's wider picture. But in what form will standards 'come along' such that we will, on their basis, recognize our previous beliefs to be false? Presumably, we will recognize them because the stakes will change, and what we accept as intersubjectively warranted will evolve in various ways. But how, on Rorty's terms, could this reveal our previous beliefs to be false? Only, I think, in the sense of subjectivity quoted earlier: in the sense that they prove to be 'beside the point' of the conversation as that stage of its development. Now this is a sense of 'false' perfectly consistent with the correlate sense of true, as (simply) what we currently regard as being good for us to believe – in the sense that fascism may become tomorrow's 'truth of man'. But this sense of 'false' is in no way the corollary of 'true' as 'ahistorical' which Rorty wants to abstract, and so to neutralize. Nothing, it seems to me, could be 'ahistorically' false on pragmatist terms. And this, precisely, is what keeps Rorty's formal version of 'truth' empty, and means that Thompson's assistance of his case is beside the (Rortian) point. For Rorty, truth does not intrude on, or inform, practice. Therefore it is utterly irrelevant, in a deep sense, to our practices that 'slavery is wrong' is so absolutely, ahistorically right.

So it seems that extricating truth from 'mere justification' does not, in fact, inform an understanding of the 'real-life' affirmation of solidarity and agreement as Rorty otherwise presents it. And so it becomes difficult to discern why Rorty has distanced himself from his earlier injunction to 'settle back into "relativism"'. In reslanting his truth-talk in *CP*, Rorty contrasts his own use of truth as a compliment, an approbative term, with the view he attributes to the Platonist: 'There is truth-or-falsity about _____, regardless of the state of our knowledge or the availability of procedures for inquiry'.[174] Truth as disquotational is not, then, truth *about* something. As soon as it is ascribed to something with substantial import, it becomes a tool, and so incorporated into the justificatory practices from which ahistorical truth remains distinct. That is how 'truth' gains its critical force, and a causal power: by not being 'truth'. Thus while 'if a proposition is true, it is true in all possible contexts', that too is just one more reminder of our finitude – of the fact that 'we shall never know all about all possible contexts, and therefore may always be wrong in our attribution of truth to propositions'.[175]

Thus if truth, as Rorty contends, cannot be incremental, bitty, relative or achieved in degrees, then objectivity-as-intersubjectivity has no relation to truth. The work of piecemeal redescription does, though, relate to understanding: 'the more descriptions that are available, and the more integration between these descriptions, the better is our understanding of the object identified by any of those descriptions'.[176] We can conclude, then, that understanding has nothing to do with truth: that it can rub along quite well enough with descriptions of the object (perhaps the fascist's, perhaps the proponent of slavery's) which achieve the needs a given community has under its present self-description.[177] Intersubjectivity takes place at a level cleanly removed from the world. Given that the diremption between subjectivity and the world, and the attendant scheme–content distinction, are supposed by Rorty to be the very product of worries about universalism, it is worth reiterating that this retains half the positivist picture: the scheme without the content.

For Rorty, then, the problem of relativism is dissolved by the removal of the world to which our beliefs might be relative. Without it, they can only be relative to each other – an unpernicious form of relativism, for Rorty, since (as we will see in Chapter 3) it requires no commitment to the claim that different justificatory practices are necessarily, immutably, incommensurable. As fabrics, our final vocabularies are always ripe for integration with descriptions arising from other such practices – as long as the goals of the two communities might coincide. For Rorty, in the end, reverts to the view of truth as expediency in meeting the goals of a community, however fuzzily conceived. Thus, 'if the other guys have different beliefs from ours, and if we are trying to accomplish the same goals, then one of us just *has* to be inferior to the other'.[178] Inferior as regards their utility in reaching goals which, as we've seen, will be the product of descriptions which themselves are freely optional.

This solution to relativism – the abnegation of the vertical – seems to me to gain its force from an original misprision. This lies in Rorty's assumption, following Putnam, that the mere entertaining of any form of vertical relation must assume the existence and attainability of a

God's eye view. Putnam presents this as a view of all languages from outside of any given language, or a view of intersubjectivity as if we were not subjects ourselves, from 'outside our own skins'.[179] This allows Rorty to make out that the mere entertaining of a substantial account of truth must presume that the world can 'propose a language for us to speak', and that this is just a hangover from theism.[180] It goes hand in hand with the idea of unsituated mirroring of the world as a whole – the world as it really is, independent of our mirroring faculties. Thus, again, he can endorse Putnam's point that 'Relativism, just as much as Realism, assumes that one can stand within one's language and outside it at the same time.'[181]

But it is the assumption that belief in a reality independent of our descriptions and interests entails a God's eye view that ushers in the denial of such a reality – and with it, the attendant problem of relativism. Yet Rorty does not, in fact, ever show that realism of this kind implies a God's eye view.[182] In his various exchanges with Putnam, he consistently presses home the point that dropping epistemology and metaphysics – the dissolution of the world – enables us to 'move everything over to cultural politics, from claims to knowledge and self-evidence to suggestions about what we should try'.[183] But there's a sort of elision here. *Why* is a reality independent of the sphere of intersubjective warrant the corollary of the idea that we must be God to see it? Such an assertion by-passes the very possibility that realist assumptions of a fairly disenchanted sort are taken for granted in our most mundane activities – not as God's eye viewers, but as makers of cups of tea, or watchers of football, or users of public conveniences. In so doing, we are assuming that the way things are provides grounds for action. Our practices are not cleanly separable, in this sense, from the world in which they (given that we are not God) inevitably take place.

Rorty, though, in saying that there is no difference that makes a difference between objectivity and intersubjectivity, is claiming that our practices can be separable from reality, and understood as unconstrained conversation, *without remainder*. He thus invokes what Terry Eagleton calls the 'tedious bugbear' involved in the claim that without a God's eye view 'we are left with an array of partial perspectives, any one of which is as good as any other' in terms of its relation to 'reality'. This, as Eagleton points out, 'is simply a kind of inverted metaphysics'.[184] It is to claim that culture, or conversation, is not just the fount of all descriptive wisdom, but the fount of reality (in any substantial sense) as well. We shall look further in Chapter 4 at why, for all its influence, this might be a mistaken inversion of the order of priority between practice and language.

Meanwhile it is arguable that Rorty's particular metaphysical inversion entails not a scrapping of the appearance–reality distinction, but its collapse into the first component. Scheme without content, discourse without intrusion by the world, means conversation without (as Farrell puts it) the shadow of a world to make our descriptions, or our understandings, *about* something other than themselves. As Farrell points out, this leads to a realm of (inter)subjectivity characterized by 'the empty running of a syntactic engine', in which conversation becomes 'patterns of noise in a vacuum'.[185] The effect that this has, I would argue, is to take our practices out of practical engagement with the concrete, unless the concrete is considered only as a discursive context. It is to assume that language comes prior to practice, and that it is only by reference to the 'narratives that hold our culture together' that we may 'do our stuff'.

The argument of this chapter has been informed by a 'background' misgiving: that it is the assumption that the mirrorless world is thereby itchless, or frictionless, which is most problematic about Rorty's 'postmetaphysical' perspective. At points in the chapters that follow, we shall see that is not the debunking of Cartesianism which causes the problems. Rather, it is the fact that Rorty does not really leave dualism behind, but tacks the shortcomings of pragmatism onto the saved half of its resilient shell. In the next chapter, we look at Rorty's account of long-term historical vocabulary change: at how one good thing leads to another, and how progress is really a redescriptive affair. Without wanting to pre-empt things, we might see that account, too, as invoking a problematic frictionlessness between language and object – or between descriptions and the concrete, embodied, material practices which one might expect to be the prime focal point in a duly disenchanted world.

## 2 • Redescription, Truth and Progress

In the previous chapter we saw how Rorty seeks to deflate, disenchant and deromanticize language, and so dissolve the gap between language and object. Our descriptions of the world, on this account, constitute (if not the world itself, then at least) the ways in which we interact with it. 'True' descriptions do not mirror the world, or 'represent' it, but rather make it comprehensible, useful, adaptable to human purposes. And so *nothing* resists redescription: 'anything can be made to look good or bad, important or unimportant, useful or useless, by being redescribed'.[1] This chapter extends the case for seeing redescription as the pivotal aspect of Rorty's recent thinking, the mark of its originality, and the source of many of its most problematic aspects.

Part of Rorty's business in *Philosophy and the Mirror of Nature* is to dispel any sort of 'hierarchical distinction between the search for "objective knowledge" and other, less privileged areas of human activity'. In its stead, he proposes a distinction between 'normal discourse' and 'abnormal discourse'. This directly invokes Thomas Kuhn's depiction of progress in the natural sciences, in which 'normal' standards of what counts as a problem or a question, and what counts as a good solution to any such problem, periodically give way – under pressure of accumulated 'abnormal' currents and anomalies – amid a paradigm shift towards another set of widely agreed-upon norms and assumptions.[2] Under normal conditions, says Rorty, 'everybody agrees on how to evaluate everything everybody else says'. Normal discourse, then, is, 'any discourse (scientific, political, theological, or whatever) which embodies agreed-upon criteria for reaching agreement'. Abnormal discourse, being that which lacks such criteria, 'is what happens when someone joins in the discourse who is ignorant of these conventions or who sets them aside'.[3]

Several things follow. One is that 'rationality' or 'correspondence to the way things are' become compliments paid to successful *normal* discourse. To congratulate abnormal discourse on its correspondence to reality would be a mistake: 'like complimenting a judge on his wise decision by giving him a fat lip; it shows a lack of tact'.[4] A second is that discursive progress requires abnormal discourse. Rorty couches this in terms of edification: 'the project of finding, new, better, more interesting, more fruitful ways of speaking'. Edifying discourse, good at being abnormal, invokes the shedding of former normalities by the power of its strangeness.[5] The edifier's nightmare is the freezing over of culture that would result if 'some given vocabulary . . . will deceive [us] into thinking that from now on all disourse could be, or should be, normal discourse'.[6] A third is that, because abnormality depends on a pre-existent normality, edifying discourse can only be reactive: can only perform the function of sending an existing conversation off in new directions. And a fourth is that, on Rorty's reading of the Kuhnian picture of intellectual progress, it applies to *all* fields of discourse, and to all successions of vocabularies. In common, there is no element of 'rational' decision-making (or of Hegelian sublation) engaged in the switch from one vocabulary to another. Thus:

> Europe did not *decide* to accept the idiom of Romantic poetry, or of socialist politics, or of Galilean mechanics. That sort of shift was no more an act of will than it was a result of argument. Rather, Europe gradually lost the habit of using certain words and gradually acquired the habit of using others.[7]

An effect of this conclusion – to raise a point to which we will shortly return – is that, for all its avoidance of Hegelian teleology, Rorty's picture seemingly echoes that of the later Hegel in characterizing the present as simply the best available alternative: Leibniz's 'best of all possible worlds'.[8]

Though it applies across the board of cognitive endeavour, science provides us with the readiest example of the effects of abnormality, precisely because it best provides us with readily isolable habits of discourse which when practised for long enough become firmed up, taken for granted, 'normal'. And then there will be undercurrents – exotic, strange or just difficult to describe in conventional terms – in which the very question of what constitutes 'normal' practice is indeterminate and up for grabs. From such undercurrents come those unpredictable leaps forward which Kuhn calls scientific revolutions and which for Rorty demonstrate two things already alluded to. First, that there are no important differences between science and historiography or literary criticism as regards the ways in which hermeneutic stability is sought and reached. And, secondly, that the cultural pre-eminence of science is to be explained by its utility rather than its having some privileged access to 'the way things really are'. Scientists invent ways of looking at the world which are useful for certain purposes, poets for others. For Rorty, as for Kuhn, the real *work* gets done under normal conditions, in which we are less concerned with the imperative to find newness. The mechanics function most smoothly when we are least interested in finding alternatives. 'In normal physics, normal philosophy, normal moralizing or preaching, one hopes for the normal thrill of just the right piece fitting into just the right slot, with a shuddering resonance which makes verbal commentary superfluous and inappropriate.'[9] But a precondition of this work staying useful is the emergence of revolutionary purveyors of abnormality. And such purveyors are dealing in a sort of literature. Important, groundbreaking physics (and metaphysics) 'has always been "literary" in the sense that it has faced the problem of introducing new jargon and nudging aside the language-games currently in place'.[10]

To put this differently, a precondition of progress in scientific knowledge is the existence of literary invention. If rigour, agreement, rational argument, and so on are the necessary attributes of science which gets things done, they themselves are traceable back to the success of abnormal descriptions which have become normal. This process is one of invention, rather than attention to detail. Latterly, in the wake of *PMN*, Rorty weaves in metaphor as the key to the process – and metaphors as the 'new terms' which facilitate redescription. With a sense of human history as 'the history of successive metaphors' we could see that the making of worlds becomes preliminary to our successful living within them. Duly, we would come to 'see the poet, in the generic sense of the maker of new words, the shaper of new languages, as the vanguard of the species'.[11] But this is not a process of steady inferential incorporation. It is the product of ruptures:

> revolutionary achievements in the arts, in the sciences, and in moral and political thought typically occur when somebody realizes that two or more of our vocabularies are interfering with each other, and proceeds to invent a new vocabulary to replace both. . . . The gradual trial-and-error creation of a new, third, vocabulary – the sort of vocabulary developed by people like Galileo, Hegel, or the later Yeats – is not a discovery about how old vocabularies fit together. That is why it cannot be reached by an inferential process – by starting with premises formulated in the old vocabularies. Such creations are not the result of successfully fitting together pieces of a puzzle. They are not discoveries of a reality behind the appearances, of an

undistorted view of the whole picture with which to replace myopic views of its parts. The proper analogy is with the invention of new tools to take the place of old tools. To come up with such a vocabulary is more like discarding the lever and chock because one has envisaged the pully, or like discarding gesso and tempera because one has now figured out how to size canvas properly.[12]

In what follows I explore the dimensions and implication of this picture of progress – or process, if that sounds less teleologically loaded – by redescription. It is a process in which vocabularies are initiated, are taken up, come to dominate, then outlive their usefulness and die. Rather than a 'rational' process, it is a process by which one description of the rational is replaced by another of greater utility, and so on.

I would argue that what is most problematic about Rorty's account is the delimiting of options to the two alternatives just given – finding pieces for a jigsaw, or the invention of tools – and the commitments Rorty makes in opting for the second. The resultant position represents an uneasy coupling of functional and romantic explanations. This arises from the need to allow both for the solidity of convention as the basis of interpretive stability, *and* for radical non-continuity, originality and newness, in our redescription both of ourselves and of the world. Rorty re-inserts inventiveness within his disenchanted universe by making it an aspect of *performativity*, rather than expressivity or representation. Section 2.1 offers an outline of Rorty's definition of metaphor, and shows the work it does in his account of intellectual and social progress – raising some reservations about its role in that account. Section 2.2 looks at how redescription works on the level of self-creation, and concludes that Rorty's arguments on this score are amongst his least convincing. Comparing his 'non-reductive physicalist' view of selfhood with Judith Butler's model of performative subjectivity, I argue that both of them are guilty of a similar lack of nuance in their treatment of the interrelations of language, reality, agency and materiality.

## 2.1. Expanding logical space: poetry and progress

Rorty wants to dispatch the idea that there are structural constraints – imposed by the structure either of the mind or of the world – on the historical progression between worldviews. The introduction of *metaphor* as 'the growing-point of language', and thus a prime source of changes in belief is crucial to this exercise.[13] It allows the conception of intellectual history as a horizontal process, rather than as the clashing of vertical, veridical claims. Very early on, in a 1961 discussion of Peirce, Rorty pinpoints *analogy* as a source of 'real illumination', especially once we admit that the goal of *complete* illumination would require somehow knowing the criteria for such completeness in advance.[14] In his 1980s work, a fleshed-out conception of *metaphor* takes a central role in the explanation of belief acquisition and vocabulary change.

Ignoring the temptation to search for advance criteria, he suggests, allows us to 'think of language, logical space, and the realm of possibility, as open-ended', which in turn allows us to 'abandon the idea that the aim of thought is the attainment of a God's eye view'.[15] Rorty's picture of discursive progress is one in which worldviews are supplanted for contingent, non-rational reasons. 'You never know,' as he puts it, 'when your favourite necessary truth may not be *aufgehoben* – made obsolete by a new vocabulary, in which it can no longer be stated.'[16] Realms of possibility are structured by nothing more than vocabularies currently in use, and their capacity to disclose a new set of possible worlds for us to explore.[17] The point here, then, is a basic reiteration of the anti-God's eye view, anti-metavocabulary thesis. It is put in basic, indeed rather crude, Darwinian terms: there are no overarching criteria which provide for our choosing to progress to a new, better vocabulary; vocabularies get chosen or discarded because they look better or worse when compared to other vocabularies.[18] To think differently is to appeal to some ahistorical 'beyond' from which to formulate such overarching criteria:

> the image of climbing out of our own minds – to something external from which we can turn and look at them – needs to be replaced. The alternative image is that of our minds gradually growing larger and stronger and more interesting by the addition of new options – new candidates for belief and desire, phrased in new vocabularies. The principal means of such growth . . . is the gradual enlargement of our imagination by the metaphorical use of noises and marks.[19]

Thus, in a break from the Kuhnian story, Rorty is suggesting that we are talking less about *revolutions* between vocabularies than about *evolutions*. The survival of vocabularies is a function of their meeting of given needs and purposes; the enlargement (rather than the transformation) of 'our imagination'. This enlargement is not diagnosable according to any pregiven standard or evaluative viewpoint.

Progress, then, is change in ways of talking.[20] Vocabulary change depends on the arrival of dissonant, unanticipated redescriptions which disrupt the rules of existing ways of understanding the world. None of these changes, or vocabularies, will be final; none will resist being supplanted by the next unpredictable arrival. The rules by which the supplanting will take place are themselves unavailable a priori. If we could know them in advance, we would already have the kind of ultimate handle on logical space which would deny the very possibility of novelty. We cannot delimit the shape of intellectual progress in advance in this way. No vocabulary is complete enough for the job; none offers us the kind of catch-all purchase on reality which would mean that its central tenets could not themselves be thrown into crisis by a future twist in vocabulary. All such twists will by definition seem weird when encountered within the parameters of an existing, entrenched mode of description. The twistiest may seem absurd or insane, as well as wrong. But when it comes to innovation, that's the way of things:

> when Christians began saying 'Love is the only law', and when Copernicus began saying 'The earth goes round the sun', these sentences must have seemed merely 'ways of speaking'. Similarly, the sentences 'history is the history of class struggle' or 'matter can be changed into energy' were, at the first utterance, prima facie false. . . . But when the Christians, the Copernicans, the Marxists, or the physicists had finished redescribing portions of reality in the light of these sentences, we started speaking of these sentences as hypotheses, which might quite possibly be true. In time, each of these sentences became accepted, at least within certain communities of inquiry, as *obviously* true.[21]

Rather than a truth-claim, then, 'The earth goes round the sun' is best understood as a metaphor. Metaphors are thus both closer to home (as tools of routine practical use) and, while at their most powerful, beyond current horizons: 'lots of the expressions used in everyday public problem-solving were, once upon a time, startling metaphors – bits of world-disclosing discourse which nobody, at first, knew how to argue about, or with'.[22] They are the standard vessels of unfamiliarity. Metaphor is 'an essential instrument in the process of reweaving our beliefs and desires; without it, there would be no such thing as a scientific revolution or cultural breakthrough, but merely the process of altering the truth-values of statements formulated in a forever unchanging vocabulary'.[23] On a macro level, Rorty's 'metaphor' is thus itself a metaphor for scientific and cultural change.

A particular model of metaphoricity is being invoked here, which departs at a certain point from its classical counterparts. On the Aristotelian account, metaphor is a kind of deliberate misnaming, through which new meaning is created from old: 'ordinary words convey only what we know already; it is from metaphor that we can best get hold of something fresh'.[24] Viewed this way, metaphor works by juxtaposing the unfamiliar with the familiar to shed light on something up to now obscured. This fits nicely with the tenor of Rorty's affirmation of metaphor's productive powers. But it sharply restricts the nature of that productiveness by returning us to the scheme–content relation, in assuming that metaphor's novelty lies in its freshly directing us to (helping us 'get hold of') already existing aspects of reality.

There is an epistemological issue here too. Traditional models of metaphor assume the relation between the fresh and the ordinary to be something technical: a mechanism inherent in the nature of metaphor itself, underwritten by some sort of set of conditions determining the nature of successful figurative language. In the same way, 'traditional' theories of metaphor work on the assumption that the metaphorical consists in the juxtaposition of two separate and distinct meanings, or the creation of one meaning 'out of' another. Thus the task for any adequate theory of metaphor is to examine the relationship between the metaphorical and literal dimensions of the figurative utterance – to explain how (as in the Greek derivation of the term, *metaphora*) meaning is 'carried over' from one dimension to the other.[25] The main focus here has tended to be on how it is that 'metaphorical meaning' is generated out of the literal, customary meanings of metaphors' component signifiers. On Rorty's view, the mistake here is twofold: to presume in the first place that our understanding of the way metaphors work can be enhanced by viewing those workings as mechanical and formulable, and then to posit a separate something called 'metaphorical meanings' which are generated out of the stable, literal, customary meanings of their component parts. These are mistakes not because there are no such literal meanings, but rather because there is no *meaning* to be identified as metaphorical.

Rorty follows Davidson in suggesting that we understand metaphoricity not in terms of *meaning*, but in terms of *use*. Thus, a metaphor is 'a use of language as yet insufficiently integrated into the language-game to be captured in a dictionary entry'.[26] As such, the distinction between the literal and the metaphorical is not a distinction, or a productive tension, between two sorts of *meaning*, but simply a distinction between familiar and unfamiliar *uses* of language. On these terms, the literal is that which we can accommodate within existing vocabularies, and the metaphorical is that which stimulates us to come up with a fresh vocabulary. Because they are unfamiliar, uncategorized marks and noises, metaphors are ruleless: they are leaps in the dark. They do not have some inbuilt capacity to 'reveal hitherto aspects of the world, or to make clear and definite the nature of the conceptual space we currently find ourselves in. They transform that space.'[27] There is no rigorous system of analogy linking the conventional with the as-yet unthought, or the expected with the unexpected. Surprises, by definition, are not predictable.

But nor, by themselves, do they extend the realm of possibility. Invoking Davidson, Rorty argues that the novelty of metaphors lies not in their meaning, but in their use:[28]

> In his view, tossing a metaphor into a conversation is like suddenly breaking off the conversation long enough to make a face, or pulling a photograph out of your pocket and displaying it, or pointing at a feature of the surroundings, or slapping your interlocutor's face, or kissing him. Tossing a metaphor into a text is like using italics, or illustrations, or odd punctuation or formats. All of these are ways of producing effects on your interlocutor or your reader, but not ways of conveying a message.[29]

We might say that, on the Rorty/Davidson model, metaphoricity is *performative*, in J. L. Austin's sense of the term. Like 'I promise . . .', a performative utterance for Austin is one in the making of which some further act is performed.[30] He contrasts this with *constative* statements which 'describe some state of affairs', purport to state some fact, and so can be true or false.[31] Performatives state by doing. Saying 'I promise' *constitutes* promising: it does not designate something already-existing, but brings my promise into being. The utterance is itself the act. Similarly, 'I name this ship . . .' is not a description of an action, but the action itself.

Pausing here for a moment, it is significant that while Austin begins his account by treating performatives as a sort of aberrant subspecies of constative utterances, he ends up having to reverse the terms, and make constatives a particular instance of performative utterances. This is because as soon as you allow that performatives need not be so explicit as 'I promise' ('I will pay you tomorrow', which sounds like a constative statement, will do just as well), the distinction between the two is fudged and blurred. Thus, 'This desk is brown' might be an abbreviated or roundabout way of saying 'I hereby affirm that this desk is brown' – a performative utterance that accomplishes the act of affirming to which it refers. Hence his subsequent distinction between the 'locutionary' act (the act *of* speaking a sentence), the 'illocutionary' act (the act we perform *by* speaking a sentence), and the 'perlocutionary' act (an act accomplished by performing the illocutionary act). Hence saying 'I promise' is locutionary, promising is illocutionary, and the effect of my promising on my interlocutor is perlocutionary. As Jonathan Culler notes, though, for all the hedgings, the thrust of Austin's insight survives in his highlighting of the 'active, creative functioning of language'.[32]

Thus metaphoricity for Rorty depends not on what the words in question *mean*, but on their *force*, or what they are used to do: the thoughts (or 'tingles')[33] they provoke and the analogies they enable us to construct. Davidson sees no sense in the idea 'that associated with a metaphor is a definite cognitive content that its author wishes to convey and that the interpreter must grasp if he is to get the message'.[34] To presume that there is a conveyed, unpackable message is like attributing to a joke or a dream some statement that with the right interpretation one could restate in ordinary language. It is to miss the point: as Davidson puts it, 'Joke or dream or metaphor can, like a picture or a bump on the head, make us appreciate some fact – but not by standing for, or expressing the fact.'[35]

This 'making us appreciate some fact' is not so much an uncovering of some antecedently existing feature of the world as a creative gesture. As Clive Cazeaux puts the Davidsonian position, 'metaphor is an agency within the world which actually creates *what we think of* as being the world'.[36] In Davidson's example: 'Once upon a time, rivers and bottles did not, as they do now, literally have mouths'.[37] The metaphoricity of these terms on first usage was not indicative of a double meaning: the words just mean what they mean. Rather, it is the product of the jarring effect of the unfamiliar juxtaposition of familiar words. To have a meaning is to have a place in a language game. Metaphors do not: they are unparaphrasable in terms of the existing furniture of a vocabulary. Hence the slap-in-the-face analogy:

If one had wanted to say something – if one had wanted to utter a sentence with a meaning – one would presumably have done so. But instead one thought that one's aim could be better carried out by other means. That one uses familiar words in unfamiliar ways – rather than slaps, kisses, pictures, gestures, or grimaces – does not show that what one said must have a meaning. An attempt to state that meaning would be an attempt to find some familiar (that is, literal) use of words – some sentence which already had a place in the language game – and, to claim that one might just as well have said *that*. But the unparaphrasability of metaphor is just the unsuitability of any such familiar sentence for one's purpose.[38]

There seems to be a difficulty with this account, to which I shall return shortly. It is roughly this: Rorty is claiming here that Copernicus's claim *made no sense* – not that it was strange-sounding, but that it could not be accommodated within the existing vocabulary. Quite how his descriptions *could* be, never mind would be, received by an audience to whom they were meaningless is a question I shall leave for now.

So on Rorty's Davidsonian account metaphors are not definitively *linguistic*, still less semantic, but are a sort of generic vehicle of surprise and dazzle. Because they have no fixed place within a language game, they cannot be subject to rational appraisal, be proved or disproved. When confronted with a metaphor one can only, as Rorty puts it, 'savour it or spit it out'. On this reaction, on the palatability of the metaphor at stake, hinges its whole potential to be something useful, its chances of becoming a candidate for literal truth: 'If it *is* savoured rather than spat out, the sentence may be repeated, bandied about. Then it will gradually acquire a habitual use, a familiar place in the language game. It will be just one more, literally true or literally false, sentence of the language.'[39] The prima facie false becomes, on the condition that it is savoured and not spat out, the literally true. Metaphor is thus the very locus of the meeting (or making) of the new. It is *because* its effect is performative rather than message-bearing that it does the work it does in expanding 'logical space'.

Because metaphors begin their careers outside contemporary cognitive horizons, they enable those horizons to be expanded. As creative gestures, they are aspects of the poetic rather than the cognitive. But it is in losing that poetic charge, in becoming more than 'mere metaphors', that they become compelling enough to be candidates for belief, for literal truth. It is in being literalized, in becoming 'dead' metaphors, that they enlarge logical space.[40] This is, as one would expect, a social process. What smooths the way for some metaphors – 'rivers have mouths', 'all men were created equal', 'diversity should be celebrated not eradicated' – to become dead, and so useful, is a process in which private invention coincides with some wider public need. Your lovingly crafted metaphors will stay socially useless, and so historically neglected – unless their vibrancy happens to chime with, hook up with, strike a chord with currently vibrant social purposes.[41]

We might, though, argue that is in this three-way conjunction of aesthetic invention, the transition to 'deadness' or literalness, and collective needs that Rorty's 'metaphor' metaphor comes unstuck. That is to say, it is the way these three factors intersect and combine which makes trouble for Rorty's deployment of the term. His own depiction of the nature of metaphor means that it cannot do the work he requires of it. In exploring why, it is worth looking first at the very idea of 'dead' metaphor. And at an initial question: if metaphors, while still 'alive', are wholly non-cognitive, then can they really function as the magic, necessary ingredient of successful redescriptions?

*Non-cognitivity?*

When Rorty refers to metaphor as 'a call to change one's language and one's life, rather than a proposal about how to systematize either', he makes (as we have seen) a strong claim about metaphor's non-cognitive status.[42] Until it gains a place in a pattern of justification of belief, a metaphor will be as meaningless, in Rorty's phrase, as 'thunderclaps and birdsongs'.[43]

But again: if metaphors are wholly non-cognitive, it is hard to see how they can function as the necessary ingredient of our descriptions and redescriptions. To put it bluntly: thunderclaps do not describe. Nor do slaps in the face, or, to use Davidson's example, bumps on the head. They are, as Rorty admits, 'mere stimuli, mere evocations'.[44] They might just express something, between interlocutors. Certainly, on Austin's account of performativity, a slap in the face could, against the right backdrop of concrete social contexts and functions (say, at a certain stage in the marriage ceremony), stand for a 'no'. But to make two rather obvious points: first, if they did so express a meaning, they would no longer be meaningless; and secondly, expressing some sort of meaning is not, by itself, to describe. So description (and, one would presume, redescription) must follow only once a metaphor itself has been savoured, and not spat out. Hence spinners of metaphors are not themselves redescribing.

But this suggests that to be redescriptive, metaphorical language must have stopped being metaphorical. Which is odd, on one level, given the association of abnormal (metaphorical) discourse with redescription, and normal discourse with (I suppose) just everyday, 'normal' descriptive work within the parameters of a given language game. To make sense of this, we could put things in terms of a three-stage process. Thus: (1) metaphors strike us somehow (being a thunderclap, slapping us in the face or whatever); (2) we forge redescriptions on the basis of those strikings; and (3) the 'normal' work gets done once those redescriptions have done the job of changing the contours of the language game in which we are operating. But in this case, *redescription* must be cognitive, since it is (to state the obvious) describing.

So let us say redescriptions *are* cognitive – it is just that they arise from non-cognitive beginnings. But at this stage, the analogy between metaphors (made of words) and an out-of-the-blue thunderclap seems to break down. The main problem is that a slap in the face would be the biggest surprise to someone who (let us say) had so far yet to meet another human being. A metaphor cannot be a surprise in this way. It can never be completely new, because, being at least *expressible* in language, it can never arrive from outside all known communicative space. We might say here, with Derrida, that newness arises in terms of 'iterability' – the readiness of any piece of language to be lifted out of the context in which it first appears and 'grafted' into new and different contexts which will render its sense, to this degree, new and different.[45] Thus, the arrival of a metaphor in a new context (or, in Derrida's terms, a new 'interlocking chain in which it is caught or given') will mean – since repetition is always, however slightly, different because the moment and scene have changed – that it takes on a certain sort of 'newness'. But this gives little help to Rorty's case. This is partly (as we shall see shortly) because of his insistence upon the transition from metaphorical 'liveness' to literal 'deadness' as a condition of the utility of metaphors as descriptive tools. But in any case, it leaves his case for the initial meaninglessness of metaphors undone: insofar as metaphors are expressible in language, they cannot be *strictly* meaningless, if by this we understand 'as meaningless as an unforeseen, unsourced bump on the head'.

A related point follows. Let us say, with Rorty, that finding an unclassified something at the bottom of the ocean is a bit like being confronted by a new metaphor because both *give us cause* to interpret things in new ways. Thus, that unclassified something does not *itself* tell us anything, or end up expressing literal truths, but as soon as it encounters a ready-woven set of beliefs it will be explicable somehow, possibly causing us to reconsider those existing beliefs, and look around for analogies.[46] And the point of the analogy with other sorts of surprise is just to emphasize the rulelessness of the redescriptive process: its open-endedness. Hence Rorty's claim that 'How do metaphors work?' is no better a question than 'What is the nature of the unexpected?' or 'How do surprises work?'[47] Perhaps the analogy need only go this far to do its job.[48]

But if indeed the analogy does work to this extent, metaphors *as such* can have no special power to help us express what come to be literal truths. Or to put it the other way around, everything phenomenologically surprising would take on metaphorical status. In other words – again – there is nothing particularly significant about the fact that metaphors, unlike unclassified ocean-bed lumps, happen to come in the form of words. Or else there is, in which case Rorty has to argue that words can be *meaningless* to the extent that found objects can be. And in this case, there seems to be nothing to explain how it is that metaphors, unlike ocean-bed lumps, can come to express literal truth. It is just not obvious why Copernicus's statement that the earth goes round the sun is non-cognitive like a sudden kiss. The statement was certainly a redescription of sorts: a redescription of the relationship between the earth and the sun. But it was not *metaphorical* like a sudden kiss sense, precisely because it was descriptive. It may have been, as Rorty says, prima facie false, to the extent that it did not connect with the fabric of familiar sentences as currently woven for Copernicus's audience. But in order to *be* prima facie false, it must have been making an epistemic claim, must have said something about the world with which its audience could agree or disagree. Sudden kisses are not false. They might be culturally incomprehensible, incendiary, offensive, joy-inducing or morally wrong. They might indeed send one off looking for better interpretive tools with which to make sense of one's recent, sudden-kiss-receiving, experience. But this is not the same as being false. Nor (as it happens) is it the same as being meaningless – at least not in the sense that unclassified things at the bottom of the ocean are meaningless.

Now maybe, again, this is a diversion, since all Rorty seems to need to claim is that metaphors *cause* us to describe things: to be 'perlocutionary', in Austin's sense. As long as the meaningless sound *has the effect of* triggering a useful redescription, it is a success. Cognition, Rorty will say, is not always *re*cognition: one can react creatively to a given meaningless stimulus such that insight is precisely *created* rather than reflected or transferred or revealed. Hence his claim that the relation between events and metaphors (and then metaphors and redescription) is strictly causal, like a sudden kiss, our surprised reaction to it and the *post-hoc* reconsideration of one's relationship to the bus conductor with whom one was talking. But this returns us to the fuzziness of Rorty's use of causality highlighted in section 1.1. If metaphors are causally induced, and then proceed to cause redescriptions, in this kind of determinate, patterned way, then the role of *understanding* becomes muddied, and perhaps occluded.

To elaborate on this: a final point. Redescription can only be a *ruleless* process if there is nothing which directs or constrains the uses to which metaphorical redescriptions are put. The point of Rorty's placing of redescription at the heart of his picture of the progress of human knowledge is to displace the idea that *anything* – the world, or our conceptual apparatus – provides advance parameters for the path which that progress will take. Its course is dictated purely by the utility of the contingently thrown-up metaphors which have marked its path. If they are useful, they are retained. If not, they are not. This helps loosen the grip of an alternative picture: that of a steadily fuller or tighter grasp on 'the way the world is', attained by better and better representations of it afforded by human cognitive activity. But in dislodging this picture, and making progress not rational but affective, or reactive to the experience of contingent novelties, Rorty denies that *reasons* can be involved in the transition from one vocabulary to another. It is impossible within his scheme for a metaphor to work and be wildly *wrong*, since working is the only sort of 'truth' we are going to be able to identify.

To put this differently: Copernicus's sun-and-earth story has worked. It has worked not because it 'reflects' 'reality', but just because it works, in terms of its fit with contingent needs and purposes. A metaphor, on Rorty's terms, cannot be encountered, savoured, successfully utilized and powerful and still be a worse metaphor for cognitive purposes than those which it has supplanted in being taken up.[49] A vocabulary cannot be *worse* than its predecessors. Why not, if there are no preordained rules determining (for instance) the steady progress of humankind towards more and more successful redescriptions? Why not, unless we are prepared to invoke a fairly crude form of teleology in which we proceed along predestinate grooves towards metaphors of greater and greater utility?

To an extent, the Darwinian slant of Rorty's account of vocabulary change does nudge towards such a teleology. To make the history of redescriptions tightly analogous with natural selection, Rorty might freely affirm that the success of vocabularies is directly parallel to the survival of the fittest species. One vocabulary outdescribes another, or entrenches itself more readily, and so vanquishes the alternatives. But pushing the analogy is not, in fact, much help. It simply exacerbates the problem just mentioned: that, since successful 'working' is our only criterion of truth here, the beliefs most widely distributed, or most fashionable, must be the truest. And, well, they are *not*, necessarily. As an obvious, if cheap, example: in contemporary America, opinion polls consistently reveal that a majority of people favour creationism over evolutionary theory as an account of human development. The teaching of Darwin has, in places, been removed from school curricula. Asked which theory is *true*, Darwinian Rorty would have to admit that statistics call the result in favour of creationism. He might object that if we asked the sorts of people whose job it is to consider these things – natural scientists – we would get a different answer. But this would assume – wouldn't it? – that scientists have some sort of privileged conversational role; that by dint of their profession, they offer more reliable comments when asked questions about the origin of species.[50] And Rorty cannot allow this.[51] So in the end he really cannot offer any sort of way of distinguishing how we tell which redescriptions have proved truer than 'it depends who you ask'. And as we saw in 1.2, Rorty isn't happy to reduce truth to outright subjectivism.

I turn now to another problematic aspect of the transition from metaphoricity to literal truth.

### Dead metaphors and the politics of redescription

For Rorty, then, a metaphor, once it becomes part of logical space, ready to be cognitively appropriated and so propositional, duly *dies*.

There is, of course, a pedigree to the Davidson/Rorty account of metaphorical deadness – although it is a problematic one. Nietzsche's depiction of truths lurks here: 'illusions of which one has forgotten that this is what they are – metaphors which are worn out and without sensuous power; coins which have lost their pictures and now matter only as metal, only as coins'.[52] Viewed this way, the transition between metaphoricity and literalness is strictly a temporal or historical (diachronic), rather than a more formally semantic or epistemic (synchronic) affair. Use of 'deadness', rather than fadedness, was, so it is said, coined in Fowler's *Modern English Usage*, which features a scale running from 'stone-dead', via 'dead', 'three-quarters dead', 'half-dead or dormant', to 'live'. The scale signifies the degree to which we are aware of a metaphor's metaphoricity: the more we have forgotten that it is being used instead of a literal alternative, the deader is the metaphor.[53] This seems consonant with Rorty's picture, in which this process, because necessary for metaphors becoming useful, is nothing to mourn. Because 'dying' in this sense is necessary for utility, it is liable to be first step to outright obsolescence as an explanatory tool. As examples of metaphors which have outlived their usefulness, Rorty gives a list including 'the suprasensory world, God, the moral law [and] the authority of reason'.[54] Not all metaphors are dead and useless. The best – like, I suppose, the idea that metaphors might be the trigger for redescriptions – will retain their usefulness, and remain (another one) tools of progress. But whether useful or not, the crux is this: all metaphors that are conventional are dead.

Metaphorical deadness is a puzzle, though, for a string of reasons. One of them is this: that as soon as you pick up an old metaphor and inspect it for signs of deadness, it becomes (in any case) alive again. Or at least, it does insofar as you can appreciate its once-metaphorical status. Take 'rivers have mouths', to use Davidson's own example. If rivers *literally* have mouths now, in the same sense that they have bends and tributaries, then there must be no 'tingle' of metaphoricity involved at all in the mention of the term. But the reason why Davidson uses it is, presumably, precisely because it pulls one up short: like being told that the Latin word *comprehendere* means (literally) 'to grasp', it directs us to an etymological dimension to which we may have become blind or inured. Now it seems to me that as soon as we are so directed, the metaphoricity becomes 'live' again. Otherwise, any once-neologistical description, like 'the sun has risen', would do equally well. It won't. The sun *does* rise, in a way that rivers do not (literally) have mouths. Or if it does not, and each is equally metaphorically charged, then *neither* is dead. Or if both have undergone the transition from metaphoricity to deadness with equal smoothness, then they must both have been equally metaphorical to start with – as indeed must *all* novel uses of language. This curiosity is a symptom of the simple equation of metaphoricity with newness, or unfamiliarity, and literalness with oldness, or familiarity. The sedimentation of mouth-possessing rivers and rising suns into familiar language use deprives us of any means of distinction between the respective qualities of their provenance. And at their first appearance they must, simply, have been equally meaningless to their audience. Equally, anything in conventional language which strikes us as metaphorical just cannot be, since language *as used* is literal.

To leave the point here for now, Rorty's use of metaphor as the index of descriptive change seems drastically short on nuance – and, indeed, to have shorn the term of much of what gives it rhetorical force in his account. For he is simply talking about the transition from (any) unfamiliarity to (any) familiarity. The very comparison depends on our recourse to metaphors which have become literal. Which is just the language we happen to be using. It is a transition which – for all his emphasis on the contingency of descriptive success – is accomplished with a certain sort of *inevitability*, in as much as the index of familiarity is, in the end, simply the passing of time. All of which is a departure from pure contingency in favour of a sort of iron rule: for if we are using language at all, it is, for Rorty, *necessarily* the product of exactly the sort of process he describes. Our decriptive terms can have arrived in no other way.

A further problem follows. Rorty and Davidson's picture must rely on the entire process from meaninglessness to deadness happening on an entirely purposive, deliberate plane. Not only is there no possibility of discrepancy (or indeed correspondence) between redescriptions and the 'way the world is'. Nor is there any possibility that the meanings of terms like 'the earth goes round the sun' are anything other than those which the conventional, consensus definition would affirm – which is to say, what has proved useful. To use another example: 'She has passed away'. As rivers have come to have mouths, then 'passing away' must simply, on this account, have come to have 'dying' as one of its meanings. While 'passing' and 'away' might retain prior meanings in isolation, when combined they deaden down those prior meanings and become a different sort of tool. They must – otherwise there would be exactly that distinction between the prior, literal sense of words, and a metaphorical sense generated from their combination, which the Rorty/Davidson picture sets out to disavow. In other words, it is the transition to deadness itself which secures and guarantees a metaphor's literalization within a given language game. Once its place is indeed secure, it is fitted to the needs and purposes its usefulness for which have been the condition of its literalization. And thus, it becomes 'true'.

Rorty's story, then, cannot account for any residual metaphoricity amongst descriptions which we now accept as true. One can put this differently: that if, as on Nietzsche's terms, truths are dead metaphors ('illusions of which one has forgotten that this is what they are') then we must – I suppose – be residually aware of the metaphoricity of the terms we are savouring or spitting out. But this itself requires a distinction between the literal and metaphorical words we are using, a distinction which we must be able to apprehend. If we are using them, and such a distinction can be had, then to say that all descriptions which have a sensible place within a language game must have passed into literalness is disorientating, to say the least. David Cooper suggests that how one conceives of 'dead metaphors' depends on whether one thinks they are like dead bodies, which are certainly still bodies, or like dead husbands, who are, for better or worse, no longer husbands.[55] On Rorty's terms the latter must apply: metaphors must be transfigured into something else on dying.

But on anyone's terms – and certainly on his – the slow death of metaphors, if death there is, must sometimes be a fairly indeterminate affair. And here is another level of difficulty. To paraphrase a remark of Samuel Wheeler's, while metaphor may slide insensibly over into the literal, it is difficult to imagine that falsity could slide insensibly over into truth.[56] 'The earth goes round the sun' was, after all, 'prima facie false'. It has since made the grade as common sense. Now, as Rorty writes:

> what we call common sense, the body of widely accepted truths, is, just as Heidegger and Nabokov thought, a collection of dead metaphors. Truths are the skeletons which remain after the capacity to arouse the senses, to cause tingles, has been rubbed off by familiarity and long usage. After the scales are rubbed off a butterfly wing, you have transparency, but not beauty – formal structure without sensuous content. Once the freshness wears off the metaphor you have plain, literal, transparent language – the sort of language which is ascribed not to any particular person but to 'common sense' or 'reason' or 'intuition', ideas so clear and distinct you can look right through them.[57]

Leaving aside the jarring anomaly of 'transparency' as something for antirepresentationalists to set their heart on, the point here seems clear enough. If contemporaneously Copernicus was dealing in strange, powerful, beautiful, tasty metaphors, he is now, anachronistically, a speaker of straightforwardly literal truths. His metaphor about the earth and the sun has reached the safety of dictionary-level status, has become tingle-free and non-poetic.

But if 'finding' truths is, at root, a matter of making new metaphors, and such metaphors are something separate from, and temporally prior to, literal truth, there are spanners in the works of the transition. Rorty will not admit that anything other than the quirks of cultural history could account for the long-term credibility of a metaphorical statement. But what exactly has this got to do with 'truth'? The death of a metaphor must on any terms be a less than precisely monitorable drift from novelty to clichédness, or loss of figurative charge. But can 'truth', on any definition, be in the same sense a matter of degree? Can it slide, in the style of Fowler's definition, along a scale from 'stone-false', via 'false', 'three-quarters false', 'still bearing traces of metaphor', 'awaiting the final piece of literalization', to 'true'? Is there, at least roughly, some point at which the 'prima facie false' turns into the 'literally true'?

This depends (again) on what we understand by 'true'. Rorty addresses a dimension of this question in the passages from 'Feminism and pragmatism' already highlighted in 1.2. To requote: 'It was of course *true* in earlier times that women should not have been oppressed, just as it was *true* before Newton said so that gravitational attraction accounted for the movements of the planets'; '"Slavery is absolutely wrong" has *always* been true – even in periods when this sentence would have sounded crazy to everybody concerned'.[58] But as we saw there, this is truth in a strictly empty sense: Rorty will not allow a *substantial* sense of 'true' which avoids collapse into what happens to be justifiable to one's given audience. Not least, this is because, if truths are the 'skeletons' of metaphors remaining after the waning of their unfamiliarity, then it's difficult to see how true sentences have *always* been true. They are the upshot of contingent savourings and utilizations. Bear in mind that 'History is the history of class struggle' did not for Rorty just *seem* to be false on first utterance. It *was* false. The same must duly have applied to Newton's 'Gravity explains the movements of the planets'. Without a categorical distinction between the nature of these sentences' claims (one that Rorty cannot provide, and would not want to) it is hard to see how he could explain this other than by saying: 'the prima facie false becomes the literally true, by which I mean *eternally* true'. Remember that 'warranted assertions' (all assertions being moves within a game, and the warranted ones being 'the ones we normally call true') are 'warranted in as many various ways as there are topics of discourse'. So '2+2 = 4' and 'Sherlock Holmes lived in Baker Street', both being warranted, are true in exactly the same sense.[59] Meanwhile, 'Gravity explains the movements of the planets' has always been true. Does this figure?

Yes and no. Rorty wants to maintain a distinction between the literal and the metaphorical (in terms of use) while depriving 'truth' of any sort of explanatory usefulness other than as a compliment we pay to appropriate or successful decriptions. One benefit of this – if it comes off – is that it neutralizes the threat of infinite, spiralling regress which threatens the Nietzschean model. According to this, however 'firm, canonical, and obligatory' a metaphor becomes, it never quite stops being a metaphor. Hence, truth is (as it were) metaphorical 'all the way down'. The problem for this account is that if truth reveals its own grounding in metaphoricity, then at some point this claim itself has to insist on its own non-metaphorical, literal grounding somewhere *outside* the endless metaphoricity and illusion of truth-speak. In other words, it needs to sneak in a rehashed version of the literal/metaphorical distinction which *isn't* simply temporal and pragmatic. How else do you talk literally about the metaphoricity of all redescription?

One way out of the spiral might be to go with its flow rather than seek any sort of resistance. This, on one reading, is Derrida's quest in 'White mythology', taken as a questioning of the presumption that metaphor is (as he puts it elsewhere) 'a transfer from the sensible to the intelligible'.[60] From this angle, Rorty's mistake lies in his pragmatic delimiting of description's metaphoric charge. 'How', wonders Derrida, in an echo of Rorty's own suspicions of ocularcentrism, 'could a piece of knowledge or a language ever be properly clear or obscure?'[61] Derrida does two things in this piece which unsettle Rorty's cheerfully melioristic account of the transition to literal truth. One is to pursue the line that the very distinction between the literal and the metaphorical is itself irredeemably metaphorical, to the extent that (for instance) any subsequent distinction between 'living' and 'dead' metaphor – itself, of course, rather conspicuously metaphorical – must presuppose some natural or original difference between the literal and the metaphorical. And this itself must duly have arisen from a metaphorical construction, since 'metaphor has been issued from a network of philosophemes which themselves correspond to tropes or figures'.[62] So the 'living'/'dead' distinction must rely on an appeal to some kind of putative escape from its own figurative genesis. In which case, circumscribing metaphor, delimiting it, finding a principle by which to determine when it 'starts' and 'stops', is impossible without forceful exclusion of the metaphorical dimension of this same project – or without the sort of philosophical apparatus required to diagnose and control the very concept of 'metaphor' in the first place. Hence Derrida's characterization of metaphor as 'a history with its sights set on, and within the horizon of, a circular re-appropriation of literal, proper meaning' – and his suggestion that this is a doomed quest given the destabilizingly metaphorical character of the conceptual tools at its disposal.[63]

Rorty's reading of this piece, as it happens, is that it 'shows us what happens once you become obsessed with the idea of the metaphorical–literal distinction, which is something more than a temporary and relative distinction between the familiar and the unfamiliar'.[64] Happy enough – since truth for pragmatists is 'made rather than found' – to relinquish the idea of *original* literal meaning, Rorty presents this as the *outcome* of the redescriptive process. Metaphors, being simply literal sentences used in surprising ways, either stop being surprising, and thus stop being metaphorical, or are left, unused, as a 'cabinet of curiosities' to which we may return if interested but will otherwise leave alone.[65] But even on his own account, he runs into a problem thrown up by Derrida's analysis. His insistence that there is only a diachronic, and never a synchronic, distinction between the literal and metaphorical, means that normality – convention, culture, the history of vocabulary change – itself absorbs and neutralizes metaphorical charge. But it is less than clear that this enables Rorty to avoid the spiralling Nietzschean regress. For it leaves a stubborn niggle: how exactly does metaphor figure in the construction of Rorty's own account of metaphor? Is suggesting that metaphor consists in a distinction between the familiar and the unfamiliar itself a familiar noise or an unfamiliar one? Is it normal discourse or abnormal discourse? What looms here is the sort of 'performative contradiction' which Habermas diagnoses in the work of those post-structuralists who conduct a radical critique of 'the rational' which itself relies upon the tools furnished by the tradition being debunked.[66]

If one reads 'dead metaphor' as equivalent to normal discourse, and 'live metaphor' to abnormal, there is no accounting for the replacement of a given vocabulary save the dwindling of its vitality, or savourability. Two things follow: that successful redescriptions cannot be wrong (or indeed 'right' in anything other than a short-term, performatively efficacious sense), and that their obsolescence cannot be taken as a sign of their deficiency as explanations or the solving of problems. They simply get old, and are nudged aside by newer versions. It is a curious double effect, removing both epistemological and ontological gaps in one gesture. Because a founding aestheticism (the savourability of meaningless metaphors) drives the process, redescription stays governed by the aesthetic. It is, in the end, a process of fashion-ability, in two senses. First, it consists of the refashioning of old vocabularies to fit new (metaphor-induced) insights.[67] And secondly, the acceptance of those refashionings is itself a question of the useful-ness of subscribing to beliefs because they are currently widely held in the fields in which one wants to get ahead.

Given that the analogy with Darwinism does not seem to hold for Rorty's account of vocabulary-change, it might seem that we are left with a fairly straightforward sort of cultural determinism. I return in Chapter 4 to a lurking issue not so far considered: his ruling out of court those sorts of 'avant-garde' redescriptions which seek to 'make all things new at once', and so work revolutionarily rather than evolutionarily. But a cognate issue arises now, too: are, for Rorty, the *only* constraints on what we say and do cultural, or descriptive? This is, in part, the question of human beings' relationship to material constraints. Addressing this question requires exploring, in rather more depth and detail, the relation between redescription and selfhood.

### 2.2. Self-redescription

The 'spectre' of the Cartesian subject, as Slavoj Žižek has depicted it, haunts recent academic discourse, if only in the sense that there is an ongoing competition to be the one finally to kick over its lingering traces.[68] Being constantly reinstated as a punchbag so that it might be pummelled anew from some different angle, it has served all sorts of dialectical purposes, and been the background villain of all sorts of pieces: the colonization of society by the logic of science, masculinist reason, Eurocentric imperialism, and others besides.

Good reasons lie behind the demonizations, whether or not con-sonant with Rorty's own objections in *PMN*. In its treatment in recent philosophy, the Cartesian self has been revealed as a curiously dis-placed figure, cut adrift from the world our knowledge of which it purports to explain. As Charles Taylor presents it, it gains control, and asserts itself, through *disengagement* from the world, and from others. In the process, it gets stuck within the world of its own ideas, and cut off both from the concrete, material world and from other moral agents. It detaches us from the intentional aspect of our experience – that is, what makes it an experience *of* something – and requires that we withdraw into a world not of what we actually experience (a tooth that aches, for example) but to an ontological locus in the mind itself.[69] What Taylor depicts as an unsituated, 'punctual self' – an agency separate from everything merely given in us – has often been presumed to be necessary to explain self-responsibility and free will.[70] But it depends on the maintenance of a strict, problematic substance dualism which, as Elizabeth Grosz has put it, 'three centuries of philosophical thought have attempted to overcome or reconcile'.[71]

Against this backdrop, much of Rorty's thought on selfhood is pushing at an open door. He describes the self as 'a network of beliefs, desires, and emotions with nothing behind it – no substrate behind the attributes'.[72] In so doing, he might be seen as providing a physicalistic alternative to Cartesian dualism – dissolving the mind–body problem simply by removing the realm of consciousness and insisting that everything goes on at the level of physical processes. This would be an accommodation with naturalism, and with the Darwinism with which Rorty strives to hook up his pragmatism. Rorty defines naturalism in different ways at different times. Here is a sample:

> the view that *anything* might have been otherwise, that there can be no conditionless conditions . . . Naturalists believe that all explanation is causal explanation of the actual, and that there's no such thing as a noncausal condition of possibility.[73]

> the claim that there is no occupant of space-time that is not linked in a single web of causal relations to all other occupants; and that any explanation of the behaviour of any such spatio-temporal object must consist in placing that object within that single web.[74]

> a picture of human beings as chance products of evolution . . . [which sees] everything as constituted by its relation to other things, and as having no intrinsic, ineluctable nature. What it is depends on what it is being related to (or, if you like, what it differs from).[75]

Well enough aware that part of the baggage of naturalism might be the sort of reductive physicalism which would allow us to describe human beings *purely* in terms of particle theory, Rorty seeks non-reductive versions of both naturalism and of physicalism. Following on from the second quote above, he describes reductionism in terms of a place where naturalists need not go: an 'insistence that there is not only a single web but a single privileged description of all entities caught in that web'.[76] Thus, against the reductionist, Rorty insists that there is never one, all-commensurating vocabulary which could capture the nature of human beings, just as there isn't such for any other 'occupant of space-time'.

On this basis, he can make the following claim: that 'the human self is created by the use of a vocabulary, rather than being adequately or inadequately expressed in a vocabulary'.[77] It is the juxtaposition of this claim with Rorty's depiction of redescription, and with his empty realism, which I will explore in what follows. In so doing, I pursue a number of points which will receive greater attention in subsequent chapters. First, that Rorty's account of self-redescription tends towards ontological commitments which sit uneasily with his claim that there no properties or attributes which are definitively human. Secondly, that in his discussion of redescription and selfhood a repressed dualism returns to haunt Rorty's thought, one which he resolves very much in the style of Descartes, by retreating to a world of free invention untethered by material constraint. (A third point, latent here but pursued further in 4.2, is that contained within Rorty's formulations above is the possibility of an alternative formulation which admits that relationality is – for want of another term – *in the nature* of human beings. If this isn't a necessary feature of being human, then the claim that 'everything is constituted by its relation to other things' becomes empty itself.)

*Self-creation: whose project?*

A richly indicative switch of terminology takes place between *Philosophy and the Mirror of Nature* and *Contingency, Irony, and Solidarity* as to the hero-figure of the redescriptive process. In the former, it is the 'edifying philosopher': a conversational partner possessed of the 'practical wisdom' required both to engage with the conversation, and 'send it off in new directions'.[78] In the latter it is someone similar, but redescribed: the 'strong poet'. This figure, similarly, shares a Sartrean fear of being pinned down by a final description, and reduced to existing *en soi* rather than as a prospecting and self-liberating *pour soi*. The 'strong poet' is Harold Bloom's alternative to what the earlier Rorty might have described as the 'normal' critic: the figure who seeks and endorses continuities and shorings-up, rather than lurches into the unknown. Poets seek the unfamiliar. For Bloom, poetry since the 1600s has been driven by 'the anxiety of influence': 'each poet's fear that no proper work remains for him to perform'.[79] Driven by this existential unease with settled descriptions, Rorty's strong poet ('the maker of new words, the shaper of new languages') becomes 'the vanguard of the species'. If history is 'the history of successive metaphors', then it is the metaphor makers who make history.[80] But not just at a 'macro' level. For strong poets, being those who feel most deeply the anxiety of influence, will react with due horror at finding *themselves* to be instances of the continuous, to have 'shoved around already coined pieces' rather than having 'impressed one's mark on the language'.[81]

Rorty no longer couches it in these terms, but this fear – the fear that, without having imposed a novel vocabulary, one 'will not really have had an I at all', being merely a rehearsal of some familiar, already-existing type – retains an unacknowledged Sartrean inflection. This is instructive, I think, for Rorty's characterizing of selfhood seems to me to run straight into the problems encountered by the early Sartre's – and in turn, by that of Descartes, whose influence Sartre failed to shed. They rehearse a sort of nineteenth-century dilemma, arising from the twin, but divergent, attractions of Darwinism on the one hand, and Romanticism on the other. Rorty's *via media* consists in a deflation of the Romantic view of a legislating, centred self in favour of a model of causal contingency – as meanwhile he retains the rhetorical resources of the Romantic emphasis on the powers of redescription, of 'making' rather than 'finding'. In the process, back-handedly, he reinstates Sartre's gaps: between self and world, mind and object, self-creation and material world, etc., even while denying any such gaps. In deflating the world in favour of endless redescribability, he cuts the self adrift from the concreteness to which both he and Sartre purport to return us.

This is a big claim, and an odd one, given that Rorty's 'non-reductive physicalism' requires that we regard the self as centreless, and its orientations contingent – and so directly reject the picture on which Descartes and Sartre fall back. According to Rorty, that picture goes something like this. The world by (or in) itself is devoid of moral import. The self is what bestows this. The self consists (as in Kant's account) of some kind of ineffable core which 'has' beliefs and desires, some of them necessary, some of them contingent. Under non-reductive physicalism, any such distinction between Self and World is replaced with 'the distinction between an individual human being (described in both mental and physical terms) and the rest of the universe'. There are causes of the acquisition of beliefs, and reasons for the retention or change of beliefs, but there are no causes for the *truth* of beliefs. This leaves out the idea of (as it were) a constitutive 'inside', commonly called 'consciousness', which refers to the way things look from within the individual human being. Our using language is not a reflection of such consciousness: 'ability to report [their psychological states] is not a matter of "presence to consciousness" but simply of teaching the use of words'.[82]

He goes on:

> once we drop the notion of 'consciousness' there is no harm in continuing to speak of a distinct entity called 'the self' which consists of the mental states of the human being: her beliefs, desires, moods, etc. The important thing is to think of the collection of those things as *being* the self rather than as something which the self *has*. The latter notion is a leftover of the traditional Western temptation to model thinking on vision, and to postulate an 'inner eye' which inspects inner states. For this traditional metaphor, a non-reductive physicalist model substitutes the picture of a network of beliefs and desires which is continually in process of being rewoven (with some old items dropped as new ones are added). This network is not one which is rewoven by an agent distinct from the network – a master weaver, so to speak. Rather, it reweaves itself, in response to stimuli such as the new beliefs acquired when, e.g., doors are opened.[83]

Rorty acknowledges that this picture is 'hard to reconcile with common speech, according to which the "I" is distinct from its beliefs and desires, picks and chooses among them, etc'. But such is life: 'we must think with the learned while continuing to speak with the vulgar'. Just using common speech is not enough to commit oneself to 'the view that there is, after all, such a thing as the "True Self", the inner core of one's being which remains what it is independent of changes in one's beliefs and desires':

There is no more of a center to the self than there is a center to the brain. Just as the neural synapses are in continual interaction with one another, constantly weaving a different configuration of electrical charges, so our beliefs and desires are in continual interaction, redestributing truth-values among statements. Just as the brain is not something that 'has' such synapses, but is simply the agglomeration of them, so the self is not something which 'has' the beliefs and desires, but is simply the network of such beliefs and desires.[84]

I quote these passages at length because I think they give as succinct, direct and cogent an expression of this perspective as exists in Rorty's *oeuvre*. Rorty's denial of centred selfhood recalls, in a 'linguistified' idiom, Hume's futile search for an impression of a unitary, continuous self behind the 'theatre' of passing perceptions which we confront on introspection.[85] While Hume's subject is 'a bundle of perceptions' in a state of 'perpetual flux and movement', Rorty's subject is a shifting network of linguistically mediated beliefs and desires.

The Kantian insistence that the 'I think' – the transcendental self – must accompany all my representations can, Rorty thinks, be (rather strongly) redescribed as a recognition that we never have single, isolated, beliefs or desires; that to have one is to have many; 'that to have a belief or desire is to have one strand in a large web'. It can, I suppose, be reconceived on a horizontal rather than vertical plane: there is no substrate beneath or above those beliefs (or, I suppose, in the strict Kantian sense *before* them, as a condition of their possibility), but just *relations between* beliefs. Thus there is no 'inside', or common human core, which accepts or resists 'external conditioning'.[86] There are simply relations between beliefs and desires – a network which 'is constantly reweaving itself ... not by reference to general criteria (e.g. "rules of meaning" or "moral principles") but in the hit-or-miss way in which cells readjust themselves to meet the pressures of the environment'. Again: a person 'just *is* that network'.[87]

And yet, in another articulation, a schism emerges in Rorty's studiedly anti-dualistic portrayal of selfhood. The tension figures throughout, but it emerges most poignantly when he wonders what happens to agency once we go down this road, 'and begin to think of the self as a self-reweaving, *and thereby self-creating*, web of beliefs and desires'.[88] A basic, immediate question arises. If there is nothing definitive of human nature, no shared attributes, needs or capacities, and no centredness to selfhood, then *what*, or who, is doing the reweaving here? If the strong poet is one who is able to escape the clutches of given, inherited self-descriptions and reconstitute her self anew by way of redescription, then in what sense is this *her* achievement? If 'there is no such thing as getting outside the web which constitutes oneself, looking down upon it and deciding in favour of it in favour of one portion rather than another', then how does *agency* figure in our self-reweaving?[89] In fact, what emerges in Rorty's romantic emphasis on self-creation is a curiously diluted, delimited, detached and disengaged form of autonomy. The process of self-reweaving in search of novelty can indeed – as Richard Shusterman makes the criticism – be seen as 'a form of *non*-autonomy, a bondage to the new and individualistic'.[90] But it also, I think, represents a displaced rehearsal of Cartesianism's requirement that agency is secured by a disaffirmation of the bodily, of other human beings, and of concrete reality.

It does not seem that way, at first glance. If selfhood consists in the strictly reactive, 'hit-or-miss' readjustment to discursive shiftings, it would seem that – whatever its problems at this level – Rorty's account has precisely avoided any sort of dualism between discursivity and the world beyond the self. It seems to be a successful dissolution of the 'gap' between subject and object. But it is precisely because Rorty prizes self-creation as he does that he needs to make space for some kind of inbuilt (or at least potential) capacity in human beings to differentiate themselves from others – to set themselves apart. Hence his claim, as early as *PMN*, that 'man is always free to choose new descriptions (for, among other things, himself'.[91] On his own account, this is because, human beings having access to the tools of language, we alone among species have the capacity to change ourselves through redescription.

But two problems emerge here. One is that – as Norman Geras has extensively argued – Rorty must, to make this claim, slide back into *some* sort of acknowledgement of core human characteristics. It seems a rather curious blind-spot in Rorty's constructions that he does not see this as running against his insistence that there is nothing that is definitively human: that 'socialization, and thus historical circumstance, goes all the way down'.[92] But blind-spot it nonetheless is. As Geras shows, Rorty treats this claim to a series of tacit qualifications until very little of it, in fact, remains.[93] I will return to this point in sections 3.1 and 3.2. For now, it will do to mention a salient aspect of the process of retraction. Geras isolates five stages in the process, from straight denial of any such thing as human nature to (it would seem) straight retraction of that straight denial. But even at the earliest stage, in the bluntest denials, a tension emerges. Take two quotes:

There is no human nature which was once, or still is, in chains. Rather, our species has – ever since it developed language – been making up a nature for itself.[94]

There is nothing to human beings except what has been socialized into them – their ability to use language, and thereby to exchange beliefs and desires with other people.[95]

'Man is always free to choose new descriptions', then, because of a historically contingent capacity to use language – which, presumably, is what sets him apart from ferrets and rocks. But something about this does not hold up. For Rorty's claim to stick, it must be the case that there is nothing about human beings which gives us a potentiality for language which isn't shared by rocks. If there were, then this would become an aspect of a shared human nature. A riposte, I suppose, might be that given the particular history of human beings – compared to that of rocks – we *happen* to have developed language, whereas rocks have not. And that given the nature of language, this has wrenched us apart from other species and objects in a way which has led us to think that we are somehow special, or endowed with something – rationality, or morality – which sets us apart from everything else which exists. We are not thus set apart. It has been pure chance, all along.

But this is not really an answer. Even to have *happened* to develop language, human beings must have had the *potential* to do so. One might insist that this does not separate us from rocks, and that rocks (conceivably) have this potential too – although not, it must be said, with much persuasiveness. At any rate, two fairly simple objections can be made here. First, this would be to concede a shared human potential, even if one shared by rocks. It would be to admit a nature of things of which human nature is a part. And Rorty, of course, cannot allow that there is any such nature to be captured in descriptions (useful as it may be for it to figure in them). Secondly, as Margaret Archer has pointed out, the tacking back to 'potentiality' rather than necessarily existing shared human attributes does not avoid ontological commitments: '*all* of our human properties (e.g. our capacities to walk, to reproduce, to make things manually, to become language speakers) exist only *in potentia*: adverse circumstances can jeopardise every one of them'.[96] To put this differently: Rorty cannot, in fact, take socialization 'all the way down', and make human nature *infinitely* malleable. To do so, he would have to admit that it is a contingent aspect of being human that we need to eat and sleep. He makes this very claim about our capacity for language use, but unconvincingly.

He might be on firmer ground when he claims that there is something distinctively human about the reweaving process of our selfhood which is (for all that) purely contingent. It is a product of the fact that (whether or not rocks could have done this too) we have developed language. Because we have, this makes us malleable. The language we happen to have gained access to means that we cannot return to a state of stable identity, unshaped by socialization. The advent of language changes everything. Even if we (necessarily, in common) merely had the *potential* to use language once, now that our species has developed it there is nothing left in common precisely because of the nature of language. The possibility of redescription renders 'human nature' necessarily elusive. Language, if you like, is a condition of human nature's impossibility. I return to this point below, but in the mean time it is worth observing that it has not necessarily got us that far. We have returned here to a fairly banal, over-familiar and utterly pivotal point: that there must be something 'there' in order for it to be conditioned by redescription. Rocks do not redescribe themselves, nor do they respond to redescriptions with an expanded sense of self.

Paraphrasing Bhaskar, all that Rorty *can* claim is, I think, the following. The social forms in which human nature happens to be manifested will be historically specific and mediated. And the descriptions under which we will (of necessity) be aware of this nature are themselves historically particular, and subject to transformation.[97] This would allow him to emphasize contingency in the sense that the discursive tools available will condition the ways in which we perceive our own being – and that we don't ourselves, except in exceptional cases (when we're 'strong poets', perhaps?), have much control over the tools which are available. But it would not require him to deny that which is a precondition of this first claim: that human beings have the potential capacity to use language as a tool, to forge new descriptions.

Of course, Rorty goes further still in insisting that, self-regardingly, in forging those new descriptions, we effect a *change* of self, create ourselves *anew*, and so move on to what is a *different* identity, or calibration of a network of beliefs and desires. The problem with this, of course, comes as an echo of Kant's objection to Hume's denial of any ongoing, unitary personal identity. For it is not clear at all how we can be inherently endowed with the capacity for self-creation without being inherently endowed with something remarkably proximate to a 'self', in an ongoing and unitary sense. Noticeable in Rorty's characterization of what he calls 'the aesthetic life' or the 'search for self-enlargement' characteristic of good self-redescribers is that, at the same time as denying any unitary basis to the self, it relies upon exactly that.

Consider the way in which Rorty contrasts the 'aesthetic' approach with its 'ascetic', 'purity-seeking' counterpart:

> The desire to purify oneself is the desire to slim down, to peel away everything that is accidental, to will one thing, to intensify, to become a simpler and more transparent being. The desire to enlarge oneself is the desire to embrace more and more possibilities, to be constantly learning, to give oneself over entirely to curiosity, to end by having envisaged all the possibilities of past and future. . . . The principal technique of self-enlargement will be Hegel's: the enrichment of language. One will see the history of both the [human] race and oneself as the development of richer, fuller ways of formulating one's desires and hopes, and thus making those desires and hopes – and thereby oneself – richer and fuller.[98]

Freud, says Rorty, 'allows us to see every human life as a poem . . . as an attempt to clothe itself in its own metaphors'.[99] This evades the lure of purity by helping us see the self as something multiply constituted, populated by a range of decentred voices. But though we may have multiple voices in our Freudian unconscious, they are all, ultimately *ours* – no one else's, and subject to no one else's direct control. The choice as presented – between purity and enlargement – is couched as if these were options for the same self: that we could either seek the anchorage of centredness or the free-wheeling openness of decentredness. Favouring one option must, of course, be a pragmatic move: it is *better* (not truer) to look at yourself this way. Better (in a circular way) because, if self-creation is your aim, self-enlargement is the best way to achieve it. And the best way to achieve self-enlargement is by embracing, and adopting, novel ways of seeing oneself: it is to be able to say, with Nietzsche and Walt Whitman, that the paradigm life is that of the exemplary self-redescriber 'who can say of the relevant portion of the past, "Thus I willed it", because she has found a way to describe that past which the past never knew, and thereby found a self to be which her precursors never knew was possible'.[100]

Now the problem with all of this is that, again, Rorty's vision of self-redescribing poets turning their lives into epic narratives sits too uneasily with his emphasis on the centreless flux of undirected reweaving which he takes to characterize the self. It is not, I think, mere linguistic happenstance that Rorty speaks in singularities and units when presenting the options quoted above. The desire to *purify oneself*, to *enlarge oneself*, to *give oneself over to curiosity*, to see *one's own history* in terms of richer descriptions; all of these imply, indeed require, both a capacity for self-reflection and, a fortiori, a discrete, unified and (most importantly) continuous self which *decides* to purify or enlarge, and carries out the mission. But Rorty provides for no such constancy, and in fact has denied it at the outset. Of course, consistency of argument need be no priority for the decentred, endlessly self-recreating empty locus of experience which Rorty himself, like the rest of us, will on his terms be. But in any case, this is a point at which his rhetoric falters: without a self which is (in some definitive sense) capable of self-enlargement, or indeed self-redescription, the life of self-enlargement is neither an option, nor something which in itself makes any coherent sense. There is no self there to be enlarged. Nor can there be any shape to life's epic poem: for, as Archer notes, this sort of life needs some kind of constant narrative voice in order to hold it together as *a life*, rather than several. 'It neither remains one if the different voices disavow their common anchorage in one and the same human being (in the same body), nor is comprehensible as a story if the various chapters are written in incommensurable vocabularies whose radical novelty defies translation.'[101] Without an aspect of selfhood which can actively aspire to novelty, which can recognize the oldness of its familiar self-descriptions and seek new ones, which can recognize that these new ones *are* new in relation to the existing weave of beliefs and desires, which can forge them into something which feels idiosyncratic and purposive – without all this, how do we account for the process?

*The unlikely spectre of Cartesianism*

It seems that Rorty, in seeking to stake freedom on the capacity to reconstitute the self in terms 'the past never knew', makes two crucial assumptions about the possibility of agency. One is that it must have a crucial link to newness: that, in other words, one would not be self-creating if one used existing lives or languages as the reference-points of our self-description. Redescription here means *novel* description, not just in the sense of difference, but in the sense of originality. It is a sort of post-linguistic turn equivalent to existentialist authenticity: a way of breaking the crust of conventional, received descriptions and forging a self which is distinctively, uniquely 'me'. Thus, like Nietzsche and the early Sartre, Rorty equates autonomy with radical individualism – and agency with floating free of structural constraint.

This is the first point at which his account bears unexpected Cartesian traces. In his objection to the claim that there is a 'substrate behind the attributes', or a centred self, Rorty is directly rejecting the tendency among liberal political philosophers to present subjectivity as something 'nonrelational' and 'swinging free of its environment' in the way required of the 'rational choosers' in Rawls's social contract.[102] As we will consider further in section 3.1, he seeks to displace the idea that liberalism relies upon the sort of 'unencumbered' self rejected by communitarian critics.[103] But despite all this, he employs a fairly straightforward methodological individualism in which there are no structural constraints of any kind on our capacity for private self-creation, our pursuit of self-enlargement. There is, again, 'no "inside", or common human core, which accepts or resists "external conditioning"'.[104] But there are, at start and finish, isolable, atomized, human 'selves' which, in the process of redescription, will with luck become ever more discrete and distinct. Moreover, there are (at least in the official version) no *internal* constraints on this process. Like poems, like works of art, our selves make their own progress, untethered by any essential core.

And yet Rorty's description of linguistic behaviour as tool-using, of language 'as a way of grabbing hold of causal forces and making them do what we want, altering ourselves and our environment to suit our aspirations' suggests that there is a lurking difficulty here.[105] We saw in Chapter 1 that Rorty's claim to have avoided linguistic idealism is difficult to credit unless he is prepared to admit the sort of dualism with which he wants no truck. To make a similar point, again: he resolves the question of the materiality of things – including our own bodily being – precisely by retreating to a world where that materiality cannot intrude. Either vocabularies work on a separate ontological plane from 'material reality', or there really is no such thing. Take, for example, the role of metaphor in self-redescription. This is presented as an entirely individualized affair: the budding redescriber encounters a metaphor, savours it or spits it out, and does or does not find it a useful tool for his purposes. The meaning of the metaphor is defined in terms of its use-value. It is constrained by nothing. In other words, if I *decide* that there is use and purpose and self-enlargement to be had from redescribing myself as having a different gender, or racial origin, or physical stature, or native tongue, or as not suffering from claustrophobia, there is nothing about me – *even* in the case of my physical stature – which stops these being valid redescriptions. This might be 'altering myself to suit my aspirations'. Nothing in the causal forces which have allowed me so to redescribe myself resists the success of the redescription. As a good nominalist, Rorty can hardly say otherwise.

But this lack of resistance is difficult to appreciate. One of the main reasons is that, curiously, it presents things as if redescription were the end of the story: that all that is needed to induce a change in my own self is to say that the change is so. As John Lysaker has put it, Rorty talks as if 'personal transformation is simply a matter of changing the words we use to describe ourselves'.[106] It is as if transformation can happen *purely* at the level of metaphoric self-redescription. It neglects the possibility of the intrusion of institutional, bodily, political, inter-subjective, or – perhaps most damagingly for Rorty – *practical* factors on the success of our own, private, self-creating project. For while it is certainly true that I might be cured of claustrophobia, it is certainly not the case that this could be effected simply by my being informed that there is, in fact, nothing to be scared of in entering an unlit, two-foot-square underground tunnel. I could redescribe the tunnel, myself, and every other relevant factor but still be stuck with a stubborn fear: something which is treatable (one would expect) only by sustained practical adjustment, by repeated experience of not being suffocated in two-foot-square tunnels. But not, in any case (unless I'm very lucky) by redescribing tunnels as jacuzzis.

The voluntarism implied by Rorty's picture of *unconstrained* re-description thus requires a forced neglecting of the body and of the socio-political world. If redescription can replace metaphysics, on this level, it is precisely by circumventing structural and bodily inhibitions on the formation of our own orientation towards the world. This is reached, I think, through two claims: that 'the human self is created by the use of a vocabulary', and that while the real world 'exists', it exists (as we saw in 1.1) only under a description. Given that the choice between descriptions is a free one, ruled only by their utility, and subject to the contingencies of metaphor creation, there is no room here for anything beyond discursive orientations themselves which might constrain the credibility (or morality) of the uses to which they are put. In emphasizing the private, interior ways in which we recreate ourselves, Rorty retreats into a realm where metaphors and vocabularies are simply at our free disposal. They thereby replace Cartesian 'ideas' as the disembodied filter through which we engage with the world. The self is thus 'thinned out' to a point where its relation to the world – and to its own bodily being – is entirely of its own (aesthetic) choosing.

Rorty's drift into linguistic idealism at this point is replicated elsewhere amongst thinkers who similarly, having made a point of rejecting the centred subject of experience, later sneak Cartesianism back in by other means. Sometimes in parallel with Rorty, thinkers of more or less postmodernist hue tend to go through a familiar series of steps. The first is to insist that there is no pre-linguistic self: that vocabularies, or discourses, provide our only access to our own supposed 'interiority'.[107] The second is to claim that because of the workings of language, which cannot be pinned down without slippage to stable, determinate meaning, reflexive access to the self is duly fractured, incoherent and multiple: we are opaque to our own gaze. The third is to claim that this means that everything is constituted by discourse. Thus there is no longer any distinction to be had between the 'given', the 'natural' or the 'pre-discursive' and the 'constructed', the 'cultural' or the 'discursively constituted'. This applies to every aspect of what we might call the 'encumbrances' of our individual identities. Thus the supposedly self-authorizing, autonomous Cartesian subject is dissolved into the chains of discursive relations of which it was supposed to be the initiator. As Jane Flax sums up the case: 'Man is a social, historical or linguistic artifact, ... forever caught in the web of fictive meaning, in chains of signification, in which the subject is merely another position in language.'[108]

The point usually drawn here is, *with* Rorty, that everything 'natural' is in fact contingent, and, departing from Rorty, that discourse is not a tool for our use, but in some sense *creates* us along with everything else. 'Lived experience' is not the possession of some prior individualized self, but a sort of process through which discourse individualizes subjects and bestows an identity which we then tend to mistake for a 'given'. Thus Judith Butler, on gender: 'Gender is not to culture as sex is to nature; gender is also the discursive/cultural means by which "sexed nature" or a "natural sex" is produced and established as "prediscursive", prior to culture, a neutral surface on which culture acts'.[109] Emphasizing the performative aspect of language in this process of creating that which it names, Butler claims that discourse is ontologically productive – and that 'performativity is the vehicle through which ontological effects are established. Performativity is the discursive mode by which ontological effects are installed'.[110]

I raise Butler as an example because her work – unlike Rorty's – has paid direct attention to the implications for our own subjective embodiment arising from a wholehearted taking of the 'linguistic turn'. She has given consistent attention to the question of how it is that our bodies are *linguistically constructed*. This makes the body into something with an ontological status which is very deliberately indeterminate – but not, as Butler insists, something that thereby is any less substantive. She refers to 'the chant of antipostmodernism', which runs: 'if everything is discourse, then is there no reality to bodies? How do we understand the material violence that women suffer?'[111] Butler insists that, while she does not want to deny 'certain kinds of biological differences', she always asks 'under what discursive and institutional conditions do certain biological differences become the salient characteristics of sex'.[112] Butler contends that matter is an effect of power: the body is thus both material *and* a social construction. As well as being material, it is an effect of regulatory norms. We simply cannot imagine the 'impossible scene' of 'a body that has not yet been given social definition'.[113] *Res extensa* is, definitively, discursive.

For all the differences between Rorty's pragmatist view of language and that of orthodox post-structuralism (to which I return in the next chapter), they do, it is arguable, share similar shortcomings in attempting to 'cash out' the status of our own subjectivity after the ontological priority of discourse has been established. In particular, both seem to install the Cartesian picture of subjectivity as the only available option for those who would like to defend any level of centredness to the self, and proceed to conclude that the untenability of Cartesianism means the untenability of the very idea of a centred selfhood. But this hides a manoeuvre by which the argument doubles back on itself to retrieve crucial aspects of the Cartesian picture.

We can see this in the way in which Butler insists that we can only have access to our own embodiment via discourse. The problem here is that positing – as she does in the above passage – 'language' as something which 'enables' (in a pretty unspecific way) violence, to the exclusion of more physical factors, is to fall into two looming traps encountered by much post-structuralist analysis. One is that of inflating 'language' into something suspiciously like God, or a sort of life-giving spirit: the ultimate source of absolutely everything which might otherwise seem to be the result of other contributing factors, including 'material' ones in a fairly mundane sense (the need to eat, or sleep, for instance). The other problem is that, through its great fear of any appeal to 'nature' as somehow inevitably involving a confirmation of the legitimacy of the status quo, post-structuralism drifts into a cultural determinism from which the very idea of constraints imposed by human capacities becomes abhorrently 'essentialistic'. The same goes for all appeals to a material reality beyond the constructions of discourse. However, this makes a crucial mistake, one which rests upon a strangely static definition of 'material reality'. To understand something as 'real', as a material aspect of our lives, is *in no way* necessarily to understand it as 'immutable', or 'unchangeable', or somehow possessing a permanent identity entirely separate from all human activity. And in parallel, arguing that there are constant human attributes need by no means require that these are manifested identically across every culture, historical epoch or situation within society – that those attributes are non-malleable or asocial. Nor need it require that they arrive, unmediated, naked to our gaze and so will always be known under the same, ahistorical description. The assumption seems to lurk behind Butler's analysis that, as Toril Moi has put it, 'if something is not discursively constructed, then it must be natural'. 'Natural' becomes the devil's language because, on this account, 'nature is taken to be immutable, unchanging, fixed, stable, and somehow "essentialist"'.[114] The mistake here is twofold: that whatever is 'real', or not simply discursively constructed, must somehow be fixed and stable; and that whatever is 'constructed' must somehow be easily changed. (This is a point to which I return in Chapter 4.)

The same mistakes, I think, derail Rorty's account of self-creation. Not wanting to admit that there could be anything 'essential' about our being, Rorty swerves in the direction of a denial that there could be anything like material constraints on the way we might be. And similarly, he denies any primary role for the (non-linguistic) experiences of the thinking subject, insisting that 'the enrichment of language' is 'the only way to enrich experience'.[115] But this is to repeat the Cartesian journey in two key respects. One is to assume that to admit that embodiment might have anything intrinsic to do with being human would be somehow to deny the power of language to make things new, by placing a constraint on the scope for our own self-redescription. Yet this leads Rorty to the downright unfeasible conclusion that metaphoric redescription can, by itself, without the intrusion of practice or (indeed) any requirement of veracity, transform one's 'self' in terms of a reweaving of one's previously central beliefs and desires. He ends up there, I suspect, because of a sense that to admit the constitutive role of embodiment in being human would be to collapse things back into a Cartesian physical world: mechanized, and with no space for poets. Yet this presumption avoids the many and deep contributions of twentieth-century phenomenology to the understanding of the role of our embodiment in our dealings with the world.

The other Cartesian echo lies, relatedly, in the Rortian ontological ordering of things. Like Butler, Rorty seems to want to insist that we are in some sense primordially linguistic beings, without actually couching this in terms of an ontological claim.[116] This simply must be the case for his various claims about the centrality of language to self-transformation to hold good. Thus, just as for Descartes ideas are necessary to our being while the bodily is contingent, for Rorty, as for Butler, language becomes the precondition of us being what we happen to be like. This is to fall back on the empty realism discussed in Chapter 1, whereby Rorty relies upon causal relations to hold his story together but makes them relative to a description. This runs parallel to Butler's insistence that it is by discursive or cultural means that 'the natural' is produced and established as 'prediscursive', or prior to culture. The effect of both, I think, is to winch subjectivity and discourse away from a material world which remains sublimely beyond their grasp. It is, in Taylor's terms, to disengage subjectivity from the world, and from others: this is precisely how Rorty's subject, by employing preferred self-descriptions, gains control over the progress of her own life, and renders it an artwork. And just as the Cartesian subject gets stuck within a world of its own ideas, so Rorty's (and Butler's) subject withdraws not into a world of what we 'actually experience' but to an ontological focus on vocabularies themselves. All of which makes them vulnerable to Taylor's charges against the original 'punctual self'.

In the process, Rorty resurrects a sort of dualism – between language and object – which, as we saw in 1.1, he has made it his business to reject. Despite his insistence that there is no order of priority between the two, and that all there is is causal interaction between an organism and its (linguistic) environment, he slides into the assumption that it is the tools of language (as the source of 'consciousness') which enable us to impose ourselves on the world, and on ourselves. The curious upshot of this is that Rorty, pragmatist though he may be, denies the very possibility that practice may be prior to language, that language is an aspect of practice. A possibility not considered is that our self-consciousness arises not as an effect of discourses of self-consciousness, or the contingent success of a description of ourselves, but from our embodied practices in the world. In these terms, we can reject *both* the Cartesian picture of the non-worldly *res cogitans* as being definitive of the human, and its postmodern equivalent, where discourse determines being – or multiple discourses engender a plural (though equally deterministic) experiential flux. We can reintroduce a form of realism which is by no means committed to denying the historicity of knowledge, or to the affirmation of a hypostatized, unchanging reality, or to the claim that the world 'speaks' truths to us rather than their being the properties of sentences.

On the one hand, Rorty wants to insist that culture goes all the way down: that *everything* is altogether a social construct, saturated in discourse, and that the comparison of vocabularies is an entirely *horizontal* process. Thus history is the history of vocabulary change, neither constrained nor weighed down by reference to a non-discursive world. And the process of subjectivity is a matter of the adoption of shifting self-descriptions, again unconstrained by anything 'given' in our experience of selfhood. Yet on the other hand, Rorty needs to generate a solidity and fixity to both these processes, to ground them in a way that can account for the fact that vocabularies have progressed in this way, and not in another. In terms of history as a whole, this requires that he tethers redescription to a process of normalization: the deadening of metaphors, the survival of the fittest (most useful) vocabularies. Thus history is not random flux, and has a sort of pattern: as Jonathan Rée observes, while Rorty scorns the idea that the world can tell us what language games to play, 'he seems willing to let the survival and extinction of vocabularies dictate to us instead'.[117] But the way in which Rorty frames this pattern is such that we cannot have been wrong in adopting metaphors which proved to have utility. And the admission that a determinate force – the logic of the survival of the most useful – dictates the progress of vocabulary change is such as to allow in an extra-discursive factor at the root of the process. Coupled with his reliance on a non-cognitive account of metaphor, this takes Rorty's depiction of intellectual progress to the edge of an outright irrationalist determinism.

If a similar spectre haunts his account of selfhood, he tries to fend it off with the insistence that human beings, as language users, can forge their own self-descriptions. Thus, again, he places a premium on the new as being (apparently) good for its own sake – a corrective, perhaps, to the pragmatist's reliance on normality and convention as the source of the justified and good. But in denying that there is any sort of centredness to being such a self, this account is in danger of collapsing under the weight of its own requirements: that a reweaving of a network of beliefs and desires in response to the stimuli provided by new metaphors might somehow in itself account for the integrity and continuity required by the possibility of living one's life as a work of literature. This requires a post-hoc methodological individualism, one which salvages the atomized, self-creating poet from the clutches of all-the-way-down socialization. And this in turn requires a curious wrenching of poets away from any structural or historical process not of their own making. They become ideal types of self-creation, whose genius, as Kate Soper remarks, 'for weaving entirely novel patterns of belief is apparently unrelated to the social context in which they find themselves and unaffected by the vastly differing conditions of education and acquisition of subjectivity it makes available to differing individuals'.[118]

This is a criticism – of elitism, or obliviousness to human need beyond that for poetic creativity – which Rorty, as humanistic liberal, has tried to meet in his explicitly political philosophy. His move into this area begins with a series of articles in the 1980s, mostly collected in *ORT*: 'The priority of democracy to philosophy', 'Postmodernist bourgeois liberalism' and 'Solidarity or objectivity?' are landmarks in this sense. It finds its culmination in *CIS* – a work which, although it has been supplemented since, constitutes the fullest, most final articulation of Rorty's normative allegiances. It is to this aspect of his work that I will now move on.

# 3 • Liberal Ironism

It is good to be loyal to what you believe in – that, however, may be tautology. Loyalty to what is wrong, outmoded, reactionary is mischievous. To that in general all will agree, even the reactionary.[1]

There is nothing wrong with liberal democracy.[2]

In the previous chapters we have seen various senses in which Rorty seeks to de-ontologize and de-epistemologize *limits* (to language, selfhood, and so on) and redescribe the scope for enlargement as delimited only by socio-historical contingency. As we have also seen, there is a premium on novelty and change for its own sake throughout Rorty's work. Yet in its overtly political key, that work is routinely dismissed as being inherently conservative in its implications. This is largely, and notoriously, because of the split he institutes in *Contingency, Irony and Solidarity* between private irony and public hope. Since pragmatism is, true to the spirit of Dewey, 'a philosophy of solidarity rather than despair', Rorty has needed to enable piecemeal social engineering even while allowing for wanton, limitless private self-creation.[3] In this spirit, he submits that 'J. S. Mill's suggestion that governments devote themselves to optimizing the balance between leaving people's private lives alone and preventing suffering seems to me pretty much the last word', and suggests that 'Western social and political thought may have had the last conceptual revolution it needs'.[4] Given that these comments come next to each other, the implication is that we need not move beyond eighteenth-century liberal-utilitarian assumptions.[5] Certainly, the prime contentions of Mill's *On Liberty* surface more or less intact in Rorty's claims that 'if we take care of political and cultural freedom, truth and rationality will take care of themselves', and that freedom can be understood negatively, as 'leaving people alone to dream and think and live as they please, so long as they do not hurt other people'.[6]

Whether we can see Rorty's work as a snug-fitting addendum to the liberal tradition is not, however, altogether clear. This is partly because of the place of redescription in his project. It seeks both to redescribe political liberalism in an appealing way, and to install redescription as a general rubric for the practice of progressive politics. Anti-foundationalist yet with a premium on personal freedom, it has often been presented (sometimes by himself) as a sort of synthesis of core ingredients of the liberal and postmodern schools.[7] This chapter explores the contours of this synthesis, and finds that to the extent that Rorty's thinking bears it out, it foregrounds key deficits and lacunae in both movements. It moves through three stages. First, in 3.1, I consider implications of Rorty's invoking of Wilfrid Sellars's 'we-intention' as an index of the scope and substance of moral action, via a comparison with Lyotard's (parallel, in some senses) attempt to formulate an ethics freed from 'modern' imperatives. In 3.2 I discuss the possibility of salvaging a viable conception of universalism from the twin assaults of pragmatism and postmodernism. And 3.3 explores the arguments of *Achieving our Country,* where Rorty traces and crtiques the political disengagement of the academic left.

### 3.1. Expanding moral space: liberalism, ironism and solidarity

> Universality requires that I respect humanity in others and in myself, while justice relates to the idea that people's relations between themselves and with things can be impersonally defined and that that definition includes me. We shall allow ourselves to stress this point, because the ethics of the twentieth century have quite simply buried and forgotten it, seeking a more noble doctrine. May I be forgiven my lack of finesse: preoccupation with nobility is a luxury which, in the current state of things, is not within everybody's reach.[8]

> Universalist philosophers assume, with Kant, that all the logical space necessary for moral deliberation is now available. Historicists . . . [say] that moral progress depends on expanding this space.[9]

This section compares Rorty's work and Lyotard's as parallel seekings of a 'more noble doctrine' than universality. It reads them as culminations of what Le Doeuff calls 'the ethics of the twentieth century', if by this we understand the burying of universality in the belief that it is both misconceived and dangerous. And it suggests three things about Lyotard and Rorty: that they neither escape from the logic of universality, nor show that this is possible, nor, in the end, show why it is desirable.

To begin with, a brief delineation of what Rorty means by liberal ironism – the mindset which defines the 'utopia' he sketches in *CIS*. The emblematic figure, the ironist, is 'the sort of person who faces up to the contingency of his or her own most central beliefs and desires – someone sufficiently historicist and nominalist to have abandoned the idea that those central beliefs and desires refer back to something beyond the reach of time and chance'.[10] She accepts the absence of a metavocabulary and rejects the idea that it is possible objectively to privilege one or other of the languages in which she and her fellow citizens habitually define themselves.[11] She recognizes that there is no non-circular way in which to justify the beliefs she holds most dear. She entertains 'radical and continuous doubts' about her own 'final vocabulary': the set of words which she uses to justify her actions, her beliefs and her life.[12] This applies to her description of her own political and moral responsibilities.

But as the ironist becomes *liberal* ironist, so she privatizes her sense of irony. Her belief that there is no non-circular defence available to liberalism can be set aside when she turns her attention to matters public. Because she is a liberal, her first *public* concern is to help create the sort of solidarity which the stable practice of liberal democracy requires; to extend the reach of the conviction that for Rorty is what makes her a liberal – that 'cruelty is the worst thing we do'.[13] In the absence of the metaphysical resource of a theory of a common human nature, this *enacted*, *created* (rather than 'discovered') solidarity provides something which 'stand[s] beyond history and institutions' on which the liberal ironist can stake her public hopes: an ungroundable desire 'that suffering will be diminished, that the humiliation of human beings by other human beings may cease'.[14]

The liberal ironist thus subscribes to what Rorty elsewhere calls 'bourgeois liberalism' – a liberalism which eschews the universalisizing ontological, epistemological and moral commitments of its Enlightenment forebear in favour of 'the attempt to fulfil the hopes of the North Atlantic bourgeoisie'.[15] There is nothing to be responsible to except the inhabitants and guiding vocabularies of actual or possible historical communities. A self-image as liberal ironist requires that one's version of moral philosophy takes the form of a cashing out of an answer 'Who are "we", how did we come to be what we are, and what might we become?' rather than an answer to the question 'What rules should dictate my actions?'[16] Leaning on Sellars's version of morality as a matter of 'we-intentions', Rorty installs the core meaning of 'immoral action' as the sort of thing '*we* don't do'.[17] Thus, 'those who act badly are those who behave contrary to the project which makes us the community we are'.[18] A sense of solidarity derives from a shared contextual perspective – one which gains its purchase through the contrasting of our 'we-intentions' with those of other historically contingent communities, and the sharper mutual definition which derives from that contrast.

And yet Rorty seeks to retain a notion of transcultural 'human solidarity'. This is enabled by a sense that there is nothing about the (initially) intra-societal extension of the 'we-intention' which makes it incompatible with urging that 'we try to extend our sense of "we" to people whom we have previously thought of as "they"'.[19] We need not presuppose a persistent 'we', a transhistorical metaphysical subject, in order to tell stories of progress.[20] Hence the scope for retrieval of Enlightenment liberal hopes without the metaphysical baggage:

> The view that I am offering says that there is such a thing as moral progress, and that this progress is indeed in the direction of greater human solidarity. But this solidarity is not thought of as a recognition of a core self, the human essence, in all human beings. Rather, it is thought of as the ability to see more and more traditional differences (of tribe, race, customs, and the like) as unimportant when compared with similarities with respect to pain and humiliation – the ability to think of people wildly different from ourselves as included in the range of 'us'.[21]

Moral progress is thus reconceived on an attitudinal (rather than action-based, or institutional) footing: it is 'an increase in our ability to see more and more differences among people as morally irrelevant'.[22] Theoretical argument having no privileged access to rhetorical force, this solidarity is most likely to be encouraged instead by narrative genres: journalism, the comic book, the drama-documentary and, especially, the novel.[23] It is fiction, be it by Dickens or Orwell, Laclos or Nabokov, which most effectively draws our attention to the kind of suffering endured by people to whom we had not previously attended, and the kinds of cruelty which we ourselves are capable of. It is fiction which enables us to redescribe, and so enlarge, our own sense of moral implication in the world. Meanwhile, justification of the merits of liberal democracy – toleration, free inquiry and so on – will be purely horizontal. It 'can only take the form of a comparison between societies which exemplify these habits and those which do not, leading to the suggestion that nobody who has experienced both would prefer the latter'.[24] While privately unconstrained by anything other than their ability to employ novel metaphors in self-redescription (and seeking novelty for its own sake), in the public sphere the liberal ironist signs up wholeheartedly to the value of *convention* for its own sake.

In his 1980s turn to political philosophy, then, Rorty reorients his meta-description of the relation between progress and novelty around a strict public/private divide. Whereas in *PMN* he pits against each other the systematic (constructive, argument-offering) and edifying (satirizing, parodic) critic, by *CIS* he is splicing him together in the idealized figure of the liberal ironist. This must involve a certain tethering of the edifying impulse, in terms of its public reach. For edifiers, on the original model, 'destroy for the sake of their own generation', to stave off the freezing over of culture that would result if 'some given vocabulary . . . deceives people into thinking that from now on all discourse could be, or should be, normal discourse'.[25] In *CIS*, Rorty seems to install as part of his 'ironist's utopia' exactly the sort of fixity and closure in the public sphere that his championing of abnormal discourse would be expected to preclude. In the process, a tension becomes entrenched between Rorty's romantic and pragmatic tendencies.[26] The abnormal, previously heroic, becomes removed to the private plane of individualistic, anti-social, narcissistic novelty-seeking. The normal, rather than temporally preceding the lurch into abnormality which brings on a shift to the installation of a fresh set of conventions, now (in the ideal state) *coexists* with the abnormal, as its corollary in the public sphere. Irony is 'inherently a private matter': 'I cannot . . . claim that there could or ought to be a culture whose public rhetoric is ironist'.[27]

And thus it is that *CIS* is so ripe for the charge that it rules in (indeed requires) the sort of piecemeal engineering that would shore up the liberal polity while explicitly ruling out (as inadmissably ironic) any submission that would demand the transformation of that public sphere. Thus private open-mindedness twins up with public intolerance. A radical redescription can only gain credence if it fits in with the bourgeois liberal outlook. If it purports to reveal 'real' discrepancies between the narratives which hold liberal culture together and deeds done in its name which belie the tenor of those narratives, then it can, all too conveniently, be dispatched as 'metaphysical'.[28] Thus the 'freezing over of [political] culture' seems to be exactly what is required in the Rortian ideal scenario.[29]

But there is a sense, still, in which the renovating powers of redescription are retained as the prime mover of moral and political progress. They come into play most conspicuously when it comes to extending the reach of the 'we' around which conventions, normal discourse, 'liberal values', etc. will cluster. Redescription, political in any case, takes on a direct role in the meeting with otherness: of expanding the reference of 'us'. It is precisely at this stage that Rorty invokes the power of narrative genres to expand our sense of solidarity. Thus, I would argue, Rorty transposes the meeting with novelty involved in a community's taking on a new vocabulary to the inter-cultural plane. Other cultures become the 'beyond' of our enlarging sense of the familiar and normal.

Crucial here, though, is Rorty's pragmatic resistance to the idea of 'radical alterity' as it features in much postmodernist discourse. In what follows I want to compare the two approaches in terms of where they leave us on the question of (to speak Rortian) the extension of the 'we' that constitutes 'the community we are'. I take Lyotard's work of the late 1970s and early 1980s as emblematic of what postmodernism means epistemologically, ethically and politically. This is largely for the sake of argument, although there is something, I think, in Calvin Schrag's comment that Lyotard is 'clearly the most postmodern of the postmodernists'.[30] One hesitates, now, to venture definitions of a term which may well be beyond use. For my purposes here, I will borrow Zygmunt Bauman's summary of its basic moral import. Postmodernism, he says, having concluded that 'morality is un-universalizable',

> opposes a concrete version of moral universalism which in the modern era served as but a thinly disguised declaration of intent to embark on . . . an arduous campaign to smother the differences and above all to eliminate all 'wild' – autonomous, obstreperous and uncontrolled – sources of moral judgement.[31]

Bauman points to a general awareness that modernity's 'all-human ethics', its aim to find both form and substance for a global moral practice, has been 'bound to evict and supplant all local *distortions*', so that, in effect, 'modern societies practice moral parochialism under the mask of promoting universal ethics'.[32] As Bill Readings fleshes out the point: 'the metalanguages of our modernity consistently propose a universal rule of justice or equity that silences any argument structured on other principles, any heterogeneous language game'.[33]

Lyotard is as thoroughgoing an advocate of heterogeneity and dissensus, and debunker of totalizing theory, as anyone writing in the late 1970s and 1980s. His exploration of a distinctively postmodern approach to justice thus runs more or less contemporaneously with Rorty's own 'political turn'.

## 'Escaping' the modern: 1. Lyotard

In *The Postmodern Condition*, amid a general endorsement of 'a form of legitimation based solely on paralogy', Lyotard suggests approvingly that 'consensus has become an outmoded and suspect value'. While made about science, the point has a general epistemic resonance: when it comes to the legitimation of validity claims of any kind, universal applicability or acceptability are beside the point, both in fact and in principle. However justice itself, in principle or as an idea, 'is neither outmoded nor suspect'. And thus

> We must . . . arrive at an idea and practice of justice that is not linked to that of consensus. A recognition of the heteronomous nature of language games is a first step in that direction. This obviously implies a renunciation of terror, which assumes that they are isomorphic and tries to make them so. The second step is the principle that any consensus on the rules defining a game and the 'moves' playable within it *must* be local, in other words, agreed upon by its present players and subject to eventual cancellation. The orientation then favours a multiplicity of finite meta-arguments, by which I mean argumentation that concerns metaprescriptives and is limited in space and time.[34]

This passage is worth quoting in full because it contains all the key motifs of Lyotard's subsequent thinking. Here is a cruder summary: consensus as a goal is epistemically dubious and morally terroristic, because the different language games that constitute inquiry stand to each other in relations of *incommensurable* alterity, such that they cannot legitimately be judged from outside by any common measure. Claims made within different language games (by the rules of which utterances 'can be defined according to the uses to which they can be put') are unarbitrable by any common standard.[35] What constitutes social reality is a multiplicity of language games, or what Lyotard will later call 'genres of discourse', which are in a state of continuous, ineluctable conflict.

Most notably in *Just Gaming* and *The Differend*, Lyotard seeks an authentically non-totalizing rehabilitation of the idea of justice: a 'metaprescriptive' duly 'limited in space and time'. He seeks a protection of the heterogeneous without appeal to 'a type of discourse . . . common to an entire political tradition' which presupposes that 'if the discourse that describes social justice is . . . true, then the social practice can be just insofar as it respects the distribution implied in the discourse'.[36] Proposed as substitute in *Just Gaming* is a justice pitted against the very idea of a teleological or redemptive politics governed by what he elsewhere calls the 'logic of result'.[37] Dilemmas and antagonisms should not be seen as temporary inconveniences, more happily dissolved away by reference to a logic which 'dominates the social practice of justice and subordinates it to itself'.[38] Indeed, the mission is to undermine the very legitimacy of ever speaking for others, ever overriding the alterity of language games by importing one way of speaking into a debate not strictly its own – be that in the form of enunciating universal prescriptions ('infatuation itself and absolute injustice') or simply telling the oppressed what is good for them.[39]

In *Just Gaming*, the idea of justice must remain unrealized, in the form of a horizon always distanced or receding from current practice. Rather than supplying specific contents for specific prescriptions, it 'just regulates our prescriptives, that is, guides us in knowing what is just and not just. But guides us without, in the end, really guiding us, without telling us what is just.'[40] Judgement must take place without criteria, without 'going through a conceptual system that could serve as a criterion for practice'.[41] Sound judgement is that which evades concept and principle and relies instead on intuition, imagination and invention. Doing justice becomes 'a matter of experimentation rather than correspondence to models'.[42] One is always caught up 'within opinion', 'in a story' – and one cannot escape the story to 'take up a metalinguistic position from which the whole could be dominated'.[43]

But while prescriptions are 'not of the order of knowledge', are *felt* rather than derived from descriptions, there is a sort of prescription which Lyotard would have us feel.[44] It is this: 'One must maximise as much as possible the multiplication of small narratives.'[45] Hence there is a value valuable for its own sake, and it is heterogeneity. A recognition of 'a multiplicity of justices' is thus accompanied by 'the justice of multiplicity'.[46] Thus, universalism re-emerges in (perhaps) a negative form: in the prescription to enhance heterogeneity.

The stakes are similar in *The Differend*, although their framing is slightly different. Here, a 'phrase' (understood as an 'event', a happening) is 'consituted according to a set of rules (its regimen)'. Examples of different regimens would be reasoning, describing, showing and so on. A phrase belonging to one regimen cannot be translated into another. The most that can happen is that phrases are linked together in a genre of discourse, towards a given purpose (without their thereby referring to a world beyond discourse; since each phrase is an event, it is open to an infinite number of equally right responses, unconstrained by any 'reality' beyond). But while linking on from phrases is necessary, since one sentence will always follow another, 'how to link is not': there are no rules for linkage.[47] A 'differend' is 'a case of conflict, between (at least) two parties that cannot be equitably resolved for lack of a rule of judgement applicable to both arguments'.[48] It arises where 'the regulation of the conflict . . . is done in the idiom of one of the parties while the wrong suffered by the other is not signified in that idiom'.[49] Hence 'the problem': 'Given 1) the impossibility of avoiding conflicts . . . and 2) the absence of a universal genre of discourse to regulate them . . . to find, if not what can legitimate judgement (the "good" linkage), then at least how to save the honor of thinking'.[50] If phrases collide, the absence of a neutral tribunal to evaluate them means in effect that every new phrase can simply obliterate the previous one. If the two phrases belong to different genres of discourse, then their competing claims are unarticulable in the logic of the other. So every 'linkage' of one phrase to another is potentially a victory: a conjuring away of the old phrase by the new. Those conjured away will, as Lyotard puts it, 'remain neglected, forgotten, or repressed possibilities'.[51]

Lyotard has by now dropped the term 'language game' because it implies what he calls the 'humanist prejudice' that 'there is "man", that there is "language" and that the former makes use of the latter for his own ends'.[52] No: 'Humanity is not the user of language, nor even its guardian; there is no more one subject than there is one language. Phrases situate names and pronouns . . . in the universes they present.'[53] The workings and bumpings and obliterations of phrases happen unconstrained by either human intentions or the world. Yet this displacement of the human subject is a move which is, I think, reversed in due course. For the (apparently) morally neutral mutual misrecognition of sentences is not, in itself, of direct ethical relevance. Even if not as their 'owners', human beings have to be reconnected to phrases: this emerges in the various examples of differends deployed in the making of Lyotard's case. The most prominent (and infamous) is that centring on the case of Robert Faurisson, the Holocaust revisionist historian. A summary: Faurisson declares that the only witness he will accept as proof that gas chambers existed would have to be someone who was actually a victim of the gas chamber. '[T]here is no victim that is not dead; otherwise this gas chamber would not be what he or she claims it to be. There is, therefore, no gas chamber.'[54]

Now the problem here as Lyotard sees it is that, to this extent, Faurisson is right. There is no way of proving on Faurisson's own terms, namely those of the cognitive genre dealing with 'establishing the facts of the human past', that gas chambers did indeed exist.[55] To do so, we would have to make some other appeal. But given that one genre is strictly untranslatable into any other, the best that we can do is acknowledge the particularity of each phrase as an event. What we must *not* do is subume that particularity under the imposition of some exterior genre: while inside a genre of discourse, 'the linkages obey rules which determine the stakes and the ends', between genres 'no such rules are known'.[56] To assume the position of knowing such rules would be to subscribe to some or other 'metanarrative', and so lapse into the terroristic logic which for Lyotard is father to the extremities of modern history: most prominently among them, the Holocaust itself. The social dominance of the cognitive genre – that which Faurisson invokes in requiring first hand experience of the gas chambers as the only acceptable proof of their existence – is itself the problem. Its rules will not furnish us with the chance to rebut Faurisson. Playing by its rules, the claims of Holocaust survivors can only be silenced.

But there is a problem here, if the only things we can be sure exist are phrases and if phrases' happening bears no special relationship to human subjects. In his straight antihumanism Lyotard must maintain adherence to the Heideggerian insistence that, rather than the subject, 'it is language that speaks'.[57] Thus 'the people are only that which actualizes the narratives . . . by recounting them, but also by listening to them and recounting themselves through them'.[58] For Lyotard's concern is not simply the fact that some sentence which says 'Gas chambers existed' might lie obliterated in the wake of a heavy succession of cognitive counter-claims. He is also (presumably) concerned about the silencing of Holocaust *survivors*. It is precisely their relationship to the phrase, their chance of articulating it and being heard, which is at stake. Hence the reintrusion of the subject – and of a rather modern-looking appeal to some kind of universal 'right' for the silenced to express their interests.

To expand on this point. Lyotard wants to bring about a 'new' form of justice, one which 'bears witness' to the conflict of incommensurable claims to knowledge which makes up social reality. What this requires in effect is – in *The Differend* just as in *Just Gaming* – the location of a philosophical ethics with the (eventually) quite explicit normative goal of opening up a space for hitherto occluded discursive genres. But in this case, as Axel Honneth makes the point, 'Moral protection of the particular would then mean the politically effective attempt to provide all *subjects* with the equal chance to publicly articulate their interests and needs.'[59] We can, for instance, only recognize a differend in the first place if we can already assume that all those involved in a conflict have had some sort of chance to articulate their views – if some phrases have been uttered by some subjects. Occluded phrases thus seem to have been denied some sort of recognition that they have some right to; otherwise, where would the injustice in their occlusion lie? In other words, without (a) the intrusion of a 'humanistic' sense in which human beings do indeed *use* language, and (b) moral universalism, it is hard to understand what the injunction to bear witness to marginalized language games in the face of their exclusion by some sedimenting consensus is supposed to mean. Thus Lyotard's call for an idea of justice to which we can appeal 'without going through a conceptual system that could serve as a criterion for practice' goes unanswered in his own depiction of a postmodern justice. In some senses, as we have seen, his ethics amounts to little more than a rehearsal of the themes of classical liberalism, shifted to the plane of the linguistic and then, sneakily, back again. Certainly there is a consonance between Lyotard's search for a universal prescriptive to outlaw all universal prescriptives and liberalism's problem of how to find a ground for the claim that there is no superior idea of the good life which is not itself, as a claim, constitutive of an idea of the good life.

It is one thing to contend, with Bauman, that the practice of universalism has veiled and furthered more dubious causes: colonialism, pro-free market ideology, or whatever. But it is a huge step from there to argue that there is something *necessarily* violent about all universal judgements, all notions of political redemption – and that one could instead base a critical, emancipatory politics on a claim of irreducible difference. Lyotard's own failure to escape from issuing universal prescriptives would itself, on this logic, lead to a slipping back into that very violence. And in its prescriptive content, it would seem to render all ethical projects equivalent in their particularity, and so in their entitlement to protection and flourishing. It would also, for that matter, render all attempts at influencing genres of discourse beyond the one from which one calls them into question *equally* guilty of ethical transgression. Banning cigarette advertising would represent a flagrant intrusion of the health/scientific genre of discourse into areas where it does not belong, and make Benson & Hedges the victims of their own special differend. The rhetoric of famine relief – let alone challenges to human rights abuses in other cultures – would doubtless be as culpable. And so on, and so on: the unsustainability of outright relativism seems hardly to need rehearsing here. But the sustaining of a credibly emancipatory position without recourse to universalism at any level is, I think, an equally fragile enterprise. The theme of universalism – and the need for a nuanced understanding of its different senses, rather than a blanket rejection – will be taken up in further depth in 3.2.

## 'Escaping' the modern: 2. Rorty

If Lyotard's postmodern ethics does not, in the end, expunge itself of modern motifs, what about Rorty's pragmatist version? I would argue that – for better or worse – it represents a more consistent articulation of the political/pragmatic position which follows from Lyotard's founding epistemology. With a change of terminology, Rorty would be happy to endorse the following: 'narratives . . . determine criteria of competence and/or illustrate how they are to be applied. They thus define what has the right to be said and done in the culture in question, and since they are themselves a part of that culture, they are legitimated by the simple fact that they do what they do.'[60] What Lyotard retains, however tortuously, and Rorty dispatches, is the idea that, on this basis, questions of truth might still be matters of justice as well. As I shall argue, this represents a sort of honesty on Rorty's part.[61] It avoids, as he must, the distinctly 'philosophical' conceit that a radical undoing of traditional epistemology is somehow, in essence, politically explosive. Rather, for Rorty (being truer, on this point, to Wittgenstein), it leaves everything as it is.

In a brief 1985 exchange in which, for the most part, Lyotard seems exasperated by his counterpart's philosophical insouciance, he identifies 'a differend between myself and Richard Rorty'. 'My mode of discourse is tragic,' as he later puts it. 'His is conversational. Where is the tribunal that can say which of these two genres of discourse is the more just?'[62] Thus, in a typical enough move, Lyotard discerns a *necessary* rupture, a paralogy, in respect of which the idea of a 'neutral' adjudication can only be an imperialistic affront. As Norris has it, Lyotard's (claimed) justice of incommensurability amounts to:

> a version of the Wittgensteinian (language-games) argument joined to a post-structuralist doctrine of the 'arbitrary' sign, of truth as a product of

linguistic or discursive convention, and of the subject (the knowing, willing or judging subject) as likewise nothing more than a transitory figment of the obsolete humanist imaginary.[63]

Now on these terms, the relation with Rorty's thinking on related issues might seem a fairly tight one. No more for him than for Lyotard is the notion of 'criteria' 'in point' when it comes to the movement between one language game and another.[64] And equally for him, of course, 'you can only elaborate a question within some language game currently under way'. But the crucial difference, first off, is that Rorty sees no *ethical* dangers in the appeal to such criteria, and has only the *pragmatic* worry about their being a fifth wheel. If neutrality is unattainable, its seeking is a waste of resources.

Rorty confesses that he finds the topic of 'otherness' (sensitivity towards which is definitive of much post-structuralist concern about recourse to 'universality' and 'totalization' in ethics) 'a bit baffling'. This is because, 'as a good pragmatist', he is 'uncomfortable with notions of uncommunicability, with the idea that some special sorts of things (God, the inside of another human being, the experience of the oppressed) are impossible, or at least very difficult, to put into language'.[65] Otherwise one risks slipping back into metaphysics, and positing language (with the later Heidegger) as a force whose workings are somehow 'always already' beyond our control. For Rorty, language is not 'always already' anything. It is a tool, neutral in itself, and as meaningless as birdsong until we put it to good purpose. The tool-using aspect of things takes Rorty away from Lyotard, and back in the direction of a sort of disenchanted humanism. In 2.2 we saw how Rorty has sneaking recourse to a vision of the freedom of the autonomous subject to (as it has been phrased by one commentator) to 'interpret any way we like, to simply pick up and use optional vocabularies, to enter into a variety of discursive practices'.[66] Stricter postmodernists recoil at this apparent exaltation of the Enlightenment rational subject, master in its own house. Rorty does not, it seems, because so to recoil is to slide into some necessitarian account of the relationship between human beings and language, such that one has to stand in some primordial relation to the other.

He thus resists the prioritization of the phrase in any ontological sense. In a 1961 article he notes the illegitimacy of moving from 'there is a sign behind every sign' to 'there are nothing but signs'.[67] There will always, in pragmatism, be a reference to *action* as that which 'renders harmless' the indefinite horizontal 'regress of rules, habits and signs standing behind rules, habits and signs'.[68] Thus *practice* is what prevents the slide into necessaritarianism about language: since the meanings of sentences depend on their use, we should not get too carried away about their particularity. In principle, at least, uses can always travel. On this basis, one might expect Rorty simply to dismiss the Lyotardian notion of strict incommensurability between discursive genres.

But Rorty can seem to waver on this question.[69] In *PMN*, he writes that 'the pragmatic approach to knowledge ... will construe the line between discourses which can be rendered commensurable and those which cannot as merely that between "normal" and "abnormal" discourse'.[70] Hence, 'we can get epistemological commensuration only when we already have agreed-upon practices of inquiry'.[71] And still more emphatically: 'to look for commensuration rather than simply continued conversation – to look for a way of making further redescription unnecessary by finding a way of reducing all possible descriptions to one – is to attempt to escape from humanity'. What is needed is a 'protest against attempts to close off conversation by proposals for universal commensuration through the hypostatization of some privileged set of proposals'.[72] There are enough consonances here to suggest that, from different trajectories, Rorty and Lyotard both arrived in their respective books of 1979 at an affirmation of the importance of the flourishing of heterogeneity. And indeed there is a hint there, in Rorty's association of *humanity* with incommensurate conversation, of an ethical injunction (or 'protest') – in line with Lyotard's – to avoid recourse to metanarrative 'hypostatizations'. Noticeable at the same time, though, is that Rorty is not appealing either to a hypostatized incommensurability: he points out not the radical alterity of language games, but that the work which must be done to render them commensurable is piecemeal and radically situated. In other words, it takes place within a given context, enabled by the provisions of the language game from which we start out.

In any case, by the time of their 1985 exchange, any such ethical dimension to our relation to incommensurability has been relinquished. Rorty argues as to 'cultural differences' that they 'are not different in kind from differences between old and ("revolutionary") new theories propounded within a single culture'.[73] As an extension of the case in *PMN*, this would suggest that, since the difference between old and new is incommensurable, so is that between different cultures. But he avoids Lyotard's appeal to a condition of impossibility of relating the incommensurable to the already commensurated. Just because there is no single commensurating language, known in advance, which will 'provide an idiom into which to translate every new theory, poetic idiom, or native culture', this does not entail that 'there are unlearnable languages'.[74] To assume the second is to assume, in line with Lyotard's appropriation of Wittgenstein, that there are only 'islets of language, each governed by a system of rules untranslatable into those of the others'.[75]

Against this, Rorty insists that Lyotard's stance is indebted to the scheme/content dualism toward which Davidson and indeed Wittgenstein are rightly dismissive: 'only the language–fact distinction will make sense of the claim that incommensurability is something more than a temporary inconvenience'.[76] There are no such things as 'linguistic islets' just as there is no such thing as a 'conceptual scheme'. To think this is to fall back into the 'Cartesian fallacy' of 'seeing axioms where there are only shared habits'.[77] We simply could not tell 'when we had come against a human practice that we knew to be linguistic and also to be so foreign that we must give up hope of knowing what it would be like to engage in it'.[78] Davidson's Principle of Charity has demonstrated that 'any two beings that use language to communicate with one another necessarily share an enormous number of beliefs and desires'.[79] Thus, writing later: 'the very idea of incompatible, and perhaps reciprocally unintelligible, language-games is a pointless fiction, and . . . in real cases representatives of different traditions and cultures can always find a way to talk over their differences'.[80]

This, then, is crucial to Rorty's retention of the sense of moral progress cited earlier: 'an increase in an ability to see more and more differences among people as morally irrelevant'.[81] Contra Lyotard, moral progress is thus, quite affirmatively, in the direction of consensus. There is no metaphysical harm done by the spinning of cosmopolitan stories aimed at including more and more of humanity in some ongoing story. The trick is not to appeal to given aspects of human commonality in the process, or a 'one big thing', something 'true and deep', that unites us. Rather, we should see moral progress as 'more like sewing together a very large, elaborate, polychrome quilt'.[82] Thus are those that once were 'them' incorporated into a larger, thriving 'us'. Where for Lyotard such a movement would be inherently imperialistic, for Rorty it is the meliorative achievement of a greater scope for the 'we-intention' that provides our moral context.

So again: while Lyotard is wary of the terrorism involved in what he calls 'the manufacture of a subject that is authorized to say "we"',

Rorty can cheerfully affirm that the reference of the word 'we' should extend to as many people as possible. 'We should stay on the lookout for marginalized people', and 'we should try to notice our similarities with them, to *create* [rather than to "recognize" as given] a more expansive sense of solidarity than we already have'.[83] From a view of incommensurability as a 'temporary inconvenience' comes a hope for future convergence which for Lyotard, insisting on the particularity of each phrase as an event, and of each discursive genre, would be a call for the elision of that particularity. And the occasion for him to invoke his (universalistic) call for an equal right to free expression. For Rorty, while claims can only be made within some already operating language game, this equates to 'within some community, some group whose members share a good many relevant beliefs'.[84] But in fact, in its way, Rorty's case is underpinned by covert universalism just as much as Lyotard's is.

Rorty's claimed rejection of universalism is, at root, an empiricist one. It derives from the same sort of (specious) dichotomy which arises from the positing of a God's eye view as prerequisite for transcendence of the given, for critique in any worthwhile sense. This dichotomy is summed up nicely in an opening sentence from Michael Walzer's *Spheres of Justice*:

> One way to begin the philosophical enterprise – perhaps the original way – is to walk out of the cave, leave the city, climb the mountain, fashion for oneself (what can never be fashioned for ordinary men and women) an objective and universal standpoint. Then one decribes the terrain of everyday life from far away. . . . But I mean to stand in the cave, in the city, on the ground.[85]

True to this framing of the options (the dubiousness of which I return to below), Rorty opts for number two. We must start from a 'we', from a 'for us'. And '"For us" means, roughly, "inside our language games, our conventions, our form of life, our standards of legitimation"'.[86] And 'immorality' means 'the sort of thing "we" don't do'. But there are no limits save conversational, pragmatic ones on expanding the reference of this 'we'. This is part of redescription's job. But stopping there for the moment: immorality does not, in fact, in an empirically given sense, mean 'the sort of thing "we" don't do'. Rorty's appeal to the given practices of one's community cannot ensure that those practices are in line with the purpose of his appeal – and in fact they are not. For when – in contemporary America, say – people claim that racial discrimination was wrong, they do not in fact, mean: 'Racial discrimination is the sort of thing that we don't do around here.' In fact, this kind of claim will mean something like: 'Racial discrimination *is* the sort of thing that people do around here, and that is why I am identifying it as a wrong.' Rorty would seem to be implying that to reject aspects of the common practices of one's own 'we' is somehow strictly meaningless: that something cannot at the same time be 'done around here', and be 'wrong'.[87] And, as with the account of vocabulary change I addressed in 2.1, it seems that the trap looms for Rorty's position that it cannot account for our proceeding according to practices which might be at the same time wrong. The 'right' is coextensive with the 'given'.

Now this may, to be sure, amount to what Matthew Festenstein calls an 'excessively literal understanding' of the invocation of Sellars's 'we-intention'. It may be that his ethnocentrism centres not on the semantics of moral claims, but on 'the scope of practical reason'. When Rorty says '*we* have to start from where *we* are', his point might concern 'only the starting-point of moral deliberation'.[88] It is merely the rejecting of an Archimedean point, beyond local understandings, from which moral considerations might be derived. Practical deliberation 'must start in some particular place and time with the concepts available there'.[89] And Rorty's ethnocentrism is, as he explains it at one stage, 'the ethnocentrism of a "we" ("we liberals") which is dedicated to enlarging itself, to creating an ever larger and more variegated ethnos . . . the "we" of the people who have been brought up to distrust ethnocentrism'.[90] So maybe it is not constrained by having to appeal to what currently dominant attitudes as its only index of moral acceptability. In fact, our practical deliberation might start from the assumption that, given the values we have derived from our particular upbringing in a particular community, its own practices fall well short of an embodiment of those values. Rorty might be offering the platform for a sort of immanent critique, commendably unparochial in its long-term outlook.

But even so (and with due stress on that 'might'), difficulties remain. First, whoever thought that practical deliberation must start in *no* particular place, at *no* particular time and *without* the concepts available there? Only, I suppose, someone who presumed that moral-political decisions involve no particular people, no particular events and no concepts somehow concretely groundable in terms of human practice. Someone who cooked up algorithms and commandments for the sheer beauty of their structure and balance, without an eye on their possible 'cashing out' in the world. Since such a figure is hardly a tough target to hit, Rorty's point does not, so interpreted, amount to much. So it must mean something thicker. But if it does mean something thicker, then Rorty's case runs into fairly drastic consistency problems.

One can, to help substantiate it, interpret Rorty's case as registering communitarian objections to liberalism in a different key. Standardly, those objections go like this. Liberalism, in its methodological individualism, has posited an isolated, monadic, lifestyle-choosing self which rests on untenably Cartesian foundations. Thus John Rawls's *A Theory of Justice*, in attempting to 'generalize and carry to a higher level of abstraction the traditional theory of the social contract as represented by Locke, Rousseau and Kant', issues in a formalistic emptiness which lacks purchase when applied to particular moral communities.[91] Its central, most influential conceptions – of the 'veil of ignorance', the 'original position', and 'justice as fairness' – were presented as the source and elements of a set of principles of justice to which all rational individuals in all societies would, given the chance, subscribe. Communitarian critics, conspicuously Michael Sandel, claimed that all of this was built on a deficient conception of moral selfhood. The 'unencumbered', abstracted, atomized liberal self was in fact too empty to be morally meaningful, and ignored our necessary embeddedness in particular cultural practices and forms of life. Moreover, Rawls was claiming for his theory a transcendental applicability when his 'rational choosers' were really embodiments of the contingent cultural preferences of modern American liberals.

Subsequently, Rawls faced up to these allegations, and replied, in effect: 'So what?' He spent much of his later work explaining why notions such as 'justice as fairness' figure in his theory not as 'claims to universal truth' based on 'presumptions about the essential nature and identity of persons', but rather as reasonable political suggestions with a particular set of social and economic institutions in mind. His, then, is a conception of justice which 'tries to draw solely upon basic intuitive ideas that are embedded in the political institutions of a constitutional democratic regime and the public traditions of their interpretation'.[92] This disclaimer follows from Rawls's assertion that 'what justifies a conception of justice is not its being true to an order antecedent to and given to us, but its congruence with our deeper understanding of ourselves and our aspirations, and our realization that, given our history and the traditions embedded in our public life, it is the most reasonable doctrine *for us*'.[93]

I include Rawls here not because the detail of his original theory and its subsequent tweakings are at issue, but because this qualification of its very nature and scope has, Rorty thinks, lent grist to his own mill. Rorty deems Rawls as affirming the value of liberal-democratic institutions without now pretending that this value can or should 'be measured by anything more specific than the moral intuitions of the particular historical community that has created those institutions'.[94] Being now 'thoroughly historicist and antiuniversalist', the later Rawls is for Rorty 'simply trying to systematize the principles and intuitions typical of American liberals'.[95] He is doing exactly what Rorty's committed public liberals should be doing: offering a hopeful and constructive redescription of the moral parameters and prospects of a given 'we'. The prime communitarian objection to liberalism is that it ignores our embeddedness in given cultural practices, practices which are constitutive of our ends and of our conceptions of the good rather than being simply incidental to them. If this is the charge, then Rorty, in endorsing the revamped Rawls, can hardly be seen to depart from it. To this extent, his own liberalism is heavily inflected by communitarian themes.

But while communitarian objections to liberalism's atomistic, self-interested account of the 'rational chooser' are important and telling, it is not *this* aspect of communitarianism with which Rorty's own case is most saliently resonant. For in dismantling the classical liberal aspiration to detachment and unencumberedness, communitarianism tends to lean too far in another direction: to overemphasize the force of cultural determination to the point of a ready collapse into a conservative affirmation that 'tradition comes first' (whatever the tradition), or into cultural relativism, or both. This is where Rorty's liberalism chimes in most clearly. For in insisting that the standard for our ethical and political judgements 'can only be something relatively local and ethnocentric – the tradition of a particular community, the consensus of a particular culture', he makes his liberalism relative to precisely that set of necessarily *local* determinants which communitarians counterpose to the ahistoricity of liberal selfhood and principle.[96]

Is this the 'thicker' sense of Rorty's ethnocentrism which would make it more than just a semantic point about the nature of moral claims? Well maybe, but if so he takes communitarianism further than it needs to go. He makes it a thesis not just about the *source* of practical reason, but also its *scope* – or seems to, at least, in the following, much picked upon passage:

> Consider... the attitude of contemporary American liberals to the unending hopelessness and misery of the lives of the young blacks in American cities. Do we say that these people must be helped because they are our fellow human beings? We may, but it is much more persuasive, morally as well as politically, to describe them as our fellow *Americans* – to insist that it is outrageous than an *American* should live without hope.[97]

Now Rorty presents this simply as back-up to his suggestion that 'our sense of solidarity when those with whom solidarity is expressed are thought of as "one of us", where "us" means something smaller and more local than the human race'.[98] This seems fairly uncontentious, in so far as we know some people better than others. But even granting it, it is not clear that anything in particular follows from it in terms of moral principle. Unless Rorty means here that our moral obligation goes only so far as the solidarities we have a sense of. But in fact, this is exactly what he means.[99] In invoking Sellars's 'analysis of *moral obligation* in terms of "we-intentions"' he takes 'the explanatory notion in this area to be "one of us"' – and gives as examples such references as 'our sort of people', and 'a fellow Catholic (as opposed to a Protestant, a Jew, or an atheist)'.[100] So it seems indeed that Rorty is saying: the scope of moral obligation is confined within set *limits*: geographical, linguistic or just in terms of our cultural affinities. If there were no such limits – if the reference of 'us' were indeed expanded to the whole of the human race – then the force of moral injunction is simply diluted accordingly. This is because we would be deprived of a 'they' relative to which an 'us' might have persuasive purchase.[101]

Rorty is not just, as Will Kymlicka describes it, 'making a *prediction* about the limits of practical reason'. He's not just saying 'Here's an abnormal description of what's most persuasive in moral persuasion. Let's see if it works.' Bear in mind his claim that standards for moral judgement 'can *only* be something relatively local and ethnocentric – the tradition of a particular community, the consensus of a particular culture'. This is a transcendental claim about the very possibility and limits of moral deliberation. Rorty claims 'to *know* such limits exist', claims 'to know this *in advance of the arguments*', claims 'to know that reasons will only be compelling to particular historical communities, before those reasons have been advanced'.[102] On the basis of this, he makes the further claim that we can best understand moral obligation as extending only as far as the 'we' which, in a given scenario, provides the appropriate contrast with a correlative 'they'. But what could be the basis of such a transcendental claim? An appeal to the facts of historical and cultural variation? Or to the vast divergence in forms of life and discourses of justice across the globe? Neither sort of observation is able to furnish a ruling out of the possibility that there might be context-transcendent ethical norms.

What I would contend is that Rorty is led to this claim by a tacit presumption, along the lines of the Walzer quote above, that there are only two alternative courts of appeal on offer: the *strictly* local and ethnocentric on the one hand, or the *strictly* acultural and ahistorical on the other. This is not to say that he must appeal to some crudely static or drastically local 'we', or even that the smaller the 'we' the greater the available 'constrast-effect' must become. He does not – as his centreless view of the self must entail – presuppose that a single, fixed identity is the be-all and end-all of moral jurisdiction.[103] In fact, nor does he make any sort of transcendental claim about the impossibility of our 'particular community' or our 'particular culture' coming to encompass the whole of humanity. (And given that incommensurability is only a 'temporary inconvenience', how could he?) Indeed, again: he recommends that we 'keep trying to expand our sense of "us" as far as we can'.[104] There are no necessary barriers to this, only the contingent forces of luck and persuasion.

As Geras argues, though, the possibility of a sense of 'we' capable of encompassing the whole of humanity would mean a cancellation of Rorty's premise concerning the contrast-effect as a vital ingredient of the sense of a 'we'. Either you can get there, to all-inclusivity, or you cannot.[105] Now given that (to put it no more strongly) it is not the case that in principle we *cannot* get there, then Rorty's necessitarian claims about the scope for moral deliberation and the requirement of a contrast-effect must either be jettisoned or acknowledged as precisely that – necessary claims, transcendental claims which affirm in advance the criteria for the enlargement of the 'we'. In other words, and to return to the quote at the head of this section, it is to put some prior condition, some identifiable limit, on the expansion of moral space. It is, in a roundabout way, to play by the rules characteristic of moral universalism.

How does Rorty get *here* from his taking of the second option provided by Walzer's dichotomy? Circuitously, certainly. To do so, he invokes what I would call, after Hauke Brunkhorst, a 'weak universalism'.[106] He allows for a possible pan-global moral community without suggesting that there is anything which makes us definitively human or worthy of equal respect. Or rather, he allows that Le Doeuff's universal 'respecting humanity in others' might be achieved along with the success of some given picture of what humanity is like – 'ours'. For liberal ironists are the sort of people who think, publicly, that human beings should be treated with equal respect. But they include among human beings, for these purposes, only those so far admitted into the orbit of 'we' or 'us'. By putting this (as we have seen) transcendental limit on those entitled to universal respect, Rorty's weak universalism relies entirely on ungrounded hope. As Pierre Bourdieu has observed, 'the propensity to universalize the particular case' is 'the root of all forms of ethnocentrism', even while it is 'supported by all the appearances of generosity and virtue'. On these terms, Rorty's thinking indeed bears out the fears of universalism which inform Lyotard's critique of its imperialistic implications. For the extension of the scope of morality to humanity at large will be precisely, and only that – an *extension* of of our, contingent, culture-bound moral codes and practices across recalcitrant boundaries in the name of some definitively partial account of the moral good. Thus it is the very *weakness* of Rorty's universalism which renders it imperialistic.

*Liberal ironism's splits and limits*

I mentioned that liberal ironism must depend on ungrounded hope. To the extent that Rorty's ideal citizens publicly affirm a commitment to liberalism while at the same time privately acknowledging it to be without metaphysical foundation, this certainly holds up. A central claim of *CIS* is that it is impossible to reconcile the public and private domains – a Platonic hope that would 'let us hold self-creation and justice, private perfection and human solidarity, in a single vision'.[107] Given that we *cannot* do this, we should keep self-creation as a private affair, and not let our projects of self-redescription infect a public sphere where they may, given their idiosyncrasy, work to harm others.

We have already seen in 2.2 that, in fact, Rorty does seem to make covert appeal to a version of human nature, at the level of requiring an autonomous self for the process of self-creation he describes. But there is another sense, so far not dealt with, in which he has leant rather heavily on an anthropological conceit to which his own historicism should deny him access.[108] This is in his consistent invoking, throughout *CIS*, of the power of redescription to cause cruelty – specifically, humiliation. So 'the best way to cause people long-lasting pain is to humiliate them by making the things that seemed most important to them look futile, obsolete, and powerless'.[109] Thus 'redescription often humiliates', by threatening people's capacity to view themselves on their own terms, rather than the redescriber's.[110] We have 'a common susceptibility to humiliation'.[111] Privately, I may redescribe everybody however I like. But as a liberal, 'the part of my final vocabulary which is relevant to such actions requires me to become aware of all the various ways in which other human beings whom I might act upon can be humiliated'.[112]

I want to say only two brief things here. One is that, as has been widely picked up on, Rorty here lapses into a claim about what human beings, in common are like: that is, susceptible to humiliation. The wrong of humiliation amounts, in practice, to a deprivation of the autonomy which, as we saw in the last chapter, Rorty (covertly) requires that we have by virtue of being self-redescribing beings. Now consider the following passage, from elsewhere:

> 'Who are we?' is quite different from the traditional philosophical question 'what are we?' . . . This 'what?' question is scientific or metaphysical . . . Traditional moral universalism blends an answer to the scientific 'what?' question with an answer to the political 'who?' question . . . Following the model of religious claims that human beings are made in the image of God, philosophical universalism claims that the presence of common traits testifies to a common purpose.[113]

To put it bluntly, Rorty conducts exactly the sort of exercise, in claiming that all human beings are susceptible to humiliation by redescription, that he describes the moral universalist as making. He identifies a core, definitive aspect of human being, installs it as a 'what', and then defines it as the paradigm case of cruelty, which is, after all, 'the worst thing humans do'. He thus importantly fails to avoid what he calls 'the embarrassments of the universalist claim that the term "human being" . . . names an unchanging essence, an ahistorical natural kind with a permanent set of unchanging features'.[114] The unchanging essences of 'human being' are, at least, 'to be the sort of being that can redescribe itself and others of its kind', and 'to be the sort of being that can thereby be humiliated'. Cruelty is not something about which 'we liberals' can be ironic. Rorty could not, in fact, substantially distance himself from this statement by Eagleton of (in effect) the limits constraining our redescriptions: 'All human beings are frail, mortal and needy, vulnerable to pain and death. The fact that these transhistorical truths are always culturally specific, always variably instantiated, is no argument against their transhistoricality.'[115] Thus, his limiting of the scope of redescription is based upon an ontological claim.

So when Rorty states that, having taken 'the morally relevant definition of a person, a moral subject, to be "something than can be humiliated"', the ironist's sense of human solidarity 'is based on a sense of a common danger, not on a common possession or a shared power', he is relying on slippery logic.[116] For in saying, shortly afterwards, that 'pain is nonlinguistic', Rorty is saying that there is a prelinguistic potential to be humiliated. This potential is not a 'mere' danger, or a possible effect of discourse. It is a common possession. And in any case, its *being* a danger requires precisely the existence of a shared power: to humiliate others. In the absence of this power, the danger would not arise. And cruelty is the worst thing we do. Thus, as Simon Critchley rightly points out, Rorty is in fact 'attempting to base moral obligation and political practice upon a foundational claim about human susceptibility to humiliation, upon a recognition of the other's suffering'. To this, Rorty might reply: but it is only a given constituency – 'we liberals' – that need think like this for my claim to hold, and that the claim is thereby relativized and any 'embarrassment' avoided. But even so, 'the claim has the status of a non-relativizable universal for "we liberals", with our set of "we-intentions"'.[117] Our private irony cannot detach us from the claim; if it did, rather obviously, we would no longer be *liberal* ironists.

The public/private split which Rorty calls upon here is similarly problematic. It is clear enough that it runs the danger of rehearsing the classical liberal blindspot regarding injustices committed in the private sphere.[118] That said, for Rorty, this private sphere is not, as in Mill, empirically conceived. It cannot be made to correlate *cleanly* with the domestic arena, for instance, since one's private ironizing is permitted by a diremption of the self, rather than a hard distinction between public and private actions.[119] It is attitudinal, rather than pertaining to aspects of the social structure. But what it does do is reintroduce the problem of 'harm', as conceived (vaguely) by Mill in *On Liberty*.[120] For as with Mill, it is difficult to see exactly what *constitutes* 'harmful' actions – if redescription can here be taken as an action in an equivalent sense. The trouble with Rorty's formulation is that 'the things which are most important to me' about my final vocabulary might include my cherished liberal belief that cruelty is the worst thing we do. But they might equally include my next-door neighbour's belief that all liberals should be summarily executed. Since the creation of a final vocabulary is her own private affair, there is nothing to withhold her from cherishing this belief, or indeed by organizing her life around it. Thus if humiliation does consist in making the things most important to people seem 'futile, obsolete and powerless', then she will, definitively, be humiliated by my forceful redescription of her as an enemy of the liberal virtues and thereby ineligible for membership of the same 'we' as I.

An implication of this is that, as Eric Gander argues, Rorty's focus on humiliation as the archetypal, gravest harm actually obliterates any sustainable distinction between the public and the private. The only reason why Rorty's liberal ironist must keep her private vocabulary private is that it will be illiberal – otherwise, why keep it private? But those who are susceptible to humiliation by others – all of us, as human beings – must, in fact, be characterized by our *inability* to split our selves down the middle in this way. For 'if we all could simply split our vocabularies into a private and a public part . . . it seems that we could all be free of the possibility of being humiliated'.[121] Why? Because with the capacity to be thoroughgoingly ironic about our own private vocabularies, we would be able to distance ourselves from what we hold most dear about our self-descriptions. But the very problem of humiliation must arise because we cannot in fact so do. Looked at from the reverse angle, it is easy enough to imagine scenarios in which having to keep one's private vocabulary private would itself be a humiliation. Gander takes the case of the clashing private vocabularies of a homosexual and a moral traditionalist, once both of them have signed up to the idea that humiliation is wrong. For the homosexual, being forced to keep his private vocabulary private (and so not disclose his sexual preferences) would itself be humiliating: it would be to render one of the things most important to him powerless. But for the traditionalist, in light of his alternative unique, private final vocabulary's ordering of values, humiliation would loom in continued membership of a society which publicly acknowledged homosexuality.[122] If either decided to leave the society, withdraw their citizenship and seek asylum elsewhere, then this itself would humiliate those dutiful liberals whose own final vocabularies led them to invest deeply in the flourishing of an inclusive, cruelty-free 'we'. And so on, and so on; the chains of humiliation might, quite conceivably, be endless. Humiliation – as indeed harm, in Mill's account – seems to suffer the drawback that, as a criterion of right action, its definition could never be pinned down to the extent that it would provide a standard which could, in practice, be readily and clearly invoked.

A secondary problem here (implied, though not explicit in Gander's argument) is that the first to go public with their final vocabulary will effectively set the tone by which future shapings of the public vocabulary will develop. And thus, the public vocabulary will be formed on the basis of might rather than right. It will become an agglomeration of those private vocabularies which have managed to assert themselves first, and by which subsequent contributions will be judged. This applies most especially in cases where, as Gander notes, one's private vocabulary requires public articulation in order to realize itself – as with one's sexual preferences, or one's passionate commitment to supporting Dundee United FC. Needless to say, there will be no transcendent criteria by which the overall direction of those sedimenting contributions might be evaluated, accepted, rejected, and so on. They can merely be assessed in terms of their fit with existing public discourse.

We are returned to the conventionally derived limits which Rorty's communitarian-inflected moral epistemology will engender upon being cashed out. The requirement that everyone keep private what might potentially humiliate *anyone* else would thus require that no one go public with their most cherished opinions. This itself would work to constrict rather than expand the range of 'public' conversation. And would lead, one would expect, to a contraction rather than expansion of the moral space which Rorty's historicism invites us to expand in the direction of a more inclusive sense of 'we'.

So while Rorty's universalism is certainly 'there', in a weak sense, and while this breaks his own strictures against metaphysical claims, it actually serves very little purpose other than, at best, to draw our attention to the fact that other people can be made to suffer much as we can, and in a similar way. Like Lyotard's furtive imperative to bear witness to particularity, Rorty's identification of susceptibility to humiliation as the one common human attribute he is prepared to sanction does not in fact take us beyond a fairly crude moral subjectivism – and one which seems likely to stifle, rather than encourage, the extension of inclusivity.

## 3.2. Three versions of universalism

If both Rorty and Lyotard fail to sever all links with universalism, and end up retrieving aspects of it in a different register, does this tell us that universalism is in fact unavoidable? Is it perhaps entailed in the rendering of any coherent political or ethical stance that we appeal to *some* form, however weak, of universal purchase for its implications? To argue for this conclusion would be to make a point about practical reason – and reason in general – which is, for the most part, beyond my scope here. One can, of course, make much of the standard self-referentiality problem encountered by advocates of relativism: does the claim 'truth is relative to a given culture' escape relativity to a given culture? As Rorty mentions, if such a claim amounts to 'the view that every belief on a certain topic, or perhaps about *any* topic, is as good as every other', then 'no one holds this view'.[123] The real issue, as he frames it, is between 'those who think our culture, or purpose, or intuitions cannot be supported except conversationally, and people who still hope for other sorts of support'.[124] In the second category would, of course, fall both realists and universalists.

But this seems to be a misframing of the issue – and one which serves to disguise Rorty's own ambiguous relationship to universalism. I would venture to suggest, without too much hesitation since he has done so himself, that part of Rorty's antipathy towards universalism (defined, as quoted earlier, in terms of a claim to prior grasp of the contours of logical and moral space) stems from a perception of its usage in American political rhetoric. In one 1980s piece, he directly associates the term with apologists for the Reagan presidency and the Christian-conservative right wing. The flak he gets from such people, he says, suggests to him that he must be on the right track in insisting on historicism: 'the idea that there are no "universal and objective values" to be found in "human nature"'.[125] Hence his characterization of the divide in terms of conversational or other support for 'our culture'. Conservatives are those who seek metaphysical back-up for existing codes of moral behaviour; radicals seek to block off any such recourse.

This seems to me to skew the issues. It does so in a way typical of postmodernist and other, purportedly radical, denials of common aspects of human being. The assumption here is that undermining any claim to universality is itself a radical gesture, because of the dubious purposes to which claims to universality have been put. Lyotard's blaming of 'modern' approaches to progress for Auschwitz and the

Gulag Archipelago are in point here, as are Foucault's unmaskings of the insidiously normalizing nature of modern regimes of social rationalization.[126] These are the tip of an iceberg of recent social and political theory which seeks to garner something inherently progressive from the destabilizing of categories (unmasked as effects of power, or imperialistic, totalizing reason) and the upholding of the ephemeral and fragmentary.

Three factors, among many, cast doubt upon this move. One is that universalistic underpinnings are hard finally to jettison without a collapse into straightforward parochialism. As we have seen, to avoid (as David Harvey describes it) 'ghettoizing' suppressed voices 'within an opaque otherness, the specificity of this or that language game', Lyotard himself falls back on a fairly standard Enlightenment-liberal notion of equal rights.[127] Another is that these switches of focus from the universal to the local amount to a denial of any metatheory that might grasp the predominantly universalizing processes of a globalizing age. As Ellen Meiskins Wood, amongst many others, has pointed out, 'whatever the conjunctural conditions of the current anti-universalism, the epochal logic of capitalism is clearly running in the opposite direction'.[128] Thus the retreat from universalism can actually lead to a disengagement with the historical circumstances to which Rorty would orient us in its stead. A third factor, implied I hope in the first two, is that a genuinely emancipatory politics cannot afford to sever itself altogether from every last trace of universalism. In fact, the universalizing process by which oppressive social forms entrench themselves – be they arising from the logic of capitalist economic expansion, or unequal power relations, or enforced adherence to patriarchal assumptions – can 'be countered only by another, more genuinely universalistic project'.[129]

Against Rorty's setting up of the stakes, then, I would like to defend a claim that an appropriately conceived universalism is crucial to any putatively progressive conception of the moral and political. This bears back upon the discussion in 3.1. For I take the different forms of universalism to which Lyotard and Rorty have ultimate recourse to point towards two distinct senses in which we might understand the term. To this I will add a third, sketched alternative – a model which I think best embodies universalism's emancipatory potential.

*Atomistic universalism*

Lyotard's covert universalism is of an atomistic kind – although one might also call it 'formalistic'. As such, it exemplifies many of the core features of classical liberalism. This tradition has tended to ground its advocation of tolerance of diverse conceptions of the good in one or more of four main ways, which are worth briefly delineating with a representative slogan for each. (1) *Anglo-Saxon sceptical empiricism* (Locke, Mill, Popper): since there is no right answer to questions about the good life, the flourishing of alternative answers can only enhance society.[130] (2) *State neutrality* (Dworkin, Nozick): the state has no right to impose its ideas about the good on its citizens.[131] (3) *Individual autonomy*: some factor about human beings – be it the capacity for rational selfhood or to order and execute their own life projects (Kant, Rawls), or their possession of a natural right (Locke, Nozick) – means that as agents they are entitled to pursue their chosen life projects in their own preferred way.[132] (4) *Incommensurability* (Berlin). Different values – between forms of life, and within them – are not jointly measurable on a common scale. There is no overall scheme within which competing, but incompatible, claims can be reconciled. Any claim to such inevitably suppresses alternative claims.[133]

I set these out because, whether installing the phrase as ontologically primary or reimporting human beings into his 'justice of multiplicity', aspects of Lyotard's thinking correspond to all four moments. His 'incredulity towards metanarratives' corresponds with the sceptical empiricist suspicion of what Lyotard would call 'the logic of result' (Popper's work is quite a clear antecedent in this respect). His relinquishing of a meta-position from which we might judge the respective worth of discursive genres matches up with the appeal to state neutrality. He views language games – as Kant views the subject – as fundamentally autonomous. And the appeal to pluralism based on incommensurability is as central to his system as it is to that of Berlin – the parallel being strengthened when human beings are allowed back into Lyotard's picture.

This is, of course, a drastically reductive laying out of the liberal tradition, and makes no claim to finality. It serves here only to make the point that Lyotard's thinking can be fairly readily assimilated with the principal themes of that tradition. I make this point because, to the extent that liberalism bases itself in universalism – as, for instance, with the early Rawls – its version has marked similarities to that into which Lyotard's thinking ends up slipping back. For both are characteristically *atomistic*. Charles Taylor defines atomism, humanistically, as entailing that it is possible for human beings to go it alone: that we can be fully fledged agents quite apart from any relation to society.[134] On these terms, the existence of other human beings, and my relation to them, is incidental rather than definitive of my subjectivity. We are definitively self-sufficient. On this basis, liberals have tended to conceive of freedom *negatively*: as my freedom from external obstruction in realizing my own life projects as I see fit.[135] Thus, as in Rawls's *Theory of Justice*, their attention has been focused on how to maximize the potential for each individual to realize those projects without impediment: typically, by a negative right to freedom from state interference in so doing.

The now-standard objection to this conception of rights was inaugurated by Marx in 'On the Jewish question': that so conceived, they are rights of separation from others and from the community, and so invoke a monadic, egoistic self, 'withdrawn into himself'.[136] It is reinforced in C. B. MacPherson's critique of 'possessive liberalism', arguing as it does that theorists like Hobbes and Locke have installed as self-evident aspects of human nature features which have, in fact, been fostered and encouraged by capitalist market relations.[137] It thus mistakes a contingency for a necessity. And by conceiving of human beings in possessive-individualist terms, the enforcement of the rights so derived will serve to entrench the unequal distribution of opportunities and resources within a capitalist society. So conceived and so enforced, rights represent a need to contain the consequences of inequality.[138] The gist of Rorty's objection to Lyotard's view of language games in terms of isolated 'islets' is an objection precisely to the epistemological tenability of such an ontological conception of radical separateness. As in the liberal conception of rights, Lyotard's appeal to the sanctity of atomized language games rests on the assumption that genres of discourse are, primarily, from the point of view of ethical concern, a *threat* to each other's autonomy. Hence his need to appeal to formal equal rights.

The universalism derived from this basis will, as in Lyotard's case, amount to a universal right to protection, as a monadic entity, from the threat posed by other such entities to my (or a genre's) chances of survival and persistence in the form I choose (or the genre's rules dictate). And as such, it will be purely formal – and so subject to Marx's objections to the legal institution of liberal rights in the modern state, as hypostatizing present relations at a formal level while failing to attend to the relationality of 'civil society' beneath. Thus Lyotard will seek to preserve intact existing relations between genres of discourse while abstracting from their necessary overlap. (Rorty's objections to

Lyotard's conception of language games are, then, merited – but go against the grain of his own liberal inclinations.) This hypostatization is tantamount to a call for protection of the status quo – for the forbidding of interference with given genres of discourse in the name of any purported ('metanarrative') emancipatory project based on 'the politics of redemption'.

Thus the latent universalism present in Lyotard's postmodern justice mirrors that 'bad' universalism identified by Marx as a fetter on the scope for genuine emancipation at the level of concrete lived experience. In a linguistic register, Lyotard's call for equal rights to articulation for phrases and genres of discourse is a right to articulation regardless of whether the claims made within a given genre are emancipatory or – as with the Faurisson case – definitively thwarting of progressive movements. They are a safeguarding of difference for its own sake.

*Strategic universalism*

If, then, Lyotard's smuggled-in universalism is inherently conservative, what of Rorty's own, informal version? It has emerged in the foregoing that the latter registers itself in two main ways. First, Rorty, in his appeal to self-description and humiliation as shared human attributes, does, despite his denials, make claims about the common 'what' of human being. The second sense is half negative – he does not rule out the possibility of a pan-human 'we' – and half positive: he indeed regards universal inclusion in our sense of 'us' as a worthy goal. This seems to me to amount to what we might designate a 'strategic' variant of universalism. For many, himself included, it is no universalism at all. I would suggest, again, that it is universalism in tentative form.

Strategic universalism will always be 'weak' in the sense cited earlier, in the sense that it will attempt to avoid making prior claims about the contours of 'moral space' and the range and nature of our responsibilities. But it will hold out hope of a hegemonic expansion of our current sense of 'we'. I take a strategic version of universalism to be exemplified in recent work by Ernesto Laclau. Laclau argues, against defenders of 'extreme particularism', that in fact 'the particular can only fully realize itself if it constantly keeps open, and constantly redefines, its relation to the universal'. Thus, 'the assertion of one's particularity requires the appeal to something transcending it'.[139] On Laclau's (post-structuralist) terms, it only makes sense to talk about the rejection of universality if one can talk of a fully homogeneous community beyond which there is nothing else, no remainder or residue to which particularity might be relative. As long as there is no such homogeneity, the universal remains as that which is not fully represented by current convention, by the rules of the relevant genre of discourse: as 'the symbol of a missing fullness', a 'constitutive lack'.[140] The co-existence of particularities, as Laclau argues, is actually impossible without the admission of certain shared universal values, without norms and principles which transcend the particularism of any language game. From this angle, sanctifying (as does Lyotard) the existing heterogeneity of discursive genres simply means increasing the chances of social stasis.

Laclau shares Rorty's 'historicist' understanding of moral space as being contingent, fluid and subject to future negotiation and expansion. He accuses Rorty of being 'unnecessarily defensive' in thinking that such a conception requires the outright rejection of universalism.[141] But in fact, on my reading of Rorty, he does not in fact reject universalism in an outright way, but rather reinstates it as a worthy aim of 'we liberals': a possibility to be achieved, in terms of universal equal respect, but not given in current logical or moral space. Thus his own picture, in its different idiom, coincides with Laclau's in seeing universality as historically relative but not, for all that, closed off by the assertion of particularity. But nor can universality provide an escape from that particularity. Rorty would, I think, concur with Laclau in arguing that universal principles, while purportedly transcendent, 'sooner or later become entangled in their own contextual particularism'.[142] In Rorty's words; '*we* have to start from where *we* are'.

I see as a necessary component of strategic universalisms some version of Rorty's call, in a recent article, for a dispensing with the opposition between 'loyalty' and 'justice'. This apparent conflict, he says, arises in the expectation that our family will stand by us even when we have done something wrong. It sharpens when, as a result of their standing by us, an innocent person is wrongly convicted of our crime. What Rorty insists is that such a conflict will only be felt to the extent that we can identify with the innocent person we have harmed:

> If the person is a neighbour, then the conflict will probably be intense. If a stranger, especially one of a different race, class or nation, it may be considerably weaker. There has to be *some* sense in which he or she is 'one of us', before we start to be tormented by the question of whether or not we

did the right thing when we committed perjury. So it may be equally appropriate to describe us as torn between conflicting loyalties – loyalty to our family and to a group large enough to include the victim of our perjury – rather than between loyalty and justice.[143]

Under this rubric, 'the idea of a universal moral obligation to respect human dignity gets replaced by the idea of loyalty to a very large group – the human species'.[144] If, that is, our sense of moral responsibility has extended its orbit that far. For Rorty this is, of course, a contingency, since 'one's moral identity is determined by the group or groups with which one identifies – the group or groups to which one cannot be disloyal and still like oneself'.[145] Thus, in order to construct a global moral community, 'we Westerners' need to 'get rid of the notion of universal moral obligations created by membership in the species, and substitute the idea of building a community of trust between ourselves and others'.[146] Our chances of pursuing this aim would be improved if 'we were more frankly ethnocentric, and less professedly universalist' – if we said 'Here is what we in the West look like as a result of ceasing to hold slaves, beginning to educate women, separating church and state, and so on': if we made the sources of our own moral identity look better than the alternatives.[147]

For stategic universalists, purportedly at any rate, neither the rules by which we might include in 'us' those hitherto regarded as 'them', nor the attributes of human being most important to our sense of 'us', need be necessary, or specified in advance. With Rorty, they will hold that we need to peel apart the Enlightenment liberal sense of cosmopolitanism from the Enlightenment rationalist sense that holding such a value requires us to appeal to something inherently human which is worthy of equal respect. And like Rorty they will insist that Lyotard-style formalism is unnecessary. Iris Marion Young makes a kindred point: 'universality in the sense of the participation and inclusion of everyone in moral and social life does not imply universality in the sense of adoption of a general point of view that leaves behind particular affiliations, feelings, commitments, and desires'.[148]

But this, I think, points to a problem with strategic universalism. It hinges on whether it is possible to have inclusive, participatory democracy as a goal without making appeal to factors beyond particular affiliations and commitments. I do not think that it is. This is borne out, I think, in Rorty's own conception of the issues. For, first, while Rorty (and Laclau, and Young) seek to avoid the conservative and reductive implications of 'identity politics' in its cruder formulations, they remain within the horizon of an appeal to identity as, morally and politically, the only game in town. To put this differently, while Rorty does not want to hypostatize a given 'we' and (as Lyotard's model does) put it in permanent agonistic relations with other discrete, hermetically sealed identities, he does, nonetheless, fall back on our sense of identity as defining the available options for progress. Thus when he says that 'there seems no particular reason to hope for immortality for any contemporary set of cultural differences, as opposed to hoping that it may eventually be supplanted by a new and more interesting set', or that 'we should let a hundred flowers bloom, admire them while they last, and leave botanizing to the intellectual historians of the next century', a certain constraint on these flourishings goes unacknowledged.[149] The constraint is this, as he puts it himself: 'we all start out thinking of ourselves as a member of some group'.[150] This is a foundational claim. It makes the future expansion of moral space contingent not on wild chance, but on possible resonances with 'our' common intuitions, 'our' practices, 'our' tradition. He appeals to these as historical givens.[151]

Thus the effect of his collapsing of the distinction between loyalty and justice is to assume that loyalty is in some sense foundational. It puts actual, even if not transcendental, limits on the scope of our identifications, and tethers our 'imaginative ability to identify with people whom their ancestors had not been able to identify with' to the residue of those preceding identifications.[152] Similarly, while Laclau rightly dispatches the claim that identities can meaningfully assert themselves in strict isolation, he still regards what lies beyond them in terms, merely, of further identities. The effect of this is to deprive identity, and its range and scope, of any contrast-effect with something else ('justice', as Rorty puts it) from which we might gain a critical leverage *on the morality of our own identity*.

A second point is this. If the appeal to inclusion does not imply universality in the sense of 'adoption of a general point of view', what does it imply? It is just not clear that Rorty himself comes up with a *purely* pragmatic justification for the liberalism he supports. Rorty's utopia is avowedly pluralistic: 'the inhabitants of such a culture would be more interested in the proliferation of languages, tasks, and forms of human life than in the convergence of scientific and metaphysical opinion to a single set of propositions'.[153] There may, to be sure, in the light of my previous point, be a difficulty in getting to such a point from a relatively homogeneous starting point. But notice here, at any rate, a certain prior pronouncement about the contours of moral space. Rorty makes a normative prognosis; liberal pluralism is, quite certainly, a goal he seems ready to affirm in advance. If this is a pragmatic gesture, then it must be affirmable solely in terms of its capacity better to serve our current purposes. It must have some utility. But (to return to my argument in 2.1) *either* it remains as a meaningless metaphorical horizon – a sketching of moral space the dimensions of which we will not realize – *or* it is realizable in terms of those current purposes. This will be a contingent process. It might not happen; things *might* (Rorty's 'historicism' must insist) tend in a diametrically opposite direction, towards ever-increasing homogeneity. In which case, Rorty's own prognosis will not have been proved to be more pragmatically efficacious. It will, in Young's terms, be a goal which makes appeal to factors beyond particular affliations and commitments. Would it still be worth having as a goal? Rorty must say no.

Strategic universalism's refusal to anchor itself in claims either about 'human being' or 'reality' thus leave it rigidly in hock to its own conception of the given – and especially, to the givenness of identities. Its own promise of expansion beyond the moral space bequeathed by those identities is rendered fragile by its own refusal to appeal to anything substantially common about humanity or its relation to a world of factors beyond identity. In its self-restriction to the horizontal, and relinquishing of all claims to the vertical, it becomes, in effect, a form of identity monism, and denies all other ontological levels. In the process, it finds it difficult to own up to any normative basis for its own contention that there is something 'good' about equality and inclusion. To return to Le Doeuff: it cannot account for a demand to 'respect humanity in others', because, aside from the contingent constructions of the given identity in which we are working, there is no such thing to respect. Even on a purely pragmatic basis, any call to recognize the equality of others will be rhetorically hampered by its own hollowness – which in turn, would make its chances of succeeding rather slim.

*Relational universalism*

Arguably, there is an available third sense of universalism which avoids the deficiencies of the first two. Against atomism and formalism, it emphasizes the relational and concrete aspects of human being. Against strategic variants, it insists that some such account of human being is necessary for the coherence and viability – and indeed the pragmatic efficacy – of any universalist appeal.

Surfacing earlier in our discussion of the atomistic account was the allegation of its blindness towards social structure. As we saw in 2.2, Rorty's root methodological individualism (shared with the classical liberal tradition) leads him to abstract from our embodiment, from social structures, and from economic and historical realities (in a material sense) in his depiction of the powers and role of redescription. And yet, as we have seen in this chapter, he is happy to admit *cultural* constraints on the formation of our identity. In fact, in a fairly standard postmodernist move, having hoisted the subject beyond contamination by the material, he returns it to a deep embeddedness in culture. Rorty understands culture in an empirical sense: it is the given practices of our community which limit the scope of the expansion of moral space.

What this amounts to – and this is a point I will return to in 4.2 – is a simultaneous denial of relationality, and an affirmation of relativism. These combine to deprive us of any substantial sense of 'respecting humanity in others'. Mentioned in an earlier chapter was Rorty's characterization of naturalists as seeing 'everything is constituted by its relations to other things, and as having no intrinsic, ineluctable nature'.[154] This, of course applies to human nature. But to present things like this is to use a sort of sleight of hand. For what it dangles and takes away is the possibility of looking at things from a reverse angle: namely, to claim that relationality is part of the nature of human beings. Since this will be fleshed out further later on, I will offer here only a brief sketch of the sort of conception which might be built on such a claim.

Relationality here pertains in two main directions. One is towards the world. While Rorty, Lyotard and Laclau displace relationality to the level of the linguistic, and so drive a (Cartesian) wedge between the operations of language and our engagement with the world, this conception would avoid the resultant dualism by insisting, with the early Marx, that our practical engagement with the world is both the source of what makes human beings distinctive, and *prior to language*.[155] Thus neither consciousness nor language exist in a self-referential realm of internal relationships. On the contrary: as the phenomenological tradition maintains, consciousness is always *consciousness of something*, something ontologically independent of its own formations. Our most distinctive powers and attributes as human beings are not understandable in radical disjunction from reality. With Bhaskar, this conception argues that realism is thus 'implied by our deeds, whatever our words, and then of course by our words, once we understand them as deeds'.[156] Reality here includes our experiences of our own subjectivity. This cannot be adequately understood by way of mediation through language, or some necessarily social epistemological aspect. Archer observes that 'A broken limb is something over which we can fume because of its direct restriction upon our mobility *per se*, that is regardless of it preventing us joining socially organized events. A convincing social constructionist account of a broken leg has never been encountered.'[157] It follows that practical interaction with reality can be seen as prior to our linguistic access to the world. Our conception here requires that we see ourselves, with Marx, as being, definitively, engaged in continuous practical activity in a material world. The practical relationship between us and things cannot be reduced to internal relations within language, or between ideas.

But nor are we definable purely in terms of a monologic relationship with nature or the world. The other direction of relationality is towards other human beings. For this to be a definitive aspect of human being, the liberal individual must indeed be the product of a fake atomization, and a fake universalization. It is fake because while its understanding of the individual purports to sever its connection to social relations, and conceive of the individual in the abstract, in fact the figure of the liberal individual is (to use a wildly unfashionable word) a bourgeois construct. It is ideologically loaded in two ways. First, it argues (for the sake of the desired view of the rational individual as a self-interested utility maximizer, or whatever) that individuals' relations to others are a purely contingent – and morally secondary – aspect of their make-up. Secondly, and for all that, it incorporates *given* aspects of contemporary social relations into an account which is professedly neutral. Hence – for instance – MacPherson's criticism of Hobbes that his 'scientific' conception of human nature in fact 'corresponds only to a bourgeois market society'.[158] But against Rorty, the rejection of this view of human nature, and the admission of relationality, does not negate the very possibility of firm, transcultural claims about what it is to be human. Rather, it requires that a cooperative and social aspect is crucial to realizing our potential as human beings. As has been seen, the denial of *any* such potentials to human being, and thus of the possibility of basing of normative demands on those potentials, is a harder trick to pull off than the methodology of

Rorty, and indeed Lyotard, maintains. There are, then, more than just conversational constraints on the processes of human being.

Now it might seem curious, in defending a conception of universality against postmodernist rejections, not to be appealing to the work of Habermas, whose own critique of the postmodern attempt to relinquish the aims of the Enlightenment has been so effective.[159] My hesitation here derives from Habermas's wholesale taking of the 'linguistic turn' – a turn for the worse, in so far as it brackets all 'vertical' relations between human being and the world in favour of a purely linguistic paradigm of inquiry. In appealing to a communicative model of rationality, Habermas seeks to emphasize the dialogical (rather than monological) nature of reason, instead of the interaction between 'man' and 'nature'. Thus he argues that 'rationalization', on correct construal, can mean 'extirpating those relations of force that are inconspicuously set in the very strictures of communication and that prevent conscious settlement of conflicts'.[160] It is this (universal) aspect of rationality which Habermas seeks to reconstruct in the name of a reinvigoration of the Enlightenment project. It is 'a reason that has been arrested again and again, ideologically misused and distorted, but that also stubbornly raises its voice in every inconspicuous act of successful communication'.[161]

Habermas derives his model of reason from an account of 'universal pragmatics' – that is to say, in terms of the 'general presuppositions of communicative action'.[162] Simply in using language, we are making claims of validity that are inherent in the very act of communication: namely, that what is said is (a) intelligible, (b) true, (c) justified and (d) sincere.[163] Thus 'in the validity claims, however implicit, by means of which we are obliged to orientate in our communicative actions, a persistent, albeit repeatedly suppressed, claim of reason lies concealed'.[164] On this basis, Habermas has developed a conception of 'discourse ethics' which explicitly (unlike in Lyotard's case) treats distortions and restrictions of societal communication as injustices in so far as they amount to the violations of justified claims raised by real-life human beings. The parameters of ethical progress towards more inclusivity and equality between subjects are duly couched in terms of a regulative idea: that of domination-free communication, an 'ideal speech situation' characterized by free and equal exchange between the parties involved. He thus provides for a universalistic ethics derived from the ontological priority of language in our dealings with the world, and with each other. 'Domination-free communication' replaces 'respect for human dignity' as the aegis under which society, if it does, will become more inclusive, egalitarian and democratic.

And this, it seems, is the problem. There is, as Norris points out, 'more in common than he might like to think between Habermas's "universal pragmatics" and those other versions of the linguistic or pragmatist turn' when it comes to the relation between claims made in discourse and the world.[165] By installing language as ontologically prior, even while preserving a model of human intersubjectivity which does not relegate human beings to the status of a mere effect of discourse, Habermas makes himself vulnerable to the various criticisms of 'discourse monism' raised throughout this study. Certainly, his position avoids the pitfalls of both atomistic universalism (since he emphasizes human being in its relational, linguistically mediated aspect) and of strategic universalism (since he provides standards by which progress towards inclusive equality may be judged). In its conception of reason in terms of intersubjectivity and communicative reciprocity his thinking is indeed in the service of the sort of relational universalism which we are here exploring. But there is a certain idealism lurking in his picture of progress, one which distracts from the material realm of lived social and economic relations and antagonisms. A formalistic aspect to Habermas's picture leads him to a picture in which history becomes 'the process through which the aspiration towards rationally founded consensus implicit in every speech act becomes ever more explicitly ariticulated in normative structures and moral consciousness'.[166] It may be that this amounts to a sort of 'intellectualist utopia', as Richard Wolin calls it: one which, of necessity, switches attention from the embodied, materially engaged aspects of our being.[167] In this sense, Habermas emphasizes the second direction of relationality mentioned above at the expense of the first. Because he conceives as equally misconceived all attempts — for instance, in Marx's praxis philosophy — to make central the practical relationship between conscious subject and wordly objects, he continues, as one critic puts it, 'to think without the body'.[168]

So where does this leave us? At one point, Rorty characterizes 'humanism', approvingly, as 'participation in the hopes of the Enlightenment — and specifically the hope that human beings, once they have set God and the various surrogates for God to one side, may learn to rely on . . . their own ability to cooperate with each other for the common good'.[169] A defensible universalism will be humanistic in precisely this sense. But it will be humanistic in another — for Rorty less forgivable – sense, too. Not the extravagant sense in which the primacy of the will takes complete priority over circumstance – but, against this, one which seeks a balance between the necessarily historically specific and socially mediated forms in which human nature manifests itself, and our capacity to intervene in the circumstances to which, as relational beings, we will be subject. Soper highlights

> the distinction, central to humanist argument, between the actions we choose to take and the processes we are subject to. There are differences of degree – and of kind – between the constraints upon us to breathe, to use money, to love someone, to obey the law, to join a political party or to go on hunger strike – differences which no political or philosophical discourse can justifiably overlook.[170]

It is those nuances of distinction which Rorty's strategic universalism, if thus we can indeed conceive it, must leave out of account insofar as his politics of redescription depends on the installation of a historical 'myth of the given' as the gauge of the scope and limits of future progress. For Rorty's account will not admit of ontological distinctions between the ways in which we are affected by material processes in our necessary commitment to engagement with the world. Manifesting itself simply as blank causal effects, meaningless until decribed in discourse, the cognitive input we get from the world provides for Rorty no constraint whatsoever on the ways in which that input might be interpreted through discourse, redescribed, and so on. The effect of this is to dislocate us from the world, and from others, and to pin universalist hopes to the success and force with which 'we liberals' can impose our descriptions of human equality across other, variegated interpretive communities.

Against, this, a relational conception of universalism will insist that it can certainly be understood historically, and as a project. By emphasizing the relational aspect of subjectivity it will not short-circuit things in the way suggested by Rorty's characterization of universalism as the prior, final mapping of moral space. It is not the case that we can simply move freely in the universal by sheer power of logic or affirmation. The task of this form of universalism will be to 'seek to materialize, in social relations, the universalist ideals that have hitherto been the more or less abstract, distorted, and unrealized claims of those who have struggled and who continue to struggle for emancipation from domination and exploitation'.[171] As Callinicos argues:

> Resistance to oppression can only be coherently justified by a theory that is universalistic in two senses: first, it involves a nonrelativist ethics on the basis of which the transformation or abolition of certain social relationships can be justified . . .; secondly, it seeks to establish the relationship between the different forms of oppression in order to identify the common interests which different oppressed groups may turn out to have.[172]

The first of these senses is denied by strategic universalism. Le Doeuff's 'respect of humanity in others' cannot be accommodated by a system which remains only agnostic about the possibility of extending the range of us to include the whole of humanity. The second of these senses is denied by atomistic universalism, which works to treat relations at the level of formal equality without attending to the structural, concrete conditions of intersubjective relations. A relational universalism, properly conceived, might work, as an unfinished project, to universalize in reality the equality and inclusion – economic as well as cultural – to which both Lyotard and Rorty might gesture, but cannot substantiate.

Bourdieu writes:

> There is, appearances notwithstanding, no contradiction in fighting *at the same time against* the mystificatory hypocrisy of abstract universalism *and for* universal access to the conditions of access to the universal, the primordial objective of all genuine humanism which both universalistic preaching and nihilistic (pseudo-) subversion forget.[173]

A relational conception of universality – instead, pointedly, of an outright jettisoning of the whole idea – seems to me to provide the strongest basis upon which to realize the nuances of these twin aims. I say more on this theme in the next chapter.

### 3.3. *Achieving our Country*'s difficult turn

The foregoing discussion has centred mainly on what might call the 'classical' articulation of Rorty's political philosophy, constructed through a series of 1980s articles and culminating in *CIS*. This body of work has formed the focus for most subsequent discussion of Rorty's normative stances and their implications. But it has been complemented by a series of lectures, *Achieving our Country*, in which Rorty takes stances not so much on the Western traditions in political theory, but on the way in which theorists have themselves contributed to the political climate of the modern West – in particular, the USA. The book has the tone of a kind of wake-up call to the American intellectual Left. Its overriding theme is that the academic Left in the USA has drifted into a form of 'spectatorship' in which their political reflections are cut off from the needs and concerns of the country at large. In the process, as it is put on the book's back cover blurb, 'cultural politics' has been allowed to supplant 'real politics'.

Rorty makes a narrative of this process. There is, he argues, a distinctively American left-liberalism, typified in Whitman and Dewey and in the motivations of the labour movement in the first half of the twentieth century. This is a progressive project neither self-consciously theoretical nor sceptical of romantic visions. Pushing dreams and piecemeal actions rather than world-historical teleologies, it saw classlessness and equality, and thus America's moral identity, as ongoing projects still to be achieved. It was anti-Stalinist, pro-New Deal and pro-cold war. It was rooted in practice, in participation and in reformism. Intellectuals and trade unionists worked together without schism, each bringing their own aptitudes to the project at hand.

This tradition got displaced, sometime in the 1960s, by a coalescence of historical and attitudinal factors which pointed to the bankruptcy of 'American' politics. Vietnam, especially, galvanized a new intellectual left, dissident and anti-mainstream, conceptually armed to reveal the systematics of late capitalism. Eventually this has culminated in the ascendancy of what Rorty calls the 'cultural Left', a mainly academic constituency which has concentrated largely on drawing attention to the ways in which received American history and values have occluded difference in terms of race and gender, and served to oppress as a result. And this has had concrete pay-offs: political correctness, Rorty observes, has made America a far better place.

But by and large this new Left has abdicated engagement with 'real' politics in favour of a stance of refusal: of blanket scorn for Western theory and practice and an unqualified celebration of 'the other'. It presumes that 'the higher your level of abstraction, the more subversive of the established order you can be', and retreats accordingly into a self-confirming world of endless conceptual novelty and avant-gardism, in which 'discourse' and its manipulation and disruption becomes the prime site of political attention. Meanwhile, a concomitant *in*attention to everyday economic and ground-level realities has allowed rightwing populism to sneak in and gain a foothold among the disenchanted white working class, and those feeling the effects of economic globalization the worst – an audience to whom the cultural left has very little constructively to say. It is resolutely mute about possible alternatives to the market economy, or about how to save and improve the welfare state.

Hence Rorty's distinction between the *agency* once embodied in the ethos of the left, and its present state of *spectatorship*: a turn from public activity to mocking, detached diagnosis. He argues that much that is mandatory thinking in professedly radical academic circles just is not, in terms of praxis, very radical at all – and offers illuminating thoughts on how cultural and literary theorists have, curiously, tended to mirror logical positivism in assuming that appropriate disciplinary 'knowingness' renders social hopes insignificant or naïve. Such 'knowingness', as Rorty puts it, 'is a state of soul which prevents shudders of awe. It makes one immune to romantic enthusiasm.'[174] The fashionable academic left has tended to substitute 'resentment over the failures of the past for visions of a better future'.[175] It has also become antinationalistic in what for Rorty is a pejorative sense: assuming that everything that America stands for is somehow contaminated by the misdeeds of its history, such as slavery, the slaughter of Native Americans and the pursuing of various acts of military aggression. The trouble is that such a conflation of the nation with its worst associations leads to a stepping back into spectatorship. Through this kind of overreaction, a generation of left intellectuals has found itself unable 'to formulate a political program, to join a political movement, or to share in a national hope'.[176] It lacks national pride.

In the process, ironically, the 'cultural Left' has become complicit with those on the right who themselves prioritize cultural issues, though in a rather more reactionary tenor. For there is a certain conservative incentive in 'encourag[ing] politicians, of both the Left and the Right, to specialise in cultural issues'.[177] For such issues, focused as they are on ethnic and religious differences, and 'debates about sexual mores', provide the ideal distraction from the realities of economic insecurity which confront all social classes, but pose the greatest threat to the worst off. As Rorty puts it in a contemporaneous interview, 'there's been a tacit collaboration between Right and Left in changing the subject from money to culture. If I were the Republican oligarchy, I would want a Left which spent all its time talking about matters of group identity, rather than about wages and hours.'[178] At such moments, the notes he strikes sound quasi-Marxist – and to be sure, there are real parallels between his own qualms about the climate of Left thinking since postmodernism, and those put forward by relatively orthodox Marxist commentators such as Callinicos.[179] The emphasis on the concrete, and on praxis, is (though they are understood in quite different ways) to some extent definitive of both pragmatism and Marxism in its more humanist variants.[180] But as one might expect, this thread in Rorty's thinking sits rather incongruously with its otherwise definitive themes. In fact, if there is any purchase in the general stance on Rorty's pragmatism I have been developing here, there is a sense in which, by making the complaints he does about the Left's drift towards an exclusively 'cultural' focus, he is attempting to ride two rather tricky horses at once.

Nancy Fraser has argued (specifically in a prominent debate with Iris Young, but her case has wider resonance) that the problem with the recent prioritization of the cultural in progressive social thought is precisely that it excludes the realm of political economy from a social justice conceived entirely in terms of the recognition of identity.[181] Fraser defends an analytical distinction between the politics of *recognition* – for example, 'claims for the recognition of ethnic, "racial", and sexual minorities, as well as of gender difference' – and on the other hand, the politics of *redistribution* which, in Rorty's terms, provided the pre-1960s priority for political progressives. The latter covers, for example, 'claims for redistribution from the North to the South, from the rich to the poor, and . . . from the owners to the workers'.[182] This distinction has its complexities, on which, for our present purposes, we need not dwell.[183] But in its separation of material, or economic, factors from cultural ones as separate sites of social injustice, it has already gone somewhere which on Rortian terms looks a tricky destination. For such a distinction requires some kind of separation of the horizontal from the vertical: namely, of the plane of signification (culture) from that which is not reducible to intra-descriptive relations – in this case, the economic. Now whether or not such a distinction is itself viable – and whether, for example, it is an analytical or an ontological one – is not, in a sense, the issue here. The point is that in any case, the force of Rorty's critique of the 'spectatorial Left' *depends* on it being viable. The persuasiveness of his case in *AC* (points about nationalism notwithstanding) is precisely that, in diverting its gaze to the operations of discourse and away from political economy, the Left has neglected something of crucial political importance.

Hence the riding of two horses. Rorty's own thinking, in denying the possibility of an extra-discursive reality, has, in its influence and its resonance with broader themes adopted by what he calls the 'cultural Left', *itself* been a significant contributor to the states of mind he finds politically useless. Or if that might be overstating the case, at the very least its own most significant metaphilosophical claims sit quite comfortably with those of, for instance, Foucault who thinks that 'discursive practices go all the way down to the bottom of our minds and hearts' – and, one might add, of the social world in which we move, and which progressives seek to improve upon.[184] As horse number two – Rorty's left-liberal reformism – strains against the spectatorish tendencies which 'discourse monism' might tempt us into, horse number one has already struck off straight in that very direction. To sit on both at once is, one might say, pragmatically difficult.

One way in which to make this point is to unpack a comment made by Rorty in a more recent exchange with Gianni Vattimo: 'I'm very pessimistic about the political future because I think that democracy only works if you spread the wealth around – if you eliminate the gap between the rich and the poor.'[185] This echoes a view going back, through Marx's 'On the Jewish question', to Rousseau, and further back beyond: that the quality of political culture is conditioned, in part, by the nature of economic relations. For it to be plausible, some degree of stratification of social reality seems presupposed – perhaps the kind suggested by Fraser's distinction (though she does not commit to it in ontological terms). For the conditions of democracy flourishing are not, on these terms, solely discursive: they depend, too, on material factors which stand apart from the processes of signification which Rorty describes in terms of 'horizontal' relations. Or maybe they don't. If they do, then Rorty has committed himself to an ontology which allows for non-horizontal modes of existence. If they do not, then he has committed himself to precisely the 'cultural turn' which, he argues, has led the left into a myopically exclusive focus on the discursive – the politics of identity – at the expense of the economic. The proximity of Rorty's thinking, in practical terms, to trends within postmodernism and post-structuralism from which he would prefer to maintain a sceptical distance is something to which I will return in the next chapter.

# 4 • Applications: History and Moral Practice

The arguments of the foregoing chapters have worked immanently for the most part, drawing out the politics of Rorty's work but addressing it primarily on its own terms. This final chapter sees a change in direction. Here, I will put Rorty's work in places where he himself has not taken it, exploring its implications in different ways, and with an element of 'creative appropriation' which itself might have something of the flavour of Rortian redescription. In 4.1, we look at how Rorty's pragmatism might cash out in a particular context: that of historiography and, in an ethical sense, our relations to the past. I find that, in common with varieties of positivism and post-structuralism, Rorty presents an impoverished, unsubtle view of history which in fact reduces it to the contours of an 'eternal present'. The 'thickening' of description leads to the thinning out of historicity. But following Rorty's own hunch that history is more important than the Philosophical tradition has tended to allow, 4.2 considers ways in which we might conceive of our embeddedness in concrete contexts and relations without slipping into the relativism from which, in the end, Rorty himself finds it impossible to escape. Thus the 'cashing out' of Rorty's politics of redescription takes us in directions which for him might be unexpected, perhaps uncomfortable, but nonetheless shed further light both on his on work and its implications for the negotiation of normative questions.

## 4.1. History and redescription

> Every image of the past that is not recognized by the present as one of its own concerns threatens to disappear irretrievably . . . In every era the attempt must be made anew to wrest tradition away from a conformism that is about to overpower it. . . . Only that historian will have the gift of fanning the spark of hope in the past who is firmly convinced that *even the dead* will not be safe from the enemy if he wins. And this enemy has not ceased to be victorious.[1]

In the Introduction I implied that Rorty's pragmatism seeks, in key respects, to wipe the slate clean: to 'forget' the stain of past thinking and experience in order to begin on a new footing – a sort of historical 'zero point', as Adorno once called it.[2] Here I want to address directly the ways in which the sort of 'discourse foundationalism' which I see as the 'cash value' of Rorty's work might affect our understanding to the past. Of course, Rorty's 'new beginning' does not position itself in metaphysical outer space, beyond time and chance. It roots itself very much in a time and in a place, and regards itself as 'historicist' precisely in the sense that it does not seek to play down or to escape the flux of contingency.

Rorty affirms in *CIS* that the 'vertical view downward' should be replaced, in the historiographical attitude, with 'the historicist metaphor of looking back on the past along a horizontal axis'. He continues: 'All any ironist can measure success against is the past – not by living up to it, but by redescribing it in his own terms, thereby becoming able to say, "Thus I willed it".'[3] I will argue that this gesture – 'historicist' and Romantic – amounts to a *denial* of a historicity of depth and consequence. In pressing the diremption between the horizontal and the vertical, Rorty's 'historicism' in fact empties out history to a point where in effect it begins again with each redescription. It reduces an unknowable past to an endless present.

If Rorty's pragmatism is indeed, as I argued in Chapter 1, a sort of positivist historicism, this reduction follows readily enough. Indeed, as I shall argue here, it highlights faults held in common by both the 'traditional', positivist position on historiography and its now-dominant postmodernist counterpart. I contend that the former position leads directly to the latter – and that Rorty, inadvertently, shows us how. In common, positivist, pragmatist and postmodernist treatments of historiography deny the possibility of *mis*description: the possibility that we might misremember, mystify, be *wrong* about and so ideologically manipulate the past for politically questionable purposes.[4] If misdescription is impossible, then deliberate misdescribers are not culpable. Concurrently, the scope for conceptualizing our relationship with the past becomes impoverished, and the relationship deprived of depth and nuance – in short, of its very historicity. The politics of historical redescription become an unbuttoned, free-wheeling affair: a matter, in the end, of caprice. Historiography becomes a sort of authorial conjuring, in which, as Bryan Palmer puts it, 'the past can only be created out of the imperatives of the ongoing instance'.[5] It thus severs us both from a responsibility to the past, from its materiality, and from the (constrained) range of possibilities which it bequeaths.

*Pastness*

It is often taken as evidence of a distinctively 'postmodern' condition that contemporary experience has, as Fredric Jameson has put it, lost touch with the separateness (or 'specificity') of historical reality, so that the past has been collapsed into a depthless 'eternal present'. Jameson calls this 'the waning of our history, of our lived possibility of experiencing history in some active way'. He diagnoses 'a crisis of historicity', in which 'we are condemned to seek History by way of our own pop images and simulacra of that history, which itself remains forever out of reach'.[6] Thus, there is no gap between *res gestae* and *res gestorum*: 'the way things happened' on the one hand and their appearance in memory, cultural representation or political utilization on the other.

Recently, echoing this analysis, Peter Novick has suggested that what is lost in this kind of process is the *historicity* of history:

> Historical consciousness, by its nature, focuses on the *historicity* of events – that they took place then and not now, that they grew out of circumstances different from those that now obtain. Memory, by contrast, has no sense of the passage of time; it denies the 'pastness' of its objects and insists on their continuing presence.[7]

The collapse of this gap removes complexities. The past becomes freely malleable, neutralized, a tool or prop, being purely the effect of present priorities. Our relationship to it thus becomes depoliticized, and frictionless, except with regard to the costs our orientations may incur in terms of our acceptability to our peers. As a corollary, history, and the national past, become items for consumption. The burgeoning 'heritage' industry lets us nostalgically shop around for the solidities of communal ways of living, of shared meanings and identities, which have passed and become fragmented.[8] Again, the past appears not as any kind of 'reality', but as the convenient construction of present economic, cultural or political concerns.

I present this picture in order to set alongside it Rorty's already-cited claim that 'anything can be made to look good or bad, important or unimportant, useful or useless, by being redescribed'.[9] The upshot of this claim is, for historians, often assumed to be liberatory and progressive: to furnish endless possibilities for the redescription of the past and its implications, where previously there were the unbudgeable, monolithic authorities of the historiographical tradition. I dispute this assumption. My basic case in what follows is that, by reducing history in principle to an eternal present, Rorty's historicism acquiesces in the ideological constructions referred to above. It makes too easy the possibility of 'doing justice' to – or learning lessons from – the past. It offers no critical help to any putative collective effort to sustain, or keep present, aspects of the past which would otherwise wane with the passing of time, become refashioned or forgotten – 'overpowered' and 'irretrievable', in Benjamin's phrasing.

Of course, my diagnosis here will not depart significantly from Rorty's own conception of the possibilities afforded by his work. As we saw in 1.2, he readily embraces the collapse of truth into what succeeds in being asserted, and takes it as a call to bolster our practices against tomorrow's always-possible advent of fascism.[10] This is because he sees no sense in describing truth as possessing any kind of causal power, or as an explanatory resource. But quite apart from this, his 'emptying out' of the realm of 'brute causality' beneath the endless play of redescriptions has the effect, as we saw in Chapters 1 and 2, of saturating historical change in discourse. He does not directly focus on my concern here with the relation of present agents to the events – rather than the philosophers – of the past. Discussing *that* relationship, Rorty concludes that 'We need to tell ourselves stories of the mighty dead in order to make our hopes of surpassing them concrete . . . we have to have both imaginary conversations with the dead and the conviction that we have seen further than they. That means that we need *Geistesgeschichte*, self-congratulatory conversations.' Moreover, 'honesty . . . consists in keeping in mind the possibility that our self-justifying conversation is with creatures of our own fantasy rather than with historical personages'.[11] This, I think, is a neat summary of the sense of historiography's scope that emerges from Rorty's work as a whole: it is a matter of *making* (through 'fantasy', or just redescription) rather than *finding*.

And he does indeed have 'honesty' on his side. The trouble comes when this terminus is viewed as the harbinger of untold possibilities of 'bearing witness' to the silenced or suppressed. Rather than construct a straw, for-the-sake-of-argument case based on the implications of Rorty's notion of redescription for philosophy, I will use another, real-life one – and one which does indeed see our freeing from the yoke of 'what actually happened' as exclusively a liberation.

*The past as* tabula rasa

Keith Jenkins's work provides extensive variations on a familiar enough sort of theme: that, as E. H. Carr once put it, 'the facts of history never come to us "pure", since they do not and cannot exist in a pure form: they are always refracted through the mind of the recorder'.[12] Like Rorty, Jenkins talks in terms of language (or, more generally, discursive practices) rather than the mind as history's filter, taking narrative as his basic epistemological medium. His point, though, chimes with Carr's: there is no unmediated access to the events of the past. But while Carr's point might seem self-evident, Jenkins's own formulations do not. In fact, like Rorty, he takes the point further, echoing the reminder that 'the world does not speak – only we do', and building from it a straightforwardly linguistic-idealist account of historiography. As with Rorty's denial that there is a 'language' that is 'nature's own', the case rests on denial of an extravagant anthropomorphism: the past is presented like a mute interlocutor, such

> [t]hat in and of itself the past contains nothing of obvious significance. That left on its own it has no discoverable point. That it expresses no intelligible rhyme or reason. That it consists of nothing independent of us that we *have* to be loyal to, nothing we *have* to feel guilty about, no facts we *have* to find, no truths we *have* to respect, no problems we *have* to solve, no project we *have* to complete. It is clear that the past doesn't exist 'historically' outside of historians' textual, constructive appropriations, so that, being made by them, it has no independence to resist their interpretative will, not least at the level of meaning. . . . Consequently, the past as history always has been and always will be necessarily configured, troped, emplotted, read, mythologized and ideologized in ways to suit ourselves.[13]

This seems a cogent, forthright articulation of the position which emerges from Rorty's account of our understanding always being 'under an optional decription'. It also shows an overlap of that account with post-structuralist concerns. For Jenkins's passage is a neat summation of a commonplace enough affirmation of the impossibility of historiographical objectivity. It is exemplified in conclusions drawn by Roland Barthes in 'The discourse of history':

## APPLICATIONS: HISTORY AND MORAL PRACTICE 153

> [I]n 'objective' history, the 'real is never more than an unformulated signified, sheltering behind the apparently all-powerful referent. This situation characterizes what we might call the *realistic effect*.... Historical discourse does not follow the real, it can do no more than signify the real, constantly repeating that *it happened*, without this assertion amounting to anything but the signified 'other side' of the whole process of historical narration.[14]

Similarly, Jenkins argues that Rorty's claim that 'anything can be made to look good or bad by being redescribed', once swallowed, induces the stark realization that 'shorn of metaphysical foundations, of non-terrestrial sky-hooks, we are now left with a world where there is "nothing but history" (contingency), and where the "past" we are left with – and the "history" that we use to try and make sense of what we are left with – are both interminably re-describable'.[15] And, extending the point: 'As soon as you think about it, the idea of a historicized past existing independently of our variously present-day constitutive concerns, is an absurd one.'[16] This is Novick's more wistful cultural observation made theory: there is no longer any distinction to be had between 'historicity' and 'collective memory'. For Jenkins, 'history' is, a priori, the product of historians who themselves are simply a product of their present.

But like Carr's point, much of Jenkins's case here may not, in itself, transcend the stating of the obvious. This is partly down to its rhetorical construction. As with Rorty's 'the world does not speak', the onus does seem to be on Jenkins to produce an example of a theorist of history arguing, unsarcastically, that left on its own (without humans? without language?) the past would have a single, discoverable point. To use this model as a foil is to suggest that to believe in any sort of objectivity one has to insist that history is the subjectless revelation of packaged-up truth, delivered on request to the doorstep of appropriately diligent historians and uncontaminated by any interpretive input of their own. It is, in other words, to imply that, to be 'real', history must be a sort of non-human agency itself – something, perhaps, like God – which gives us its details directly and unmediated.

Much, then, hangs on the function of those '*have*'s in the longer passage from Jenkins quoted above, in as much as they caricature a position which nobody would seriously defend in order to validate an opposite conclusion presented as the only sane alternative. As such, as is familiar enough from Rorty's own equivalent constructions, they set up a false dichotomy. Of course, we do not literally *have* to talk about the past in any particular way, as if it might interrupt and start haranguing us if we misdescribe it, or are disloyal to it, or just ignore what happened in it. To claim as much would be a bit like saying that we literally *have* to call tables tables or else they'll complain: an ultra-naive version of what philosophers call 'naive realism'. Jenkins, anyway, suggests that the vanquishing of naive realism leaves no alternative but to conclude that history is *only* our descriptions of it: 'Having no meaning-full existence independent of historians' textual embrace, being constructed by them, the past constituted as historicized text has ultimately no choice but to go along with whatever purposes are desired.'[17] Because history exists for us in so far as it is a textual creation, then, it *has no choice* but to bend itself to current social purposes. It has no choice because it cannot speak without *us*.

What Jenkins collapses here is a gap that very few people would have seriously claimed the existence of in the first place: that between the past as an independently existing entity with its own agency and motives, whose feelings we can literally hurt (a past which, as Rorty might put it, 'speaks'), and on the other hand the texts through which we gain access to that past. For Jenkins, this distinction is unsustainable. Hence, all we have are texts. Hence, 'the goal of "learning lessons from the past" is actually learning lessons from stories written by historians and others'. And so the question arises: 'If the past as history has no foundation, can anything ethical be gained from its study?'[18] And the answers follow: that 'we can now "forget history" for postmodern imaginaries *sans histoire*'; that 'history *per se* . . . just slipping out of conversations' is 'a *good thing*'; that we should now 'embrace a non-historicizing postmodernism'.[19]

Jenkins's cashing out of the common denominators of the pragmatist/post-structuralist line on the impossibility of historical knowledge is – for all its studied flippancy – faithful and instructive. It seems very difficult, once history has been 'horizontalized' and so reduced to conversation, to find a sense in which historical descriptions might be about anything besides other historical descriptions. And this, of course, is the standard post-structuralist case: that dealings with 'the past' present a prime example of exactly why there is no extra-discursive reality to speak of (after all, in speaking of it, we have made it text). The force of the case lies largely in its highlighting of a basic empirical aspect of 'doing history'. We do not survey the past directly, with a somehow passive eye, but rather reconstruct it according to 'evidence' (texts, bones, ruins or whatever – things which otherwise might seem to have differing ontological status, but are here reduced to a par) our interpretations of which will always be theory-laden. Thus, historiographically speaking, language really does go all the way down: the past, mediated to us and received in the present, cannot be viewed except from within, and through, the present's contingent, linguistically constituted, horizons of interpretation.

And so far, on its own terms, the case seems unrebuttable. But the idea that it somehow spells doom, as Jenkins suggests, for the very idea of the past's existence beyond our current descriptions of it owes its credibility, I think, to another, *uncollapsed* gap. It emerges in the stubborn, positivistic hunch that there must be an absolute breach between 'what happened' and 'how it is remembered', or between our relationship to history and the circumstances in which we forge it. This is the hunch that, to be 'really' about the past, history has to be written as if the present did not exist, and the assumption that the impossibility of this kind of 'God's-eye' perspective cuts us free from any meaningful burden of veracity. Any 'history' to which we need have an ethical relationship would have to be history from the past's own point of view, for its own sake. And there is (plainly enough) no such thing as history from its own, or God's, point of view.

From this Rortian point, there is a fairly smooth transition to Jenkins's subsequent moves. Given the impossibility of speaking in a language entirely the past's own, uninflected by present concerns, there is no sense in which the past constrains us to think about it in any given way. Hence, 'historiography' is really just a circular exercise with no referent beyond the horizons of the present – an 'eternal' present, in Jameson's phrase. Pretending that it involves anything *historical* is just a sort of self-delusion, a figure of speech, an effect of conventions of enunciation. Thus, Jenkins has it that the idea of the historical past is simply an imaginary projection, a soothing fabrication 'to help us make some sense of the apparent senselessness of existence':

> Of course, the past *per se* is not imagined in the sense that 'it' didn't actually occur. It did occur, and in exactly the way it did. But it is an imaginary with respect to the historical meanings and understandings, the significances and purposes it has been deemed to have for us, both as a whole and in its parts . . . Put simply, we are the *source* of whatever the past means for us.[20]

Now Jenkins's main target here is the idea that adequate historiography is that which writes, in Leopold von Ranke's phrase, *wie es eigentlich gewesen* – 'what actually happened'.[21] It is the positivist historian's conception of history on the model of positivism's conception of natural science – value-neutral, prejudice-free, based on sound verificationist method and rigorous examination of the past on its own terms. Compare, for instance, the following declaration, made at the first International Congress of Historians in 1900, that historians should avoid *judging* the past and simply write about what *actually happened*: 'We want nothing more to do with the approximations of hypotheses, useless systems, theories as brilliant as they are deceptive, superfluous moralities. Facts, facts, facts – which carry within themselves their lesson and philosophy. The truth, all the truth, nothing but the truth.'[22] In purported contradistinction, Jenkins has written that

> The factualist/empiricist assumption so rooted in traditional historical thinking, that if we can find 'the facts' then this will stop interpretive flux, fails because only theory can constitute what counts as a fact in the first place. When we talk about facts we always do so under a description, so that to claim that 'x' is a fact can only mean that the description it is under is adequate.[23]

Therein, for Jenkins, lies the chasm between empiricist and postmodernist views of history: the one proposing that truths link ideas with realities, and the other responding, with Rorty, that interpretations refer only to other interpretations. But in fact, *pace* Jenkins, a common thread links the two positions. Basically it is this: that 'real' history depends upon prejudice-free, judgement-free, value-neutral, scientific inquiry. For the Congress of Historians speaker cited above, this means that cultural values should be excluded from the proceedings. For Jenkins, the impossibility of history-as-science means that cultural values are all we are left with: 'facts' dissolve into the contingent descriptions by which their status is secured. But for both, facts and values belong to different realms.

For both positions there is a fundamental rupture between language and historiographical practice on the one hand and the world on the other: a rupture which is breached in both cases by the projection of a conceptual scheme in order to absorb the independence of historicity into what can affirmed about it in discourse. One commentator characterizes Rorty's project as 'thin description'; it would seem more accurate to describe it as involving the *thickening* of description and the thinning out of the world.[24] Jenkins makes a Sartre-style appeal to the sheer senselessness of the world relative to the individual knower, prior to the projection of discourse upon it and its incorporation into the horizontal to-ings and fro-ings of description. As E. P. Thompson once remarked about Althusser, the result is 'exactly what has commonly been designated, in the Marxist tradition, as idealism' – that is, 'a self-generating conceptual universe which imposes its own identity upon the phenomena of material and social existence, rather than engaging in continual dialogue with them'.[25]

The result, when it comes to the writing of history, is a sort of extreme Romanticism: the narrator is secured at the centre of the universe, unconstrained by materiality, constrained only by his/her own sensitivities to the audience for which he/she writes.[26] Jenkins's view is that truth is *essentially* and exclusively the effect of narrativity, and that if you do not think this you must think that the facts in any given case can simply be read off from the documents, or established in a straightforward positivist way without recourse to interpretive frameworks of any kind.[27] But this presumes that there are cultural constructions on the one hand (like language, values, *The Fall of the Roman Empire*, news reports, commemorative exhibitions, etc.) and the (for Jenkins, unattainable) brute reality of events on the other. As he says: 'the past . . . did occur, and in exactly the way it did'. Quite how he can claim knowledge of this is intriguing, since he insists that the past's meaning (and its existence for us) depends on our free, unconstrained descriptions of it. 'The past occurred in exactly the way it is' represents just one among an unrestricted range of such descriptions. Thus, *à la* Frege but without any appeal to logical rules, present-day 'sense' determines historical 'reference'. Hence there is the elusive 'real' on the one hand, and contingent cultural constructions on the other. Because the first is prohibitively elusive, the second are all we have. 'History' as we relate to it is a contingent creation of our own. Hence it is not something to which we can have any real sort of ethical relationship.

Again, this seems a faithful historiographical couching of Rorty's position on the role of the object which, while it exists prior to being described, thenceforth exists only under a contingent description. With respect to history, the implications become especially pronounced. 'Historiography' can exist only as a misnomer, since there is no ontological gap between past and present for it to bridge: given that history only exists in terms of our present experience of it, its pastness can only ever be ineffable. Hence, we are stuck in an eternal present, in which the horizontal workings of discourse conduct themselves unconstrained by any emergent properties of the past itself. As Berkeley had it: an idea can relate only to another idea.

*Making space for misdescription*

One *might* (as Lyotard would) conceive of the severing of all ontological ties when it comes to writing or representing history as an ethical gesture. A liberation, for instance, from the overweening intrusions of scientific thinking (and the vocabulary of 'truth', 'objectivity' and all the rest) into areas where it has overweeningly intruded too long. One might (with Rorty) insist that, in the process, our proper relationship to history becomes a matter of our proper relationship to each other, rather than to a spurious 'objectivity' to which our representations can never, in any case, be fully adequate. After all, mainstream philosophy of history has acknowledged more and more, before and since E. H. Carr, that historiography reflects the priorities of the present rather than some pregiven, inbuilt historical script. History does not write itself. We write it – and it is only within our present horizons that those writings (now, with Jenkins, lacking a referent beyond the present) can be challenged and held to account. Our relationship to history is thus open, always recreatable, and unconstrained by that spurious concoction 'the past itself'.

Again: one *might* argue that. But to draw these conclusions as if they amounted to the end of the story (and indeed, as Jenkins would have it, the end of 'history') is, as I have argued, to swallow whole an inheritance of assumptions from positivist historiography. These assumptions, in fact, sit very uneasily with any assumption that there might be something intrinsically ethical/political about our relationship to the actions and events of the past. To state the obvious, the existence of that 'something' depends on there being such a relationship: that one is not simply reducible to the logic of the other. We need not agree on the nature of this 'something' in order to agree that a viable idea of misdescription depends on it.

I argued in Chapter 1 that Rorty's pragmatism retains half of the positivist picture while scrapping the part (the empirical 'given') which was causing it problems. A similar gesture informs Jenkins's fusion of pragmatism and post-structuralism on history. After the perceived collapse of the idea of historical reference, all we have are our descriptions. Because they are constrained and obstructed by nothing about the past itself, the incongruous upshot is that the alterity of the past is rendered unattainable as its sense is reduced to our description of it. In its particularity, the historical event is bunk – or as bunk or as non-bunk as the interpretations of the texts which constitute it will allow.

Both views conclude that the past can be levelled down to a series of statements about it: for positivism, statements of verified and so incontrovertible fact, and for postmodernism, descriptive statements epistemologically on a par with each other and so as right as it is possible to be.[28] For post-structuralism especially, the very idea of history becomes a piece of illegitimate metaphysics: a totalization whose logic, when enacted, has for Lyotard produced the most extreme atrocities of modern history. My point is that, while positivism allows for the possibility of misdescription, it condemns us to a situation in which it is inevitable: nothing could tell us when we had finally arrived at the complete mapping of a given series of events. Meanwhile, Jenkins's position makes it *impossible*, precisely because there is ultimately no discrepancy between text and world: texts are *strictly* all we have, in principle, a priori. This is, of course, a *metaphysical* claim. On its basis, the very idea of doing justice, or injustice, to the past becomes simply a piece of circular self-deceit.

We can draw out the implications of the Jenkins/Rorty stance by way of Rorty's reading, in CIS, of the 'ironist' O'Brien in George Orwell's *Nineteen Eighty-Four*. Orwell takes O'Brien's arguments in 'breaking' Winston Smith towards the end of the novel as demonstrating a point similar to that which he himself makes (see 1.2) in quoting Sartre to the effect that nothing about 'human nature', or history, or truth, would prevent fascism, tomorrow, becoming 'the truth of man'. Rorty's point is that O'Brien is aware that the past, like reality, is infinitely malleable: that nothing, of necessity, resists redescription. Take the following passage, cited by James Conant as 'an argumentative gambit strikingly reminiscent of some of Rorty's own tactics':[29]

> O'Brien smiled faintly. 'You are no metaphysician, Winston,' he said. 'Until this moment you had never considered what is meant by existence. I will put it more precisely. Does the past exist concretely, in space? Is there somewhere or other a place, a world of solid objects, where the past is still happening?'

'No.'
'Then where does the past exist, if at all?'
'In records. It is written down.'
'In records. And . . . ?'
'In the mind. In human memories.'
'In the memory. Very well, then. We, the Party, control all records, and we control all memories. Then we control the past, do we not?'[30]

As I see it, O'Brien's manoeuvring here parallels Rorty's own. The idea that the past ('the world') is a place ('speaks') as if a separate empirical entity is dispatched in favour of an option presented as the only alternative: that the past is exhaustively controlled by our redescription of it. Because there is no past-as-entity against which we can hold up our present descriptions by way of comparison, there is no past understood as extricable from our present practices. As Conant himself suggests, in reconstructing an O'Brien-esque slant on history:

> The 'truth' about the past is simply a matter of how the community's memories and records as a whole *cohere* and has nothing to do with how well those memories and records 'represent the facts'. To seek an answer to the question 'What happened at such-and-such a point in the past?' is to seek a *consensus* with one's peers.[31]

The 'true' story will be the one which prevails as a result of that conversation.

The inadequacies of such a conclusion emerge, I think, when we consider a situation (hardly far-fetched) wherein at stake in that conversation is a dispute between participants that depends for its resolution on what *actually* happened in the past. An example of this would be the issue of Holocaust denial – which, as we saw in 3.1, figures in Lyotard's work as an example of the problems of historiography. In exploring the ramifications, it is worth looking at particular issues in the course of a particular conversation: the recent High Court libel suit brought by David Irving against a writer who had described him as a Holocaust denier.[32] Irving, an expert Hitler scholar, has made, in a series of books since the 1960s, three main claims against customary assumptions about the scale of the Holocaust and its execution: (i) that there was in fact no systematic Nazi plan to exterminate the Jews; (ii) that there is no proof that Hitler ordered a policy of extermination; and (iii) that no Jews were killed in gas chambers at Auschwitz.

# APPLICATIONS: HISTORY AND MORAL PRACTICE 161

The defence's case against Irving consisted of a reiteration of the claim (made in the work the author of which he was suing 'for the sake of his reputation') that he is a 'liar', a Holocaust denier, and that his work as a historian has been warped by his politics. I will not go into the details of the case or of the judgement here. I just want – at the risk of tokenizing it – to situate it *vis-à-vis* what we might now call the Rorty/Jenkins/O'Brien position.

As emerged in the trial, and is anyway public enough knowledge (advertised, for instance, on his own website), Irving has for years offered $1,000 to anyone who can produce a document demonstrating that Hitler ordered the Holocaust – in other words, that it was planned at the highest levels of the Reich, and not merely the result of the sporadic and coincidental actions of the more bloodthirsty among the lower ranks of the SS. Nobody has. Irving's tack throughout the trial, and in his rhetoric through the years, has tended to base itself on a seemingly commonsense, but more likely expediently literalist, appeal to the basic requirement of documentary evidence as verification of every historical claim.

This is a standard ploy amongst Holocaust deniers: to ask for evidence they assume to be unattainable as the only possible justification of the claim that certain core features of conventional accounts of the Holocaust existed. Take, for instance, Faurisson's claim that there is insufficient evidence that gas chambers existed at Auschwitz. 'I have tried in vain,' claims Faurisson, 'to find a single former deportee capable of proving to me that he had really seen, with his own eyes, a gas chamber.'[33] Faurisson's basic (and needless to say, cynical) point is that the only acceptable proof that a gas chamber existed and was used to kill people would be that one had seen it kill people. Therefore the only eyewitness he will accept would be a victim of the gas chamber. Now gas chambers were such that no victims survived. Therefore, there were no 'gas chambers' in the sense in which conventional history maintains: their existence as such could only be proved by the coming forward of a survivor as eyewitness, and that would disprove the claim that the gas chambers were what we assumed them to be.

This equates, Lyotard observes, to the impossibility of answering the challenge from a book publisher to name 'a work of major importance which would have been rejected by every editor and which therefore remains unknown'.[34] You can't. If you could, it would be because it had been published, a precondition for attaining 'major importance'. So the publisher is right. Much the same reductive strategy as Faurisson's operates in Irving's challenge to produce evidence of Hitler's complicity in the Final Solution.[35] It is a sort of strategic positivism: a demand for directly verifiable, physical evidence which is known in advance to be unforthcoming or unobtainable. But it is only the nature of the question posed which makes an affirmative answer impossible to provide. In the case of the Final Solution, as everywhere, this approach conveniently misses the point, asking for isolated, atomized facts in isolation from the wider context which would make those facts interpretable in the first place. In this instance, the plans for the Final Solution, rather than existing in the form of a single, comprehensive edict, are widely acknowledged to have evolved over time – as indeed has the body of historical evidence which gives rise to that acknowledgement. Such is historiographic practice: ongoing, and relating to events and processes which themselves were neither static nor atomized.

Still, Irving's strategy throughout the court case was consistently in line with the ultra-positivist approach: constantly asking for pinpointed written evidence of orders, and so on.[36] Amongst other things, what is operating in this technique is a simple collapse of ontology into epistemology: of what *is* (or was) into what can be known, or more accurately what *is* known, or textually extant. (The same logic collapses historicity into collective memory, to use Novick's terms, and intellectualizes the collapse of historical specificity into an eternal present, to use Jameson's.) To return to Carr's point, it is like deriving from the premise that 'the facts of history never come to us "pure", since they ... are always refracted through the mind of the recorder' the conclusion that 'minds' are all that we can be sure exists.

And yet this is *exactly* the move made in the setting up of the Rorty/Jenkins/O'Brien position. All three take as final the crude positivistic challenge ('Show me this place called "the past" which exists concretely, in space') and, in the face of it, back away into a position of chastened refusal: the past, insofar as it exists, is what we say it is. On these terms, as O'Brien rightly concludes, the party wins because it holds the tools of redescription and the power to assert its version of events. Beyond that version lies – in practice – ineffability. With history looked at this way, even outwith Oceania descriptions of the past can *only* be wrong in relation to other, competing, perhaps sedimented and so authoritative, accounts of the past. In effect, this is to collapse the past into a present which becomes everything, the sole existent. But a deeper notion of misdescription than simply 'versions of the past alternative to those to which we customarily cleave' is required for the punishment of Irving to be anything more than a flexing of ideological muscle, or a vanquishing of the sort of marginal, minority views which Lyotard finds everywhere to be suppressed by the logic of proof.

The anti-realist case that history exists solely in our descriptions of it, with only ineffable unverifiability beyond, relies (as Rorty would concur) on the logic of O'Brien. The obvious rejoinder here is that, as Chris Lorenz has put it, 'the mere fact that the past is only known by us through . . . description . . . does not entail the conclusion that the past *is* a description or can be regarded as such'.[37] Reduction of the past to present descriptions of it, or to put it Novick-style, the emptying out of the historicity of past events, removes the possibility of culpability for misrepresentation. It exonerates David Irving from the charge of denial, *whatever he says* and *whatever happened in the past*. A meaningful charge of misdescription requires that *right* description is at least a term of which we can make sense.

That the cash value of Jenkins's position is a severing of all responsibilities towards the actors and events of the past is fairly apparent – indeed he admits as much. That it amounts to a foreclosure of the possibility of relating to the past on terms which do not reduce it to a 'logic of the same' is not something he chooses to advertise. 'Metaphysics may be a mug's game,' as Berel Lang has written, 'but those who think they can avoid it by burying their heads in the sand are likely to wind up playing the game anyway but from the other end.'[38] In the Rorty/Jenkins/O'Brien case, this backwards metaphysics results in a false dichotomy. *Either* one must hold that historical events are merely a fictive effect of the narratives with which we recount them, *or* one must hold that, to be worthy of the name, historiography must give us the facts on their own terms, and (as if no human agency were involved) let the past articulate itself. As I have argued here, any credibility that the former claim has is directly proportionate to the extent to which one takes the second claim seriously.

What the Rorty case misses is precisely what seems to be promised by his pragmatism's suggestion that historicity might displace metaphysics: that our relations to the past are not purely constituted by, or reducible to, the ways in which we happen to describe them. The problem is that Rorty's sense of historicity sides with that of (logical) positivism and postmodernism in conceiving it as indeterminate until secured in our description of it. This 'thinning out' of the past makes it something – like the world – to which the pragmatist claims we can have no relations except those imposed upon it through our descriptions.

It is not something whose significance we can deny or abuse. Thus Rorty's own appeal to historicity is rendered meaningless except as an appeal to voluntarism. Both history *and* metaphysics are, on the logic of his case, dissolved in the present-day politics of redescription.

## 4.2. Relationality and moral space

A staple claim of post-structuralist thinking, along with that of Heideggerian or Levinasian descent, is that the very positing of subject–object relations involves a sort of violence. On these terms, the idea that the object of the subject's knowledge can be known *as an object*, as an empirical existent ('ontically', to use Heidegger's term) requires a coercive reduction of the 'other' – whether nature, or another human being – to the 'same'.[39] This entails an assimilation of the other's singularity to some sort of formal identity. Hence the worries about assuming a formal equivalence between subjects, as in the liberal tradition, which punctuate much postmodern discussion of ethics. This concern for singularity leads to a flight from firm ontological commitments and, as we have seen, a draining of historicity, understood as the concrete context in which human beings act.

This is perhaps best exemplified in the insistence among post-structuralist feminists such as Butler that the category of 'woman' as a distinct sex with given ontological attributes can be replaced by that of 'gender'. Gender (and 'sex', after its subsumption under this heading) is a matter of signification, and so disruptable and *re*-signifiable. This is because 'Sex' is not a cultural construct imposed on an already-existing body, but what constitutes that materiality in the first place: '"Sex" is, thus, not simply what one has, or a static description of what one is: it will be one of the norms by which the "one" becomes viable at all, that which qualifies a body for life within the domain of cultural intelligibility.'[40] On this picture, signifiers such as 'woman', and indeed 'human', become disconnected from any (vertical) specific referent. Both are, as Jane Flax puts it, 'deessentialized and set to play among other equally nonnecessary, nondetermined, and non-referential signs'.[41] It is this contingency which makes them ripe for challenge, subversion and change.

That this account appeals to the mistaken notion that the socially constructed is somehow not 'really real', and is thereby freely malleable, is one fundamental weakness. But it is another which is my main concern here. This is the up-front relativism characterizing such refusals to countenance the appeal to any 'reality' of our bodily being beyond or besides that which is imposed by a regulatory norm. That Rorty's thinking – for all its 'leaving the door open' for a future realization of pan-human solidarity – falls into the same category should by now be plain enough. For the insistence that such solidarity is made, or imposed, rather than deriving from a sense of shared human needs and capacities, makes human nature straightforwardly relative to the description of it which happens to be imposed in different times and places.

As I see it, this relativism arises from the insistence that we are stuck within the horizontal relationality of contexts: that reference is determined by meaning, and that meaning is an inter-description affair. This might be demonstrated by way of an example of the affirmation of horizontal relationality at the expense of the sort of vertical relationality from which, as I would argue, it is inseparable. Such an example is provided in the political philosophy of Iris Marion Young. Her work is motivated by wariness of 'a predominant tendency in participatory democratic theory to deny or think away social difference by appeal to an ideal of community'.[42] She posits the necessity, in terms of social justice, of recognizing the 'heterogeneity of the public' and affirming group differences. Her case is subtler and more textured than I have the space to convey; but here is a brief attempt. Addressing conflicts between radically different group identities and agendas, she says, many would regard a liberal individualist conception of the polity as the only legitimate option: to recognize only individuals, disregard as extraneous their attachment to a given group identity and treat their different priorities and orientations as the voluntary preferences of rational choosers abstracted from social context. This she rejects precisely for its voluntarism and abstraction.[43] Alternatively we might go for a communitarian affirmation of the sharedness of social identity, our embeddedness in forms of life the details, pulls and influences of which we have not chosen but have been inserted into by the lottery of birth and upbringing. This she rejects because it posits fusion, wholeness and unity as the ideal, and so denies the necessary differences which characterize any polity all the way down.

What Young wants to avoid is the essentializing either of atomistic individualism or of group natures. Faced with conflicts between different groups, then, we should not aim to defuse them by ignoring the importance of group identity as a constitutive aspect of what makes politics important (and so assimilate different groups by dissolving their differences as ultimately inconsequential). But nor should we proceed by separating them out from each other in an exclusionary fashion so that each group views all others as inexorably other. The first leads to the occlusion of different identities. The second leads to straightforward racism. She presents a third, alternative ideal: 'a single polity with differentiated groups recognizing one another's specificity and experience', which requires

> a conception of groups expressing a relational rather than substantial logic. Groups should be understood not as entirely other, but as overlapping, as constituted in relation to one another and thus as shifting their attributes and needs in accordance with which relations are salient. In my view, this relational conception of difference as contextual helps make more apparent both the necessity and possibility of political togetherness in difference.[44]

The conclusion, then, is that when differences between group identities are defined as derived horizontally, in terms of their interrelations, rather than vertically, in terms either of ontology or of a necessary attachment to a place or a 'real' identity, it becomes easier to negotiate a just path between the competing claims which will arise from them.[45]

Young is right, I think, to oppose a strict distinction between individual and community such that we must view the essence of the human subject *either* as atomized, isolated and self-determining *or* as the product of social factors such that any individual's identity and perspective is inseparable from the shared understandings of their community as a whole.[46] Also important is sensitive treatment of conflicts between the needs and aims of different groups, or individuals of the same group. These cannot, for Young, be adequately dealt with by pretending the groups in question don't really exist (or are irrelevant when it comes to questions of social justice) beyond the individuals which happen to comprise them. Nor can they be justly addressed simply by hypostatizing their radical separateness, treating it as sacrosanct, and refusing to decide between the conflicting values and practices that arise from different identities whatever their substance. Neither between individuals nor between groups are there static, impermeable boundaries such that there is no overlap or interrelation between them.

All of this represents a marked improvement on, say, liberal accounts of justice in terms of negotiating between the conflicting claims of radically atomized individuals, and indeed to the communitarian tendency to hypostatize communities as discrete and circumscribed givens.

The latter will tend towards an outright cultural relativism in which the constitutive norms and priorities of different communities will be taken as sacrosanct and worthy of protection whatever their content or implications.[47] Young rightly sees both these tendencies as disregarding the necessary overlap between identities. But I would argue that this interrelation holds not just in terms of the horizontal relation between different identities, but also in terms of the *vertical* relation of interaction between different individuals and *non*-cultural factors. In other words, there is not a separate, sealed-up cultural sphere within which identities are negotiated, purely reciprocally, in abstraction from material, historical and economic circumstances.[48] For Young's consideration of identity and difference solely at the level of cultural exchange of meaning – parallel to Butler's negation of the sex/gender distinction – 'depends upon the claim that forms of life end up determining political reality. Young may sanction what I called in Chapter 3 a 'weak universalism' – since her conception of identities, as the basic concern of social justice, is fluid and open-ended and so not delimited to static parameters. Her denial of the 'ideal of community', however, points to an in-principle refusal of the value of Rorty's (possible) pan-human solidarity. But she cannot, in fact, provide much in the way of resistance to a relativistic construal of her work. This is precisely because of the fact that political reality must always be assessed through a cultural lens.

To expand on this point, it is worth reconsidering Rorty's opposition, cited at the start of 3.1, between a 'universalism' which assumes as given the 'logical space' required for moral deliberation, and a 'historicism' which insists that moral progress depends on 'expanding this space'. It makes a similar appeal to the (potential) fluidity of boundaries between moral communities. But, as in Young's case, it makes an appeal to the local as the place from which our ethical/political deliberations must begin. Hence his claim that the standard for such judgements 'can only be something relatively local and ethnocentric – the tradition of a particular community, the consensus of a particular culture'.[49] Now this equates fairly readily with a defence of ethical particularism, given that it is not, as David Miller puts it, 'general facts about other individuals' which determines my duties towards them, but rather 'relational facts'. Thus, 'agents are already encumbered with a variety of ties and commitments to particular other agents, or to groups and collectivities, and they begin their ethical reasoning from those commitments'.[50] Miller's point is that 'relational facts' like these – deriving from our actual reciprocal dealings with others – determine the scope of moral duty. As Phillip Cole observes, moral principles that arise in this way have 'boundaries of exclusion' built in: 'those who are not in the relationship are excluded from the rights and responsibilities that arise from it'. Thus, from a moral point of view, 'there is no external world' beyond the scope of the bounded relational community.[51] This secures a solid foundation for an ethical relativism working precisely on the basis of a Rortian contrast-effect between a given 'us' and the 'a "they" which is also made up of human beings – the wrong sort of human beings'.[52]

And this is indeed often taken as an inevitable upshot of emphasizing the relationality of human nature: since there are limits to the inter-relations which may realistically obtain, there are limits to the scope of our moral responsibility. These limits are provided by the outside contours of a given culture, or form of life. It may be, as in Young's case, that this sort of claim goes along with a further, 'weak universalist' appeal to guarantee the sanctity of such different forms of life. For her, the very goal of their reconciliation constitutes, as with Lyotard, a sort of violence, given what for her is the *irreducible* diversity of forms of human life. The problem here is thinking that we could resolve such tensions without, as John Gray has put it, 'concomitant cultural loss'.[53]

Two immediate responses to this position strike me as instructive. One is that Miller's appeal (like Rorty's) to 'given' local relationships as an index of the scope of ethical concern rests on a reductively empiricist sense of relationality. Only those (like 'our fellow Americans') with whom we *actually* have some relationship fall within the range of our moral responsibility. But this is not practically tenable. Miller's prime concern is to defend the nation as the community to which we owe moral allegiance. Nations do not, in this strictly empirical sense, consist of all-inclusive reciprocal relations. Not even in local neighbourhoods do the inhabitants necessarily, in actuality, recognize the moral force of any such relations. As Eagleton, with apt sarcasm, responds to Rorty's invoking of 'fellow Americans' as those to whom we can most readily be persuaded to respond morally, even stretching things this far may bear traces of universalism:

> There are, after all, rather a lot of Americans, of various shapes and sizes, and there is surely something a little abstract in basing one's compassion on such grandiosely general grounds . . . Would it not be preferable for an authentic critic of universality to base his fellow-feeling on some genuine

localism, say, the city block? On second thoughts, however, this is still a little on the homogenizing side, since your average city block does of course contain a fair sprinkling of different sorts of people; but it would surely be a more manageable basis for social justice than some universal abstraction like America. One might demonstrate compassion to those in the next apartment, for example, while withholding it from those down the street. Personally, I only ever display sympathy to fellow graduates of the University of Cambridge. It is true that such credentials aren't always easy to establish: I have occasionally tossed a coin towards some tramp whom I thought I recognized as a member of the class of 1964, only to retrieve it furtively again when I realized my mistake . . .[54]

I quote this passage at length – in fact, it carries on a fair bit further in similar vein – because it demonstrates the sheer difficulty of deriving *any* consistent moral commitment from the appeal to actual, circumscribed, reciprocal relations.[55] If the duty is stronger the more proximate the relation, the process soon enough unravels and reduces to the absurd. As made by Rorty and Miller, the relationality claim seems to have little cash value beyond the firming up of a sort of moral sentimentalism – and perhaps, a confirmation of exclusionary prejudices.

So empirically given relations do not, it seems, provide much headway in understanding the scope of ethical/political judgement and obligation unless we are prepared to grant that, for some individuals, their scope might extend no further than their immediate families or even, for the especially reclusive, themselves. This leads to a second, more affirmative response. If we understand relationality not in empirical but in ontological terms, the spectre of relativism need not arise. We have already considered ways in which we might understand our practical relation to the world as prior to the socialization which Rorty sees as going 'all the way down'. If this is indeed a generalizable claim about human existence, then it evidently provides vertical purchase for the horizontal relationality to which Rorty and Young have exclusive recourse. But in conceiving relationality as having both vertical and horizontal aspects, the nature of the second aspect will have to be rethought. For if on its 'cultural' definition relationality consists solely in the relation between different significations, or descriptions, then indeed it becomes detached from the embodiment of human being to which the claim of the primacy of practice has made appeal. What impact does the introduction of the individual's vertical relationality to the world have on her horizontal relationality to other subjects?

To begin to explore this it might be worth considering a core objection to both liberal and communitarian conceptions of the individual. As emerged in the course of Chapter 3, I see key shortcomings of both positions to consist in their shared assumption of an eminently contestable metaphysical either/or. It might be couched as follows. *Either* we must conceive of the self as an isolated, punctual, monadic, lifestyle-choosing neutral archetype, *or* we must conceive of it on the Rorty/Miller model, as saturated in contingent, local relational facts which, alone and exhaustively, provide its moral and critical bearings. The options as posed suggest that to admit intersubjective relationality into the constitution of the self with anything more than an incidental, contingent role precipitates a slide into ethical particularism. At its worst, the latter entails an inherently conservative reification and endorsement of *any* integrative, traditionally constitutive way of life regardless of the oppressions – the systematic discriminations or rank economic inequities – which may provide the basic structure for ostensible moral cohesion and stability. Looked at in such zero-sum terms, the appeal of either the liberal or communitarian position seems largely to consist in its avoidance of the chief drawbacks of the other.

But from the reverse angle, this implies that either side has a portion of truth which, when combined, might point beyond the terms of the dichotomy so conceived. On the one hand, it is no doubt true that each individual is part of a multiplicity of communities which exercise a direct effect on her identities, values and loyalties. On the other hand, this does not require that she cannot always distance herself from any such particular encumbrance and assume a critical stance towards it.[56] Referring back to the dialectical 'ambiguity' which for Merleau-Ponty (and Marx) characterizes our subjective immersement in a world the nature of which we do not choose conjoined with our capacity to act upon that world as agents, it is clear that the potential for rational critique of the encumbrances we happen to have ended up with is inherent in our very nature as agents. Thus, even as situated selves we are able – and must be able, for the sake of progressive politics – to *challenge* that situatedness in the name, as Seyla Benhabib put it, of 'universalistic principles, future identities and as yet undiscovered communities'.[57]

Thus the presumed, formal, atomistic universalism of the liberal/Cartesian heritage is not, as we saw in 3.2, the only version on offer.

Nor need we assume that universality exists in any full, concrete sense. It might be seen, rather, as a potential arising from the capacity of members of the human species to direct their own practical engagement with the world. Its purchase as a critical norm exists precisely in the need to differentiate between the formal egalitarianism of liberal-capitalist societies and the possibility of a genuine egalitarianism in which everyone has the opportunity to realize their 'species being' on autonomous terms.

Our capacity so to do depends, of course, on our interrelationships with others – a relationality not just to the world, but to each other. Thus the force of universality as a critical norm will depend in part on the appeal to a possible *genuine* reciprocality the conditions of which may not yet exist. It is in this sense that the communitarian emphasis on the necessary mutuality of human being is *half* right. For it takes given mutualities as providing the only available basis on which moral and political discourse might proceed. Relativisms of all kinds – and especially so in the case of ethical particularism – require that we must take as given a *static* interrationality between agents. Thus when Rorty defines the immoral as 'the sort of thing that we don't do around here' he presumes a given, packageable, set of identities, values and loyalties which, once reified, can be readily produced as an index of right and wrong. That these are too elusive and multi-dimensional to be so packaged is rightly emphasized by Young when she refers to the fluidity of horizontal relations: the fact that no static conception of a differential identity can ever capture the multifarious overlappings between groups which are never wholly separate from one another. But the shortcomings of Young's account lie in the fact that, on its terms, it is only cultural forms of life – however non-discrete and interpenetrative – which are afforded any determinate role in the constitution of political horizons.

Thus what Young's account – because of its exclusively horizontal bearings – cannot admit is any role for situated, reflexive human beings in contributing (through their practical engagement with the world and with each other) to the cultural particularities recognition of which she takes as the basic focus for social justice. Intersubjective relationality is itself underpinned by a common aspect to human being, insofar as (at the very least) we have all gone through the same processes of practical engagement with the world: that our human predicament is at root the same. On these grounds, we can avoid the contradictions of 'weak universalism' precisely by affirming that horizontal relations between identities cannot fully be understood (or done justice to) without taking into account the vertical aspect neglected by exclusive attention to the cultural. With the vertical allowed to enter into the proceedings in the form of a claim about what it is like to be a human being, Le Doeuff's principle of equal human respect can be derived not merely from the contingent orientations of a particular ethical scheme, but from our very nature and potential as embodied subjects. It is in this sense that there is a (pre-discursive) 'humanity' to be respectful towards.

What this approach avoids is the performative contradiction entailed in denouncing the very appeal to 'objectivity' or 'universality' as inherently coercive, while at the same time making claims like 'British colonialism involved an oppressive imposition of western univeralist discourse and the forceful silencing of the other'. For some conception of human being – as more than just the effect of discourse – is necessary for the substantive and suasive power of any such judgement. A normative grounding for such a claim can only be provided, in the end, by some sort of appeal to a shared human condition – as is borne out by Rorty's own falling back on our common propensity to experience humiliation as a basis for the claim that 'cruelty is the worst thing we do'. I would go further, and suggest that this condition will be shared in the sense that we are all, individually, in the same boat when it comes to our situated engagement with the world. But it will also be shared in the sense that from this condition arises the value of mutual understanding and reciprocal respect – not as something which will necessarily have been realized at any given historical juncture or in any given community, but as something which will be required for our equal flourishing as different individuals.

It is at this point that relationality emerges in a second sense: the sense invoked by Marx and Engels's resonant phrase 'the free development of each is the condition of the free development of all'.[58] Against the atomistic univeralism criticized in 3.2, it is not the case that our relations to others are a contingent, or incidental, aspect of our makeup. If we do not, *pace* Descartes, need to renounce the world in order to ground our subjectivity, then nor do we have to renounce other subjects. While I have argued in favour of a pre-social element in our development of selfhood, this does not by any means entail that our development and flourishing is an entirely monological experience into which the existence of others need not enter as a factor. In fact, quite the reverse. The claim that the human subject is distinguished by its practical orientation to the world requires that our relations with others are, as soon as we are able to differentiate between the objective world as a whole and our fellow subjects in it, defined by a respect for them as similarly situated.

Thus while Descartes confesses in the *Meditations* that when he looks out the window all he sees, strictly speaking, are hats and cloaks which might, for all he knows, be nothing but machine-like 'dummies', Merleau-Ponty dismisses the 'fundamental prejudice according to which the psyche is that which is accessible only to myself and cannot be seen from outside'.[59] We must, in negotiating our way through the world, assume that other conscious beings are constrained and enabled by similar bodily capacities. This intersubjectivity is confirmed at the point of communication, when, by language as such or by physical gesture, understanding is enabled by 'the reciprocity of my intentions discernible in the conduct of other people'.[60] Such a reciprocity cannot take place without the assumption of a shared ontological status and bearing. It is evident too in Husserl's rejection of solipsism in the *Cartesian Meditations*. I experience others, he proposes, as actually existing, 'not as mere physical things', but as beings similarly orientated towards the world as myself. As well as being objects 'in' the world, they are also '*subjects for this world*', 'experiencing it (this same world that I experience) and, in so doing, experiencing me too, even as I experience the world and others in it'.[61] On this basis, intersubjectivity – or horizontal relationality – can be addressed without the presumption that a sense of mutuality must derive from the moral or cultural conventions of the community of which we happen to be part. Rather than being imposed 'top-down' by the rules of a given form of life, it can be conceived as emerging 'bottom-up' from a recognition of our similarities as embodied subjects – not as members of this or that community, but as members of the human species.

So far, I have laid only the groundwork for a deeper consideration both of the self's relationality to the world, and of its relationality to other selves. What I hope to have shown here is that we need not assume that the positing of any such relationality leads straight down the expressway to outright cultural relativism of the ethical-particularist type. Nor, from the reverse perspective, is it the case that the only escape from such a relativism is provided by the positing of a suspended, atomized, utility-maximizing or intrinsically self-regarding subject for whom the existence of the world, and of others, is purely secondary to its own substantial existence.

A third claim follows: that Rorty's own denial of the vertical is what deprives his emphasis on practice and the value of consensus (the extension of the 'we') of ultimate persuasive force. Endorsing Habermas's conception of communicative rationality as a means by which to junk the need for any metaphysical back-up for liberal-democratic practices, Rorty writes: 'It lets us turn from the love of truth, conceived of as a correct relation to reality, to the need for justification, conceived of as a relation to other human beings.'[62] I would argue that the idea that our relations to other people are nothing like a relation to 'reality' is one of the major misprisions of Rorty's pragmatism.

# Conclusions

> ... one has to argue for one's problems as well as one's solutions[1]

This book has followed two main lines of critical approach to Rorty's work. One addresses Rorty's solutions, and the other his presentation of the problems to which those solutions are constructed.

On the former tack we have worked immanently, in exploring how Rorty's work, in the broadest sense of the term, 'hangs together', in the broadest sense of the term.[2] My conclusion is that there are points – both internally, and those at which the fabric of Rorty's beliefs and desires touches on other, alternative fabrics – where the fabric frays. If Rorty's goal is an authentically Rortian redescription of various impetuses within philosophy since Descartes, it fails to erase the stain of tendencies among those it is most concerned to leave behind. There are nagging spectres – chiefly positivism, idealism and Cartesianism – which re-emerge, recast, in Rorty's narrative and so disrupt its coherence and force. Insofar, then, as his work does echo the tradition more strongly than he would admit, it echoes some of its more problematic tenets. But the more general point is that Rorty's thinking recommends, but does not accomplish, a circumvention of metaphysical claims of all kinds. This is the purported point and force of 'redescription', presented as a replacement for Philosophy with a capital P. But looked at thus, both Rorty's redescription of Philosophy and his case for redescription as its replacement fail. To use again the hermeneutic terms I have been deploying throughout, Rorty fails to escape the need for vertical considerations in his recommendation that we transfer inquiry to the horizontal plane.

To reinforce this point, it is worth retracing some steps. The reorientation of pragmatism to a purely horizontal plane rules out the seeking of layers beneath, or preconditions of, or some kind of ultimate, or primal, determinate point of which the indeterminate, or the contingent, might be epiphenomenal. As we saw in 1.1, he regards any such appeal to a 'ground level' as itself obscuring the inevitability of its *own* indeterminacy. Viewing things horizontally, there are no differences of kind, only differences of degree. So there is no elusive core which makes the self what it is, which defines human nature, which separates knowledge from fancy, which makes a principle morally acceptable, which makes one language different from another and so on. For Rorty, such elusive 'cores' are a figment of the philosophical imagination – goals which, despite having been on a mission since Plato, philosophy has signally failed to achieve. There is a simple way of avoiding the frustration of these failed attempts: we can choose not to try. For example, rather than 'this theory of human nature gets it truly right'; we should concentrate on saying 'this theory of human nature gives us something socially useful'. To 'go horizontal' is to understand the utility of such theories in terms of their contribution to social welfare, and their fit with our already-articulated priorities, rather than their mapping of 'the way the world is':

> For such theories are supposed to be normative – to provide guidance. They should tell us what to do with ourselves. They should explain why some lives are better for human beings than other lives, and why some societies are superior to others. A theory of human nature should tell us what sort of people we ought to become.[3]

The message of Rorty's normative thinking is precisely that the discussion of social values can, and does, swing free of all 'vertical' relations with a world independent of the descriptions through which we negotiate the politics of life. So a world without gender discrimination is *preferable*, certainly, in light of the most appealing among presently influential descriptions of our human lot; but it is not more 'natural', or more 'faithful to our humanity'.[4]

An ongoing argument in this book has been that in the delivery of this message, Rorty's project is self-undermining. At each step in our narrative, we have found places at which Rorty's own severance of description from ontology has not been achieved cleanly. And from the other direction, we have seen that, just at those points when his normative claims are most powerful, he has needed to have recourse to generalized ontological claims – most prominently, about human nature. In chapter 1, we saw how his pragmatism is constructed on the basis of the claim that 'language' and 'contexts' and 'socialization' go 'all the way down': that there is nothing *independent* of these, nothing (vertically) available against which we might compare (for example) a given normative claim. We also saw how this amounts to a kind of collapse of the 'appearance–reality' distinction into its first component. Rorty wishes to present 'conversation' as something which takes place without the intrusions of a world to which the claims presented there might be adequate, or not. But in Chapter 2 we saw that this position is one which, as Rorty goes about the work of applying it to different contexts – intellectual progress, and the development of selfhood – becomes quite hard to sustain. To account for these solely in terms of imaginative redescription begs as many questions as it answers. For us even to have the potential to be the kinds of imaginative self-redescribers which, for Rorty, is what makes us the individuals we are, certain ontological commitments must hold true. For us to be either the agents or the recipients of redescription in this way, there must be things about us which resist redescription – which are constant, or definitive, and which (in vertical terms) lie beneath, or above, the processes of construction. Rorty presents vocabulary-change as if it takes place entirely unconstrained either by the material world, by social structures, or by factors 'internal' to individual vocabulary-users. But the tensions which build up as he develops these accounts suggest, in the end, the reverse conclusion: that reality is not so easily reduced to the ways in which it has come to be described.

Similarly, Rorty's 'liberal ironism' cannot get by without furtive reliance on the kinds of ontological claim which it is designed to rule out of court. Like Lyotard's ethical and political thinking, Rorty's ends up echoing elements of the Philosophical heritage which on its own terms should be rendered anathema. He makes appeal to non-discursive factors about being human as a means to ground his own normative priorities. He endorses a form of 'strategic' universalism which, to be plausible, must depend on an inclusive account of human being such that a pan-human 'we' can be envisaged, even if it is unlikely. He slips in and out of apparently 'transcendental' claims about the parameters of moral space, and the moral significance of loyalty. But in each case, because the claims tend to be tacit rather than explicit, or implied in passing rather than expanded upon, or in any case go by without due 'unpacking', they tend to undermine the suasive appeal, and so the pragmatic utility, of Rorty's case. Why be persuaded by a call to human solidarity which, though it seems as if it is saying that this is universally achievable, also quite stridently denies that it has any firm basis on which so to do? There are alternative routes to the realization of a non-atomistic universalism. One such – that we might couch universality in terms of human relationality, and in terms of potentials which need not to have been already achieved in order to have normative force – was put forward at the end of Chapter 4.

And Chapter 4, too, attempted to identify the limits of Rorty's pragmatism by moving beyond them. In 4.1, we saw how Rorty's thinking – along with other currents that more eagerly embrace the label 'postmodernist' – develops an affinity with positivism in its lack of attention to the texture of historical events. This is a point which surfaced too in 1.1: that pragmatism mirrors positivism in reducing questions about the nature of reality to what can justifiably be *said* about reality. There is a normative concern raised by the prospect that the past might be reduced without remainder to the horizons of present interests, or of currently dominant views (reinforced by this or that process of power). It has been argued here that this is a normative concern with which Rorty's politics of redescription has real trouble dealing. Significantly, it seems to debar us from attention to the particularity (the 'otherness', as one might put it) of precisely those historical events which, in Rorty's terms, have forged the legacy of dominant discourses which our own generation has inherited, and through which we understand ourselves. The effect of this, it seems to me, is to close down the scope for future, unpredictable, novel, development rather than open it up.

There is a similar feature in Rorty's exclusively 'horizontalized' conception of relationality. Here as elsewhere, as was argued in 4.2, the horizontalizing move runs into two kinds of problems. One is that it tends to relativize norms and human orientations to contexts, in a way which carries with it the gamut of problems with which relativism is routinely associated. The second is that it seems, despite itself, to highlight the significance of vertical factors which – despite Rorty's protestations – do indeed seem to pertain. Thus to understand our potential for relationality (and so for the 'socialization' which for Rorty goes 'all the way down') is to understand a way of relating to the world, and to others, which is a precondition of such socialization, rather than simply a product of it. There are distinct ontological levels here which on a purely horizontalized view would be levelled to the same plane, even as they are implied in the very process by which the taking of such a view becomes possible.

Problems with Rorty's solutions, then, point back to more foundational, Philosophical problems which linger despite his attempts to reveal them as 'pseudo' and so circumventable. This has emerged here in the pursuing of the second main critical approach: to 'cash out' elements of Rorty's thinking in terms of implications sometimes disruptive of its own impetus, and in any case problematic in terms of wider factors which continue to demand attention. Those wider problems are, it must be said, redolent of oppositions punctuating that 'traditional' philosophical agenda which Rorty would have us set aside: idealism versus materialism, universalism versus particularism, and so on. For all its promise in seeking to put 'shared utopian dreams – dreams of an ideally decent and civilized society – in the place of knowledge of God's Will, Moral Law, the Laws of History, or the Facts of Science', Rorty's thinking fails to show how these can be secured by affirmation, rather than refutation.[5] For those very dreams of a post-Philosophical sort of social hope rely, whether they like it or not, on propositional claims about the nature of reality, about the nature of human beings, and about the relation between the two. Nor does he show that his redescription is strong enough to nudge aside those previous positions and heuristics – realism and universalism, most especially – by which (some of) the Philosophical tradition has charted its course. This is not just an academic trifle, or a piece of Philosophical nit-pickery. It is, rather, crucial to the success of any politics of redescription. If that politics itself is enmeshed in factors which it cannot simply describe away, then the nature of a viable progressive politics would seem to be rather different from that depicted by Rorty himself.

What both of these approaches have sought to expose is that Rorty's attempt at a costless circumvention of philosophical problems proves neither to be costless, nor a circumvention. His own thinking demonstrates that problems of ontology, in particular, cannot be described clean away in the transition to a new vocabulary. Both immanently and in its application to the world, Rorty's project is haunted by spectres which are never quite exorcised.

At points, he seems to acknowledge as much. In 1962, he wrote the following:

> Granted that in epistemology we redefine 'truth', 'fact', 'validity', 'knowledge' and the like, and that we have the option of redefining them in such a way as to take the wind out of our opponents' sails, there are still certain restrictions on how far this redefinition can go. Adequacy to something external to one's system, despite the difficulty of defining what this 'something' is, does seem to be a requirement; we do seem to be able to tell the difference between philosophers, who attend both to adequacy and coherence, and sophists, who attend to coherence alone. I shall call those who adopt this position metaphilosophical *realists*.[6]

It is the fact that Rorty's thinking is never *merely* sophistic, that it relies at crucial points on claims about what is external to his system (a shared selfhood, for example) which means that it never quite achieves a clean break from the concerns of the tradition. It will be clear enough from the dialectical course of the previous chapters that my own tendencies are in the direction of what Rorty here calls 'metaphilosophical realism'. (My own preferred term is that of 'critical realism', though expansion of what this means is a task best left for other work.[7])

Substituting 'redefinition' with the later Rorty's preferred term, I have argued that there are limits to how far redescription can go. Rorty himself imposes limits (of a Kantian kind) at one level: we can say nothing about the world as it is apart from our descriptions and redescriptions, except that it is ruled by causality. Rather than being a constraint, though, this functions to liberate descriptive practice: *within* our vocabularies, we can say what we like about a world which does not talk back. Meanwhile, limits re-emerge in a second respect. We cannot hope to transcend our own 'frankly ethnocentric' parameters in discussing the rights and wrongs of the treatment of other human beings. It is arguable, though, that these limits might be more accurately swapped around, or reversed. If our practical engagement with the world precedes our naming of objects, the scope of our descriptions of it is importantly constrained. If the idea of being ethnocentrically constrained to speak and think in certain ways cannot, in the end, be rendered self-consistent then openness to a moral universalism will always be an option. Both of these claims will benefit from a deeper fleshing out than there has been space to provide in this book. That they are viable grounds on which to proceed seems to me to emerge from an assessment of the impact of Rorty's own positions.

We might stress the need for so proceeding in another way, again with reference to Rorty's own delimitations. I would insist that the claim that the world, or others, can in practice be reduced to our descriptions of them, itself requires a foreshortening of the dialectic of understanding. 'Adequacy to something external to one's system' is duly ruled out of court, since that which is external to one's system will be 'as meaningless as thunderclaps or birdsongs'. Rendering it meaningful, on these terms, requires an extension of one's system – a system shored up and legitimized on terms which can only be already internal to it. Such is Rorty's conception of practice: something governed by, dependent upon, and only available for interrogation within, the language we have ended up speaking because it works. An extension of this kind can recognize no sort of principle of equal respect for that beyond our system's reach – whether an independently existing world, or human beings – except those which we might happen to confer upon them. In this sense, again, universalism and realism will provide constraints on current practices while leaving open the possibility that we might understand those practices to a deeper and more nuanced extent.

The question of 'practice' is key to the differences between Rorty's position and the alternatives I have been exploring. If Rorty's pragmatism, as a pragmatism, seeks a conception of knowledge adequately informed by the centrality of practice, it fails for five main reasons amongst the various pitfalls and lacunae encountered during this book:

1. It drifts into linguistic idealism, not a priori but as the practical effect of the terms in which it is presented. There is nothing which resists the practical imposition of a given description except its compatibility with other extant descriptions. The material world becomes an effect of discourse.
2. It cannot account for vocabulary change through history on its own anti-cognitivist terms.
3. It cannot attend to social justice without furtive reliance on supposed philosophical relics – the idea of a self prior to language, or the possibility of ethical universalism – which, at the outset, it has confined to that 'cabinet of curiosities' to which philosophers should return only with a sense of distanced nostalgia.
4. It cannot account for the very historicity which it takes as its first and major weapon against the overweening other-worldliness of the Philosophical tradition.
5. Because of all this, it cannot provide an explanation for the success of human practice itself, qua practice, whether individual or collective, in dealing with the world in which we necessarily find ourselves.

Adorno once wrote that 'the new beginning at a supposed zero point is the mark of strenuous forgetting'.[8] There will always be good reason to treat with suspicion any claim that whole parts of the philosophical landscape can, just by casting them in a different light, be finally neutralized or set aside. That Rorty's pragmatism fails to divest itself of lingering ontological and epistemological traces suggests that those issues are both messier and more adhesive than what I have called his 'politics of redescription' can allow.

This book has set out to explore what is distinctive in Rorty's approach to philosophy, politics, and the relation between the two. True to his own prioritizing of the political role of redescription, Rorty seeks a narrative to inspire. He also, more generally, seeks a more direct engagement with concrete social issues by those in the privileged position of being able to 'theorize'. A combination of both these elements will always seem seductive, though a balance between them seems crucial. As Richard Bernstein has written in sympathetic criticism, 'inspirational liberalism without detailed, concrete plans for action tends to become empty, just as quick fixes without overall vision and careful theoretical reflection tend to become blind'.[9] Rorty's priorities, in seeking a grounded, constructive, emancipatory and inspiring practical role for theoretical disciplines which become all too easily capitivated by the sight of their own navels, are hard to object to. What is more problematic is his assumption that questions about what is persuasive and effectual in bringing about progressive social change are somehow severed from those about how the world is, and about what human capabilities are like. The question of what 'works', socially speaking, is unanswerable except by reference to *some* degree of ontological and normative inquiry.

An example might be helpful here, to close. A fixation with 'what works' has, as it happens, been a hallmark of recent political initiatives in my own country. The New Labour project has been recognizably pragmatist in precisely the sense which, in the preceding chapters has been the cause of most critical concern. It has sought to redescribe political possibilities in a way which reconcile perceived dichotomies: between 'left' and 'right', 'capitalism' and 'socialism', 'state' and 'market', 'community' and 'individual responsibility', and so on.[10] The electoral success of the party under Blair may well reflect the expediency of such an approach; it will, indeed, have its elements of inspirational appeal. But as New Labour has duly discovered, such oppositions cannot be resolved simply by being described away. The economy does not become 'dynamic' just because we perceive it as such. The social world does not become more 'inclusive' simply as a result of changes in vocabulary. Military interventions overseas are not 'humanitarian' simply to the extent that they match some fresh reworking of that term's significance. Tensions between goals – for example, individual freedoms and collective security – do not dissolve simply by those goals being redescribed as complementary rather than divergent. These points are simplistically put. Still, they carry a deeper point. How do we account for these resistances? Why might it be that the description of the world in a certain way does not make it endlessly malleable for present purposes? What is the source of the constraints on what is possible, or morally acceptable? If those sources are other than description-relative then, in the end, Rorty's politics, like New Labour's, hits constraints which lie beyond its own conceptual radar. At such points, theory – whether or not we call it Philosophy – does rather seem to have its uses. Not least, it might offer us a way of trying to figure out a normative response to the ever-startling capacity of words, backed by force, to shape ourselves, our social world, and questions about how we might best live in it.

# Notes

## Preface

1. Richard Rorty, *Consequences of Pragmatism* (Minneapolis: University of Minnesota Press, 1982); – hereafter, *CP*, p. 176.
2. 'Top 100 global public intellectuals', *Prospect* 115 (October 2005), p. 25.
3. Gideon Calder, *Rorty* (London: Weidenfeld & Nicholson, 2003).
4. For the elaboration of the distinction between philosophy (as an attempt to see how different issues 'hang together') and the specialized, timelessly defined discipline of Philosophy see *CP*, pp. xiv-xv.

## Introduction

1. For uses of this term see William James, *Pragmatism* (New York: Dover, 1995), especially chap. 6, 'The pragmatic theory of truth'.
2. Ian Hacking, 'Two kinds of new historicism for philosophers', in Ralph Cohen and Michael S. Roth (eds), *History and . . .: Histories within the Human Sciences* (Charlottesville, VA: University Press of Virginia, 1995), p. 228.
3. 'After philosophy, democracy', interview in Giovanna Borradori (ed.), *The American Philosopher* (Chicago: University of Chicago Press, 1994), p. 116.
4. Ibid., p. 117.
5. *CP*, p. 92.
6. Ibid. Here Rorty memorably identifies philosophy, qua literary genre, as a 'family romance involving, e.g. Father Parmenides, honest old uncle Kant, and bad brother Derrida'. I did think of appending Rorty to this list, but found it hard to pin down an appropriate character rôle without invoking bloody patricide. Perhaps in contemporary US realist fiction he might be a clued-up son who sues his parents for divorce.
7. BUL, p. 25.
8. *CP*, p. 165.
9. Ibid., pp. 171–2.
10. Hence the titles of two of Rorty's collections of articles: *Consequences of Pragmatism*, and *Philosophy and Social Hope*. One might run these together to provide a sort of answer to the rhetorical questions they suggest: a chief consequence of pragmatism is that philosophy (or Philosophy, at any rate) has nothing particular to offer in the way of social hope.

11 'Is "postmodernism" relevant to politics?', typescript in my possession, p. 11.
12 'Against belatedness', *London Review of Books* (16 June 1983), p. 5.
13 Jürgen Habermas, 'Richard Rorty's pragmatic turn', in *RC*, p. 32.
14 Rorty freely admits the charge that he might in some ways misappropriate the work of those other philosophers he holds most dear. He has defended the strategy with a rhetorical question: 'If you borrow somebody's good idea and use it for a different purpose, is it really necessary to clear this novel use with the originator of the idea?' (*RP*, p. 190). I will not spend any time answering this question in what follows.
15 *CP*, p. 165.

# 1 Rorty's Project: Redescribing Pragmatism

1 *PMN*, p. 379.
2 'Habermas and Lyotard on Postmodernity', *EHO*, p. 169.
3 'Is Derrida a *quasi*-transcendental philosopher?', *Contemporary Literature*, 36 (1995), 184.
4 *LT*, p. 1.
5 Ludwig Wittgenstein, *Philosophical Investigations*, trans. G. E. M. Anscombe (Oxford: Blackwell, 1974), part 1, section 133.
6 In a 1982 interview, Rorty admits to taking the 'positivistic enterprise' of 'clearing away pseudo-problems terribly seriously' – 'From philosophy to post-philosophy', *Radical Philosophy*, 32 (1982), 1. It is not, as I hope to show, an incidental predilection.
7 *ORT*, p. 75.
8 *PMN* p. 12.
9 *PMN*, pp. 3, 141–3, 137.
10 John Locke, *An Essay Concerning Human Understanding* (Glasgow: Fontana, 1964), p. 111.
11 Ibid., p. 89.
12 W. V. O. Quine, *Theories and Things* (Cambridge, MA: Harvard University Press, 1981), p. 68.
13 *PMN*, pp. 49–50.
14 *PMN*, p. 12.
15 Iris Marion Young, *Justice and the Politics of Difference* (Princeton: Princeton University Press, 1990), p. 125. Young's description here makes no reference to Rorty, although in fact, in its full version, it represents a neat summary of much of Rorty's argument in *PMN*.
16 Ibid., p. 125. The 'standard lines of rejection' to which I refer here are the various critiques of the 'cogito' current through structuralist, post-structuralist and phenomenological thinking in the twentieth century.

Different forms of the rejection have, of course, surfaced concurrently in the Anglophone analytical tradition. While they emerge most obviously in Wittgenstein's appeal to forms of life (rather than the egological subject) as conferring meaning, they feature also, as Mark Sacks points out, in Saul Kripke's similarly anti-Cartesian insistence that rule-following requires the constraint of social context. The wide exposure of such views make it difficult, Sacks argues, to see how 'the analytical tradition can survive intact the consequences that follow from the demise of the egological subject'. His contention, like Rorty's, is that its default position in that tradition is a result of its own failure to wake up to some of its own most prominent conclusions. See Sacks, 'The subject, normative structure, and externalism', in Anat Biletzki and Anat Matar (eds), *The Story of Analytic Philosophy* (London: Routledge, 1998), pp. 88–107.

17  *PMN*, p. 51.
18  See René Descartes, *Discourse on Method and the Meditations*, trans. by F. E. Sutcliffe (Harmondsworth: Penguin Books, 1968, orig. 1641), meditation 1.
19  *PMN*, p. 58. Rorty argues that 'indubitability' rather than 'non-extension' must, in the end, be the mark of the mental for Descartes because non-spatiality, for all its repeated emphasis, is not the whole story: 'we would hardly think of a thought or a pain as a *thing* which was not locatable unless we already had the notion of a nonextended substance of which it might be a portion. No intuition that pains and thoughts are non-spatial antedates, or can ground an argument for, the Cartesian notion of the mind as a distinct substance (a non-spatial one)' (*PMN*, p. 63). We need the indubitability criterion so to do.
20  *PMN*, p. 61.
21  *PMN*, p. 105.
22  *PMN*, p. 218.
23  W. V. O. Quine, 'Two dogmas of empiricism', in *From a Logical Point of View*, 2nd edn (Cambridge, MA: Harvard University Press, 1961).
24  Quine, 'Carnap and logical truth', in P. A. Schilpp (ed.), *Carnap and Logical Truth* (La Salle: Open Court, 1963), p. 406.
25  The quoted phrase is Hans Reichenbach's, cited in *CP*, p. 211.
26  *PMN*, p. 6.
27  'Realism and reference', *The Monist*, 59 (1976), 339–40, n. 18.
28  John Dewey, *Experience and Nature* (New York: Dover, 1958), p. 11.
29  The quoted phrase being the title of a review by Rorty of four books about Dewey, *London Review of Books* (25 July 1991).
30  *RP*, pp. 3–4.
31  William James, *Pragmatism* (New York: Dover, 1995), p. 86.
32  That this stance on meaning does not apply so readily to the ideas of Charles Sanders Peirce, the other main figure of the 'first generation' pragmatist canon, is largely why Rorty finds his work less relevant to his own development of pragmatist themes that that of the other two. Peirce himself

is not prepared to reduce truth to purpose, as James does, and preserves a sense of a mind-independent reality which is granted a role in the cashing-out of our concepts' worth. See 'What pragmatism is', in H. S. Thayer (ed.), *Pragmatism: The Classic Writings* (Indianapolis: Hackett, 1982), p. 116, where Peirce affirms that 'that is real which has such and such characters, whether anybody thinks it to have those characters or not'. Thought will, eventually, with the fixing of correct opinion through practical trial and error, find that ultimately, those firmed up opinions will conform with the real. Thus while for James, the true is 'only the expedient in our way of thinking', for Peirce it is by way of finding out what is expedient in our thinking that we will arrive, ideally, at the truth.

33 *CP*, p. 165.
34 Charles Sanders Peirce, *Philosophical Writings*, ed. J. Buchler (New York: Dover, 1955), p. 228.
35 Ibid., p. 229. It is worth noting the resemblance between these claims and Wittgenstein's rejections, more than half a century later, of the problem of scepticism. See, for example, his *Philosophical Investigations* (Oxford: Blackwell, 1974), § 481.
36 Ibid.
37 Dewey, *Experience and Nature*, p. 3.
38 Ibid., p. 410.
39 Donald Davidson, 'The structure and content of truth', *Journal of Philosophy*, 87 (1990), 279.
40 Dewey, *Experience and Nature*, p. 410.
41 This is, though, something of a moot point. While James (whose treatment of truth is dealt with below) insists that 'the notion of a reality independent of . . . us, taken from ordinary social experience, lies at the base of the pragmatist definition of truth', he also makes claims like: 'The object's advent is the significance's verification' (*Pragmatism*, p. 79), and equates Berkeley's explanation of matter with pragmatism's explanation of truth (ibid., p. 90). The latter two claims sit rather unsteadily with the first, in a way which, as we shall see, is a harbinger of very similar waverings in Rorty's thinking.
42 This was not, needless to say, a proximity recognized by proponents of either school. Bertrand Russell is famously rude about James and Dewey in his *History of Western Philosophy*, where he describes James's pragmatism not just as 'dependent on fallacies' but as 'a form of subjectivistic madness'. See Russell, *History of Western Philosophy*, 2nd edn (London: Unwin, 1979), pp. 772–3.
43 James, *Pragmatism*, p. 30.
44 James, 'What Pragmatism Is', in H. S. Thayer (ed.), *Pragmatism: The Classic Writings* (Indianapolis: Hackett, 1982), p. 110.
45 Ibid., p. 111.
46 James, *Pragmatism*, p. 77.

47 See John Patrick Diggins, *The Promise of Pragmatism* (Chicago: Chicago University Press, 1994), pp. 133–4.
48 Max Horkheimer, 'On the problem of truth', in *Between Philosophy and Social Science: Selected Early Writings* (Cambridge, MA: MIT Press, 1993), p. 196.
49 'Totality' here being understood in the Hegelian, dialectical sense, in which whole and part must be considered in reciprocal relation. See Martin Jay, *Marxism and Totality* (Berkeley: University of California Press, 1984), pp. 201, 260–1.
50 See Theodor Adorno and Max Horkheimer, *Dialectic of Enlightenment*, trans. John Cumming (London: Verso, 1979), chap. 8.
51 Horkheimer, 'Problem of truth', p. 197. See also his *Eclipse of Reason* (New York: Continuum, 1992), in which he charges pragmatism with holding 'not that our expectations are fulfilled and our actions successful because our ideas are true, but rather that our ideas are true because our expectations are fulfilled and our actions successful' (p. 42).
52 Horkheimer, *Eclipse of Reason*, p. 52.
53 Adorno and Horkheimer, *Dialectic of Enlightenment*, p. 16.
54 Horkheimer, *Eclipse of Reason*, p. 55.
55 For the sake of exposition and coherence I have been fudging key differences between the approaches of Peirce, James and Dewey. As Festenstein observes, pragmatists themselves have typically squabbled over the sense, utility and ownership of the term – *Pragmatism and Political Theory* (Cambridge: Polity Press, 1997), pp. 2–4. Certainly Dewey saw himself as synthesizing the differing systems and attitudinal stances of Peirce and James – and, as I argue here, Rorty sees himself as synthesizing, or re-describing, certain key themes in Dewey with the lessons of the 'linguistic turn'.
56 Plato, *The Republic*, trans. Desmond Lee (Harmondsworth: Penguin Books, 1955), pp. 316–25.
57 Hobbes, *Leviathan* (Harmondsworth: Penguin, 1969), esp. chaps 1 and 2.
58 See Tony Burns, 'Materialism in ancient Greek philosophy', *Historical Materialism*, 7 (2000), for an account of Aristotle, and then Marx, as seeking to avoid both the Scylla of Plato's idealism and the Charybdis of Democritus' materialism. Marx's doctoral thesis was, of course, on 'The difference between the Democritean and Epicurean philosophy'; one 'difference' being that Epicurus, while a materialist, rejected the strict (proto-Hobbesian) causal determinism underlying Democritus's work, affirming the existence of free will.
59 Karl Marx, *Economic and Philosophic Manuscripts* (New York: Prometheus Books, 1988), p. 154.
60 See notes 32 and 41 above.
61 *PSH*, p. xxi.
62 Adorno and Horkheimer, *Dialectic of Enlightenment*, p. 3. By this stage,

they diagnose the 'rationalistic' impulses of the Enlightenment as having dissolved into scientistic, intrumental rationality after the pragmatist/positivist model.

63 *CP*, p. 34.
64 *CIS*, p. 22.
65 'Something to steer by', *London Review of Books* (20 June, 1996), 7.
66 Cf. Nietzsche's account of the stages by which the 'real world' ('attainable to the wise') is first recognized as unattainable, then abolished. Like Rorty, Nietzsche thinks that the appearance/reality distinction will perish along with it: 'We have abolished the real world: what world is left? the apparent world, perhaps? . . . But no! *with the real world we have also abolished the apparent world!*' Nietzsche, 'How the "real world" at last became a myth', in *Twilight of the Idols/The Antichrist* (Harmondsworth: Penguin, 1968), pp. 40–1.
67 *PMN*, pp. 390, 174, 167.
68 F. Waismann, 'How I see philosophy', in H. D. Lewis (ed.), *Contemporary British Philosophy* (London: George Allen & Unwin, 1956), pp. 445–6.
69 See Hilary Putnam, *Reason, Truth and History* (Cambridge: Cambridge University Press, 1981), pp. 49–50.
70 *ORT*, p. 23.
71 *PSH*, pp. 27–8.
72 *CIS*, p. 6.
73 Bob Jessop, *State Theory* (Cambridge: Polity Press, 1990), p. 294.
74 *PMN*, p. 9.
75 *PCL*, p. 219.
76 *PCL*, pp. 219–20. Note that this was written long before Rorty came across those literary-theoretical 'heroes' of his later work (Derrida, for instance, and Harold Bloom) whose own conclusions along parallel lines he will later characterize as 'textualism'. See *CP*, pp. 139–59.
77 Ferdinand de Saussure, *Course in General Linguistics*, trans. Wade Baskin (New York: McGraw-Hill, 1966). There is, curiously in some ways, no real discussion of Saussure in Rorty's work.
78 Ibid., p. 65.
79 Indeed, the explanatory diagrams used in the *Course* depict the relation between signifier and signified in vertical terms, as the bottom and top halfs, respectively, of a circle.
80 *CP*, pp. 86–87.
81 Ibid., p. 153.
82 Ibid., p. 92.
83 Rorty admits, if only Whiggishly, that 'for all my doubts about analytic philosophy, I think that the linguistic turn was an instance of genuine philosophical progress'.
84 *CP*, p. 91.
85 *PSH*, p. 83.

86 Donald Davidson, 'On the very idea of a conceptual scheme', in his *Inquiries into Truth and Interpretation* (Oxford: Clarendon Press, 1984), p. 189.
87 Ibid., p. 183.
88 Ibid., pp. 196–7.
89 Ibid., p. 197.
90 *TP*, p. 161.
91 *CP*, p. 14.
92 *ORT*, p. 168.
93 *ORT*, p. 99.
94 *TP*, p. 161.
95 'Is Derrida a *quasi*-transcendental philosopher?", *Contemporary Literature*, 36 (1995), 178.
96 *ORT*, p. 7.
97 *CP*, p. xiv.
98 Quine, *Ontological Relativity and Other Essays* (New York: Columbia University Press, 1969), p. 51.
99 *PMN*, p. 170.
100 Ibid.
101 *PMN*, p. 157.
102 *ORT*, p. 164.
103 'Reply to Dreyfus and Taylor', *Review of Metaphysics*, 34 (1980), 46.
104 'A discussion' (with Hubert Dreyfus and Charles Taylor), *Review of Metaphysics*, 34 (1980), 49.
105 *PMN*, p. 378.
106 *PCL*, p. 204.
107 'Pragmatism and law: a response to David Luban', in Morris Dickstein (ed.), *The Revival of Pragmatism* (Durham, NC, and London: Duke University Press, 1998), p. 309.
108 *CP*, p. xiv.
109 'Foucault and Epistemology', in David Couzens Hoy (ed.), *Foucault: A Critical Reader* (Oxford: Blackwell, 1986), p. 48.
110 *RP*, p. 4.
111 *ORT*, p. 9. For a fuller account of Rorty's views on relations between language and world, see my *Rorty* (London: Weidenfeld & Nicolson, 2003), pp. 24–43.
112 *LT*, p. 373.
113 *AB*, editors' introduction, p. ix.
114 Again, for a more extended discussion of this charge, and Rorty's rebuttals of it, see my *Rorty*.
115 See George Berkeley, *The Principles of Human Knowledge and Other Writings* (Glasgow: Fontana, 1962).
116 *TP*, p. 87.
117 *TP*, p. 191.

# NOTES

118 Borrowing, here, from Fredric Jameson's description of structuralism as confining us to the 'prison-house of language'. See his *The Prison-House of Language* (Princeton: Princeton University Press, 1972).
119 Jessop, *State Theory*, p. 295.
120 ORT, p. 81.
121 CIS, p. 6.
122 Ibid. Charles Taylor argues, rightly, I think, that even the most thoroughgoing realist is highly unlikely to subscribe to the 'Raving Platonism' embodied in the claim that nature has its own vocabulary – Taylor, 'Rorty in the epistemological tradition', in Alan Malachowski (ed.), *Reading Rorty* (Oxford: Blackwell, 1990), p. 269.
123 Putnam recalls Rorty, in discussion, declaring that 'Commonsense realism is just as bad as metaphysical realism – one leads to the other', and that 'That's the part of common sense we have to get rid of.' Putnam, 'Richard Rorty on reality and justification', in *RC*, p. 87, n. 11.
124 Paraphrasing here Peter J. McCormick's 'Introduction', in his (ed.), *Starmaking: Realism, Anti-Realism and Irrealism* (Cambridge, MA: MIT Press, 1996), p. xiv.
125 Nelson Goodman, 'On starmaking', ibid., p. 144. Goodman's case here echoes the remorseless circularity of Berkeley's: in response to the question, 'How could we have made the stars, when they are older than we are?', he answers: 'Plainly, by making a space and time that contains those stars'. Thus: 'when I say a world is made [by languages and symbol systems], I mean it literally. . . . [W]e make versions, and right versions make worlds' (p. 145).
126 Goodman, 'The way the world is', ibid., p. 3.
127 I first came across the term 'linguistic monism' in Judith Butler, *Bodies that Matter* (New York: Routledge, 1993), p. 6, although doubtless it has been around for longer. Butler herself uses the term in characterizing a misplaced objection to her own position. As we will see in 2.2, it is not clear that it is, in fact, misplaced.
128 ORT, p. 105.
129 For more on this latter point, see 2.2 below.
130 'Reply to Dreyfus and Taylor', p. 49.
131 ORT, p. 101.
132 CP, p. 154; 'Deconstruction', typescript in my possession, p. 29. Accordingly, Rorty seeks to strip Heidegger of the metaphysical residues of his account of Being – and his claim that 'language speaks man' – by 'cherishing what he loathes': the 'humanist outlook' which insists that language has no intrinsic nature beyond the uses to which it happens to be put. See CIS, p. 113, n. 13; also EHO, pp. 39–48.
133 See Sartre, *Nausea* (Harmondsworth: Penguin, 1965); *Being and Nothingness* (London: Routledge, 1956).
134 Ibid.

135 See Roy Bhaskar, *Philosophy and the Idea of Freedom* (Oxford: Blackwell, 1991), pp. 52–3.
136 *TP*, p. 285.
137 *ORT*, p. 84.
138 Adorno, *Negative Dialectics*, trans. E. B. Ashton (London: Routledge, 1973), p. 119.
139 Ibid, p. 185.
140 Ibid.,
141 Carrie L, Hull, 'The Need in Thinking', *Radical Philosophy* 84 (1997), p. 29.
142 Ibid.
143 *ORT*, pp. 90, 131.
144 *PCL*, p. 219.
145 See the opening paragraphs of 'Philosophy as a kind of writing: an essay on Derrida' (*CP*, pp. 90–1) as a prime example of Rorty's rhetorical technique in this regard.
146 Frank B. Farrell, *Subjectivity, Realism and Postmodernism* (Cambridge: Cambridge University Press, 1994), p. 137.
147 Ibid.
148 *RP*, pp. 3–4.
149 'Language goes all the way down', *CP*, p. xx; 'perspectives go all the way down', *TP*, p. 131; 'contexts go all the way down', *ORT*, p. 99; 'socialization goes all the way down', *CIS*, p. xiii. With all these things 'all the way down' there together it must be rather cramped. Unless, of course, they are all, in the end, reducible to, or at least a product of, *one* thing: language. This, in fact, is exactly the case I see Rorty as making.
150 *ORT*, pp. 22–3; 27.
151 *ORT*, p. 90.
152 *RP*, p. 50.
153 *PMN*, pp. 338–9. It is not the case that Rorty was oblivious to the self-contradictions involved in declaring truth to be relative in his work before *PMN*. In fact, in the 1972 essay 'The world well lost' (in *CP*) he is already endorsing the disquotational view of truth, discussed below, as a means of neutralizing the truth issue. Even so, in post-*PMN* writing and interviews he has expressed regret at not making a sharper distinction sooner between truth and justification.
154 *PMN*, p. 377.
155 *TP*, p. 2.
156 Ibid.
157 *RC*, p. 2.
158 'Realism and reference', pp. 322–3.
159 *FP*, p. 10.
160 *CIS*, pp. 5, 6.
161 Rorty, 'Is "postmodernism" relevant to politics?', typescript in my possession, p. 16.

162 *ORT*, p. 25.
163 Putnam, 'A comparison of something with something else', *New Literary History*, 87 (1985), 62.
164 *TP*, p. 3 ('the relative about which there is nothing to say' meaning, I assume, the one aspect of the holistic 'web' of our beliefs and desires about which we can say nothing).
165 *FP*, p. 14, n. 40.
166 *CP*, p. xlii.
167 Sartre, *L'existentialisme est un humanisme*, cited in *CP*, p. xlii.
168 'Pragmatism', typescript in my possession, p. 19.
169 *RP*, p. 205.
170 Simon Thompson, 'Richard Rorty on truth, justification and justice', in Matthew Festenstein and Simon Thompson (eds), *Richard Rorty: Critical Dialogues* (Cambridge: Polity Press, 2001), p. 42 – emphasis in the original.
171 *TP*, p. 22.
172 Thompson, 'Richard Rorty on Truth, Justification and Justice', p. 46 – emphasis in the original.
173 Ibid., p. 43.
174 *CP*, p. xxviii.
175 'Response to Simon Thompson', in Festenstein and Thompson, *Rorty*, p. 52.
176 *BUL*, p. 24.
177 A point worth noting, although I do not explore it here, is that Rorty's own examples of 'ahistorical' truths are always moral, or political: to do, at any rate, with intersubjective relations such as slavery. Why he himself does not choose 'the world is spherical' as an exemplar, I'm not sure – except that he may have qualms about citing even as an empty, powerless truth a 'vertical' claim about 'the way the world is'.
178 'Response to Simon Thompson', p. 54.
179 Putnam, *Realism with a Human Face* (Cambridge, MA: Harvard University Press, 1990). In this book and elsewhere, and in various replies from Rorty (most notably 'Solidarity or objectivity?' in *ORT*, and 'Hilary Putnam and the relativist menace' in *TP*), Putnam has tried to elude Rorty's ongoing attempt to claim Putnam's work as having a similar 'cash value' to his own.
180 *CIS*, p. 6.
181 Putnam, *Realism with a Human Face*, p. 53.
182 Robert Kirk makes this point in his *Relativism and Reality* (London: Routledge, 1999), pp. 139–40.
183 *TP*, p. 57.
184 Terry Eagleton, *Ideology* (London: Verso, 1991), p. 169.
185 Farrell, *Subjectivity, Realism and Postmodernism*, p. 140.

## 2 Redescription, Truth and Progress

1. *CIS*, p. 7.
2. See Thomas Kuhn, *The Structure of Scientific Revolutions*, 2nd edn (Chicago: University of Chicago Press, 1970). I avoid the issue here of whether Kuhn's project is at heart an explanation of rational progress in science, or a denial of it. Suffice it to say that, on Rorty's reading, its force and utility derive from its being the latter.
3. *PMN*, pp. 11, 320.
4. *PMN*, p. 365.
5. *PMN*, p. 360.
6. *PMN*, p. 377.
7. *CIS*, p. 6 (emphasis in the original).
8. See Voltaire, 'Candide', in *Candide, Zadig and Selected Stories*, trans. Donald M. Frame (New York: New American Library, 1961), for example p. 101.
9. *CP*, p. 105. In fact, a '*shuddering* resonance' seems not, given Rorty's general account here, to be the typical experience of 'normal' discursive practice. 'Reassuring resonance' might be more like it.
10. *EHO*, p. 99.
11. *CIS*, p. 20.
12. *CIS*, p. 12.
13. *EHO*, p. 12. Rorty identifies 'three ways in which a new belief can be added to our previous beliefs, thereby forcing us to reweave the fabric of our beliefs and desires': perception, inference (both of which leave our language – and thus the realm of possibility – unchanged) and metaphor, which adds to our language.
14. *PCL*, p. 207.
15. *EHO*, p. 12.
16. 'Is "postmodernism" relevant to politics?', p. 16.
17. *EHO*, p. 127. Rorty states that one might as well say 'invents' as 'discloses' here: 'the difference is beside any relevant point'.
18. 'Philosophy without principles', p. 463.
19. *ORT*, p. 14.
20. For more on Rorty's account of metaphor, see my *Rorty* (London: Weidenfeld & Nicolson, 2003), pp. 43–53.
21. *ORT*, p. 124.
22. 'Habermas, Derrida, and the functions of philosophy', *Revue Internationale de Philosophie* 49 (1995), p. 445.
23. *ORT*, p. 124.
24. Aristotle, *Rhetoric* 3, 1410b, cited in Terence Hawkes, *Metaphor* (London: Methuen, 1972), p. 10.

25 For Max Black, as sophisticated contemporary technician, the metaphorical utterance contains two 'subjects', primary and secondary, and works by 'projecting upon' the primary subject a set of 'associated implications' which act as a kind of 'filter' through which can be attained a new understanding of the primary subject. See Max Black, 'More about metaphor', in Andrew Ortony (ed.), *Metaphor and Thought* (Cambridge: Cambridge University Press, 1979), pp. 28–9.
26 'The higher nominalism in a nutshell: a reply to Henry Staten', *Critical Inquiry*, 12 (1986), 365.
27 'A metaphor is, so to speak, a voice from outside logical space, rather than an empirical filling-up of a portion of that space, or a logical-philosophical clarification of the structure of that space.' *EHO*, p. 13.
28 Donald Davidson, 'What metaphors mean', in his *Inquiries into Truth and Interpretation* (Oxford: Oxford University Press, 1984), p. 245.
29 *CIS*, p. 18.
30 J.L. Austin, *How to Do Things with Words*, 2nd edn (Oxford: Oxford University Press, 1975), esp. pp. 4–11.
31 Ibid., p. 1.
32 Jonathan Culler, 'Philosophy and literature: the fortunes of the performative', *Poetics Today*, 21 (2000), 506.
33 *CIS*, p. 152.
34 Davidson, 'What metaphors mean', p. 262.
35 Ibid. Susan Haack suggests that Rorty is not necessarily committed to the 'surely incautious' Davidsonian view that metaphors cause ideas in exactly the same way that a bump on the head might cause ideas – see her 'Surprising noises: Rorty and Hesse on metaphor', *Proceedings of the Aristotelian Society* 88 (1987–8), 299. I'm not sure that I can see an important dividing line between Rorty's generous list of similes in the passage quoted above (slaps in the face, kisses, pointings and so on) and Davidson's 'bump on the head example' – except insofar as bumps on the head require no interlocutor.
36 Clive Cazeaux, review of *ORT* and *EHO*, *Textual Practice*, 6 (1992), 521.
37 Davidson, 'What metaphors mean', p. 252.
38 *CIS*, p.18.
39 Ibid.
40 *ORT*, p. 124.
41 See *CIS*, p. 37; *EHO*, p. 17.
42 Ibid.
43 *ORT*, p. 168.
44 *ORT*, p. 168..
45 See Jacques Derrida, 'Signature event context', in his *Margins of Philosophy*, trans. Alan Bass (London: Harvester Wheatsheaf, 1982), pp. 314–17.
46 See *ORT*, p. 167.
47 *ORT*, p. 166.

[48] It seems dubious, in any case, to present 'How do surprises work?' as a laughably futile question. Presumably it is meant to transfer the metaphoricity issue from the cognitive to the behaviouristic plane, thus making it a non-issue for philosophers. But this only works if you're a behaviourist. For if 'surprises' are those unexpected, dazzling events which disrupt convention and send inquiry off in unpredicted directions, there is a very real philosophical interest in figuring out how they 'work'. In fact, it's what a great deal of twentieth-century philosophy of science (Canguilheim, Bachelard, Kuhn) spent its time exploring.

[49] Alessandra Tanesini makes this point in 'The "spider's web" and the "tool": Nietzsche *vis-à-vis* Rorty on metaphor', in Peter R. Sedgwick (ed.), *Nietzsche: A Critical Reader* (Oxford: Blackwell, 1995), p. 292.

[50] Frank Farrell makes a similar point in his *Subjectivity, Realism and Postmodenism* (Cambridge: Cambridge University Press, 1994), p. 132.

[51] As he says in 'Texts and lumps', the desiderata met by agreement on what counts as objective are not specific to disciplines or areas of inquiry, but to purposes. See *ORT*, pp. 78–92.

[52] Friedrich Nietzsche, 'On truth and lie in an extra-moral sense', in Walter Kaufmann (ed.), *The Viking Portable Nietzsche* (New York: Viking Press, 1954), pp. 46–7.

[53] H. W. Fowler, *Fowler's Modern English Usage*, 2nd edn (Oxford: Oxford University Press, 1983), p. 359.

[54] *EHO*, p. 20.

[55] David E. Cooper, *Metaphor* (Oxford: Blackwell, 1986), p. 119.

[56] Samuel C. Wheeler III, 'Metaphor according to Davidson and de Man', in Reed Way Dasenbrock (ed.), *Redrawing the Lines* (Minneapolis: University of Minnesota Press, 1989), p. 122.

[57] *CIS*, p. 152.

[58] FP, p. 10; p. 14, n. 40.

[59] *CP*, p. 127.

[60] Derrida, 'The *retrait* of metaphor', *Enclitic* 2 (1978), p. 13.

[61] Derrida, 'White mythology: metaphor in the text of philosophy', in *Margins of Philosophy*, p. 252.

[62] Ibid., p. 219.

[63] Ibid., p. 270. My use of Derrida here is purely for argument's sake, to show the road strategically blocked off by Rorty's appeal to dead metaphor. As a bite-sized account, it conveniently ignores the shifting currents through the article which point in less Nietzschean directions – and towards the claim that, just as metaphor lies deeper in its conceptual apparatus than philosophy likes to acknowledge, so a certain philosophical account of metaphor is presumed in our very registering of that depth. For forceful renderings of this interpretation, see Christopher Norris, *New Idols of the Cave* (Manchester: Manchester University Press, 1997), chaps 3 and 4, and 'Metaphor, ontology, and the new antirealism', *Common Knowledge*, 6/2 (1997), 69–97.

64 HNN, p. 166, n. 3.
65 Ibid.
66 Jürgen Habermas, *The Philosophical Discourse of Modernity*, trans. Frederick Lawrence (Cambridge: Polity Press, 1987), chaps 9 and 10.
67 Redescribing, here, Rorty's comment in his 'Response to Michael Williams', in *RC*, p. 218, on 'the need to reconcile the old and the new – to reshape old metaphors and vocabularies so as to accommodate them to new insights'.
68 Slavoj Žižek, *The Ticklish Subject* (London: Verso, 1999), pp. 1–5.
69 Charles Taylor, *Sources of the Self* (Cambridge: Cambridge University Press, 1989), pp 159–64.
70 Ibid., p. 514.
71 Elizabeth Grosz, *Volatile Bodies* (Bloomington: Indiana University Press, 1994), p. 6.
72 *ORT*, p. 199.
73 *EHO*, p. 55.
74 'Taylor on truth', in James Tully (ed.), *Philosophy in an Age of Pluralism: The Philosophy of Charles Taylor in Question* (Cambridge: Cambridge University Press, 1994), p. 30.
75 *DP*, pp. 15, 16.
76 'Taylor on truth', p. 30.
77 *CIS*, p. 7.
78 *PMN*, pp. 372, 378.
79 Harold Bloom, *The Anxiety of Influence* (Oxford: Oxford University Press, 1973), pp. 78, 148.
80 *CIS*, p. 47.
81 Ibid., p. 24.
82 *ORT*, pp. 118–21.
83 Ibid., p. 123.
84 Ibid., p. 123.
85 See David Hume, *A Treatise of Human Nature, Book 1* (London: Fontana, 1962), pp. 300–12.
86 *TP*, p. 322.
87 *ORT*, p. 199.
88 'Taylor on self-celebration and gratitude', *Philosophy and Phenomenological Research*, 54 (1994), 201; my emphasis.
89 'A reply to six critics', *Analyse und Kritik*, 6 (1984), 95.
90 Richard Shusterman, *Pragmatist Aesthetics* (Oxford: Blackwell, 1992), p. 254.
91 *PMN*, p. 377.
92 *CIS*, p. xiii.
93 Norman Geras, *Solidarity in the Conversation of Humankind* (London: Verso, 1995), pp. 47–68.
94 *ORT*, p. 213.
95 *CIS*, p. 177.

96 Margaret S. Archer, *Being Human: The Problem of Agency* (Cambridge: Cambridge University Press, 2000), p. 42.
97 Roy Bhaskar, *Philosophy and the Idea of Freedom* (Oxford: Blackwell, 1991), p. 69, n. 7.
98 *EHO*, p. 154.
99 *CIS*, p. 36.
100 Ibid., p. 29.
101 Archer, *Being Human*, p. 39.
102 *PSH*, p. 77; *TP*, p. 111.
103 Rejected, in particular, by Michael Sandel in *Liberalism and the Limits of Justice* (Cambridge: Cambridge University Press, 1982), but also in the work of Taylor and Michael Walzer (see Bibliography).
104 *TP*, p. 322.
105 *ORT*, p. 81.
106 John T. Lysaker, 'The Shape of Selves to Come: Rorty and Self-Creation', *Philosophy and Social Criticism* 22 (1996), p. 48.
107 I return to the issue of whether Rorty thinks there is a pre-linguistic self both below and in 3.1.
108 Jane Flax, *Thinking Fragments* (Berkeley: University of California Press, 1990), p. 32.
109 Judith Butler, *Gender Trouble* (New York: Routledge, 1990), p. 7.
110 Butler, 'Gender as performance', in Peter Osborne (ed.), *A Critical Sense: Interviews with Intellectuals* (London: Routledge, 1996), p. 112.
111 Butler, 'Contingent foundations', in Judith Butler and Joan W. Scott (eds), *Feminists Theorize the Political* (New York: Routledge: 1992), p. 17.
112 Butler, 'Gender as performance', p. 113.
113 Butler, *Exciteable Speech: The Politics of the Performative* (New York: Routledge, 1997), p. 5.
114 Toril Moi, *What is a Woman? And Other Essays* (Oxford: Oxford University Press, 1999), p. 51.
115 *RP*, 36.
116 Though see 1.2 and 3.1 for his waverings on this matter.
117 Jonathan Rée, 'Timely meditations', *Radical Philosophy*, 55 (1990), 39.
118 Kate Soper, 'Richard Rorty: humanist and/or anti-humanist?', in Matthew Festenstein and Simon Thompson (eds), *Richard Rorty: Critical Dialogues* (Cambridge: Polity Press, 2001), p. 125.

## 3 Liberal Ironism

1 C. L. R. James, *Beyond a Boundary* (London: Serpent's Tail, 1999), p. 42.
2 Rorty, 'Solidarity or objectivity?', *ORT*, p. 34.
3 *ORT*, p. 33.
4 *CIS*, p. 63.

5 Rorty has never provided any substantial back-up for this claim – odd, perhaps, given its forthrightness, and given the well-acknowledged tensions between Mill's utilitarian and individualistic strains. That those tensions also characterize the Rortian project is something which will be pursued in what follows.
6 'Truth and freedom: a reply to Thomas McCarthy', *Critical Inquiry*, 16 (1990), 634, 635.
7 These days Rorty tends to distance himself from the 'postmodern' epithet. As he says in a 1997 interview: 'I once used it, mostly as a joke, in the title of an article called "Postmodernist Bourgeois Liberalism", because I thought it was a mildly amusing oxymoron. But unfortunately it seems to have been taken seriously. I think of the philosophical ideas that are usually called "postmodern" as having been promulgated between 1880 and 1910 by Nietzsche and William James, so "postmodern" doesn't seem the right term for them' (Interview with Sean Sayers, 18 May 1997; cassette recording in my possession). I think he is right to keep his distance in some respects, but disingenuous in others – a point I pursue through this chapter and the next.
8 Michèle Le Doeuff, *Hipparchia's Choice: An Essay Concerning Women, Philosophy, Etc*, trans. Trista Selous (Oxford: Blackwell, 1991), pp. 279–80.
9 FP, p. 3.
10 *CIS*, p. xv.
11 Ibid., p. 7.
12 Ibid., p. 73.
13 Ibid., p. xv.
14 Ibid.
15 *ORT*, 29.
16 *CIS*, p. 60.
17 Ibid.
18 'From philosophy to post-philosophy' (interview), *Radical Philosophy*, 32 (1982), 3.
19 *CIS*, p. 192.
20 *ORT*, p. 214.
21 Ibid.
22 *TP*, p. 11.
23 *CIS*, p. xvi.
24 *ORT*, p. 29.
25 *PMN*, p. 377.
26 See Nancy Fraser, 'Solidarity or singularity? Richard Rorty between romanticism and technocracy', in Alan R. Malachowski (ed.), *Reading Rorty* (Oxford: Blackwell, 1990).
27 *CIS*, p. 87.

28 A point well made by Jo Burrows, 'Conversational politics: Rorty's pragmatist apology for liberalism', in Malachowski (ed.), *Reading Rorty*, pp 332–3.
29 Some of the sting of this point might be removed were it the case – as it certainly could be – that Rorty's lack of specificity about economic relations within his 'utopia' leaves scope for there being a fundamentally more equal distribution of wealth and power than there currently is. But not that much. For (a) *CIS* abounds with comments that current Western social relations are pretty much as good as it gets, and (b) Rorty specifies no fundamental change in those relations as being required for his utopia to come into effect.
30 Calvin O. Schrag, *The Self After Postmodernity* (New Haven, CT: Yale University Press, 1997), p. 28.
31 Zygmunt Bauman, *Postmodern Ethics* (Oxford: Blackwell, 1993), p. 12.
32 Ibid., pp. 12, 14.
33 Bill Readings, 'Pagans, perverts or primitives? Experimental justice in the empire of capital', in Andrew Benjamin (ed.), *Judging Lyotard* (London: Routledge, 1992), p. 170.
34 Jean-François Lyotard, *The Postmodern Condition*, trans. Geoff Bennington and Brian Massumi (Manchester: Manchester University Press, 1984), pp. 61, 66.
35 Ibid., p. 10.
36 Lyotard and Jean-Loup Thébaud, *Just Gaming*, trans. Wlad Godzich (Manchester: Manchester University Press, 1985), p. 20.
37 Lyotard, *The Differend: Phrases in Dispute*, trans. Georges Van Den Abbeele (Manchester: Manchester University Press, 1988), pp. 91–7, 172.
38 Lyotard and Thébaud, *Just Gaming*, p. 20.
39 Ibid., p. 9.
40 Ibid., p. 77.
41 Ibid, p. 18.
42 Readings, 'Pagans, perverts or primitives?', p. 173.
43 Lyotard and Thébaud, *Just Gaming*, p. 43.
44 Ibid., p. 26.
45 Ibid., p. 59.
46 Ibid, p. 100.
47 Lyotard, *The Differend*, p. 66.
48 Ibid., p. xi.
49 Ibid., p. 12.
50 Ibid., p. xii.
51 Ibid., p. 136.
52 Ibid., p. xiii.
53 Lyotard, 'Wittgenstein "After"', in his *Political Writings*, trans. Bill Readings and Kevin Paul Geiman (London: UCL Press, 1993), p. 21.

54 Lyotard, *The Differend*, p. 4.
55 Ibid., p. 27.
56 Ibid., p. 30.
57 See, for example, Martin Heidegger, 'The way to language', in his *Basic Writings*, ed. David Farrell Krell (London: Routledge, 1993), p. 411.
58 Lyotard, *Postmodern Condition*, p. 23.
59 Axel Honneth, 'The other of justice', in Stephen K. White (ed.), *The Cambridge Companion to Habermas* (Cambridge: Cambridge University Press, 1995), p. 294; my emphasis.
60 Lyotard, *Postmodern Condition*, p. 23.
61 A point made by Seyla Benhabib: 'Epistemologies of postmodernism: a rejoinder to Jean-François Lyotard', *New German Critique*, 33 (1984), 123.
62 'Discussion entre Jean-François Lyotard et Richard Rorty', *Critique*, 41 (May 1985), 581, 583; my trans.
63 Christopher Norris, *Reclaiming Truth* (London: Lawrence & Wishart, 1996), p. 36.
64 *CIS*, p. 6.
65 Letter VI, in Anindita Niyogi Balslev, *Cultural Otherness: Correspondence with Richard Rorty* (Shimla: Indian Institute of Advanced Study, 1991), p. 86.
66 Rick Roderick, 'Reading Derrida politically (contra Rorty)', *Praxis International*, 6 (1987), 445.
67 'Pragmatism, categories, and language', *Philosophical Review*, 70 (1961), 204, n. 19.
68 Ibid., pp. 221, 22.
69 Asked in person about this wavering (in May 1997), Rorty gave a not wholly untypical shrug and suggested that perhaps he should never have dabbled with the term 'incommensurable' at all. Still, he did, and the waverings themselves are instructive.
70 *PMN*, p. 320.
71 Ibid., p. 321.
72 Ibid., pp. 376–7.
73 *ORT*, p. 215.
74 Ibid. In the 1985 exchange, Lyotard implies that Rorty misreads his position as a stance on the incommensurabilty of empirically existing *languages*, rather than genres of discourse. It is genres (rules for linguistic action) rather than languages that we cannot translate. However, Rorty's objections to the appeal to systems of rules applies, if anything, more strongly to genres within language than to languages as wholes.
75 Lyotard, *Tombeau de l'intellectuel* (Paris: Éditions Galilée, 1984), p. 61; cited in *ORT*, p. 215.
76 *ORT*, p. 216.
77 Ibid., p. 26.
78 Ibid., p. 215.

79 JLL, p. 237, n. 18; see the discussion of Davidson in 1.1.
80 UT, p. 12.
81 TP, p. 11.
82 PSH, p. 86.
83 CIS, p. 196.
84 'Thugs and theorists', *Political Theory* 15 (1987), p. 575.
85 Michael Walzer, *Spheres of Justice: A Defence of Pluralism and Equality* (Oxford: Blackwell, 1983), pp. 6–7.
86 CP, p. 183.
87 See, on this point, Will Kymlicka, *Liberalism, Community and Culture* (Oxford: Clarendon Press, 1989), pp. 67–9.
88 CIS, p. 198; Matthew Festenstein, *Pragmatism and Political Theory* (Cambridge: Polity Press, 1997), p. 116.
89 Festenstein, *Pragmatism and Political Theory*, p. 116.
90 CIS, p. 198.
91 John Rawls, *A Theory of Justice* (Oxford: Oxford University Press, 1971), p. viii.
92 Rawls, 'Justice as fairness: political not metaphysical', *Philosophy and Public Affairs* 14 (1985), 223–5.
93 Rawls, 'Kantian constructivism in moral theory', *Journal of Philosophy*, 77/9 (1980), 51.
94 ORT, p. 190.
95 Ibid., pp. 180, 189. For a contesting of Rorty's reading of Rawls, see Stephen Mulhall and Adam Swift, *Liberals and Communitarians* (Oxford: Blackwell, 1992), pp. 232–4.
96 ORT, p. 176.
97 CIS, p. 191.
98 Ibid.
99 Norman Geras, *Solidarity in the Conversation of Humankind* (London: Verso, 1995), p. 74.
100 CIS, p. 190; my emphasis.
101 Ibid., p. 190. See Geras, *Solidarity*, for extended discussion of the implications of these claims.
102 Kymlicka, *Liberalism, Community and Culture*, p. 69.
103 It is important to note that Rorty eschews communitarian attempts to a 'metaphysical' account of selfhood as inherently social in order to ground their moral and political priorities. We need no such account as back-up for our defence or advocacy of given sorts of social institutions. Even so, he argues that communitarians who so argue 'are right in saying that a conception of the self that makes community constitutive of the self does comport well with liberal democracy' (ORT, p. 179).
104 CIS, p. 196.
105 Geras, *Solidarity*, pp. 76–7.
106 Hauke Brunkhorst, 'Adorno, Heidegger and postmodernity', in David

Rasmussen (ed.), *Universalism vs. Communitarianism* (Cambridge, MA: MIT Press, 1990), p. 188.
107. *CIS*, p. xiv.
108. Rorty explicitly presents his politics as needing no philosophical anthropology, only history and sociology: *ORT*, p. 181.
109. *CIS*, p. 89.
110. Ibid., p. 90.
111. Ibid., p. 91.
112. Ibid., p. 92.
113. 'Moral universalism and economic triage', *Diogenes* 173 (1996), 3–4.
114. FP, p. 5. See again, on this point, Geras, *Solidarity*, chap. 2.
115. Terry Eagleton, *The Ideology of the Aesthetic* (Oxford: Blackwell, 1990), p. 410.
116. *CIS*, p. 91.
117. Simon Critchley, 'Deconstruction and pragmatism: is Derrida a private ironist or a public liberal?', DP, p. 26.
118. A point made forcefully by Nancy Fraser in 'Solidarity or singularity?', in Alan R. Malachowski (ed.), *Reading Rorty* (Oxford: Blackwell, 1990), and by Susan Bickford, 'Why we listen to lunatics: antifoundational theories and feminist politics', *Hypatia*, 8 (1993), esp. pp. 109–11.
119. Rorty registers a certain bemusement with Fraser's objections by insisting that his vision of the private indeed pertained not to 'the kitchen or bedroom', but to 'what you do with your solitude' – *AB*, p. 60.
120. John Stuart Mill, *On Liberty* (Harmondsworth: Penguin, 1974), p. 68.
121. Eric M. Gander, *The Last Conceptual Revolution* (Albany: State University of New York Press, 1989), p. 88.
122. Ibid., p. 89.
123. *CP*, p. 166.
124. Ibid., p. 167.
125. 'Thugs and theorists', p. 574. Rorty makes a similar point in 'Trotsky and the wild orchids', *Common Knowledge*, 1 (1992), 140.
126. See, for instance, Michel Foucault, *Discipline and Punish*, trans. Alan Sheridan (Harmondsworth: Penguin Books, 1979).
127. David Harvey, *The Condition of Postmodernity* (Oxford: Blackwell, 1990), p. 117.
128. Ellen Meiskins Wood, 'Intellectuals and universalism', *Imprints* 1 (1996), p. 71.
129. Ibid.
130. See John Locke, *Two Treatises of Government* (Cambridge: Cambridge University Press, 1960); J. S. Mill, *On Liberty*; Karl Popper, *The Open Society and its Enemies* (London: Routledge & Kegan Paul, 1945).
131. See Ronald Dworkin, *A Matter of Principle* (Cambridge, MA: Harvard University Press, 1985); Robert Nozick, *Anarchy, State and Utopia* (Oxford: Blackwell, 1974).

132 See Immanuel Kant, 'Groundwork of the metaphysic of morals', in H. J. Paton, *The Moral Law* (London: Hutchinson,1948); Rawls, *Theory of Justice*.

133 See Isaiah Berlin, *The Proper Study of Mankind* (London: Chatto & Windus, 1997).

134 See, for example, Taylor, 'The nature and scope of distributive justice', in his *Philosophy and the Human Sciences* (Cambridge: Cambridge University Press, 1985), pp. 291–3.

135 Here I invoke Berlin's influential distinction between negative liberty (as freedom from obstruction) and positive liberty (as freedom to realize my potential) – see 'Two concepts of liberty', in *Four Essays on Liberty* (Oxford: Oxford University Press, 1969).

136 Karl Marx, 'On the Jewish question', in *Selected Writings*, ed. David McLellan (Oxford: Oxford University Press, 1977), pp. 52–3.

137 See C. B. MacPherson, *The Political Theory of Possessive Individualism: Hobbes to Locke* (Oxford: Oxford University Press, 1960).

138 See Gillian Rose, *Mourning Becomes the Law* (Cambridge: Cambridge University Press, 1996), p. 5.

139 Ernesto Laclau, *Emancipation(s)* (London: Verso, 1996), pp. 33, 65, 48.

140 Ibid., p. 28.

141 Ibid., p. 122.

142 Ibid., p. 57. In drawing this parallel I am not attempting to fudge their differences, some of which emerge in their exchange in *DP*. Crucial among them, I think, is that Laclau conceives particularity and universality as being, necessarily, in a mutually defining relationship. This is down to his ultimate adherence to a Saussurian account of meaning, in which it is generated by difference between signifiers rather than as entailing any relation to a 'real world' reference. Rorty, as we have seen, sees no such necessary workings in language.

143 *JLL*, p. 224.

144 Ibid., p. 226.

145 Ibid., p. 226.

146 Ibid., p. 235.

147 Ibid.

148 Iris Marion Young, *Justice and the Politics of Difference* (Princeton: Princeton University Press, 1990), p. 105.

149 *TP*, p. 194; *CP*, p. 219.

150 'On obligation, truth and common sense', in Jósef Niznik and John T. Sanders (eds), *Debating the State of Philosophy: Habermas, Rorty, and Kolakowski* (Westport, CT: Praeger, 1996), p. 48.

151 And thus, as Richard J. Bernstein argues, Rorty substitutes a 'historical myth of the given' for the 'epistemological myth of the given' (the idea that we might have common intuitions to which we can appeal when resolving

disputes) which he seeks to leave behind. See *The New Constellation* (Cambridge, Mass.: MIT Press, 1992), pp. 243–4.
152 'On obligation, truth and common sense', p. 48.
153 *RP*, p. 32.
154 *DP*, p. 15.
155 See Karl Marx, *Economic and Philosophic Manuscripts* (New York: Prometheus Books, 1988).
156 Roy Bhaskar, *A Realist Theory of Science* (London: Verso, 1997), p. 33.
157 Margaret Archer, *Being Human: The Problem of Agency* (Cambridge: Cambridge University Press, 2000), p. 33.
158 MacPherson, 'Introduction' to Thomas Hobbes, *Leviathan* (Harmondsworth: Penguin, 1968), p. 39.
159 See Habermas, *The Philosophical Discourse of Modernity* (Cambridge: Polity Press, 1987).
160 Habermas, *Communication and the Evolution of Society* (Cambridge: Polity Press, 1991), p. 119.
161 Habermas, 'Questions and counterquestions', in Richard J. Bernstein (ed.), *Habermas and Modernity* (Cambridge: Polity Press, 1985), pp. 165–6.
162 Habermas, *Communication and the Evolution of Society*, p. 1.
163 Ibid., pp. 50–9.
164 Habermas, *Autonomy and Solidarity*, rev. edn (London: Verso, 1992), p. 58.
165 Christopher Norris, *Minding the Gap: Epistemology and Science in the Two Traditions* (Amherst: University of Massachusetts Press, 2000), p. 31.
166 Alex Callinicos, *Against Postmodernism* (Cambridge: Polity Press, 1989), p. 115.
167 Richard Wolin, *The Terms of Cultural Criticism* (New York: Columbia University Press, 1992), p. 46.
168 David Michael Levin, 'Visions of narcissism: intersubjectivity and the reversals of reflection', in M. C. Dillon (ed.), *Merleau-Ponty Vivant* (Albany: State University of New York Press, 1991), p. 76.
169 *DP*, p. 14.
170 Kate Soper, *Humanism and Anti-Humanism* (London: Hutchinson, 1986), p. 153.
171 Neil Lazarus, Steven Evans, Anthony Arnove and Anne Menke, 'The necessity of universalism', *Differences*, 7 (1995), 124.
172 Alex Callinicos, *Theories and Narratives* (Cambridge: Polity Press, 1995), p. 199.
173 Pierre Bourdieu, *Pascalian Meditations*, trans. Richard Nice (Cambridge: Polity Press, 2000), p. 71.
174 *AC*, p. 126.
175 Ibid., p. 127.
176 Ibid., p. 8.
177 Ibid., p. 88.

178 *AB*, p. 33.
179 See e.g. Callinicos, *Against Postmodernism*.
180 Marxism and pragmatism are perhaps most proximate in the thinking of the Praxis group of philosophers in 1960s and 1970s Yugoslavia. On this, see Mihailo Marković and Robert S. Cohen, *The Rise and Fall of Socialist Humanism: A History of the Praxis Group* (Nottingham: Spokesman Books, 1975), esp. pp. 35–6. On the account given here, the basics of praxis-based epistemology and ontology are noticeably close to the pragmatism of James and Dewey – and indeed Rorty.
181 See Nancy Fraser, *Justice Interruptus: Reflections on the 'Postsocialist' Condition* (New York: Routledge, 1997), pp. 189–206; also 'From redistribution to recognition?', *New Left Review*, 212 (1995), 68–93; 'Rethinking recognition', *New Left Review* (2nd series), 3 (2000), 107–20 – and her contributions to Fraser and Axel Honneth, *Redistribution or Recognition? A Political-Philosophical Exchange* (London: Verso, 2003).
182 Fraser, in Fraser and Honneth, *Redistribution or Recognition*, p. 7.
183 Fraser presents this specifically as an *analytical* distinction, rather than an ontological one. While she refers to the two kinds of injustice as having 'irreducible roots', it seems in the end that this is a claim about how we must describe them, rather than about the natures of the phenomena themselves. This, in the end, may lend grist to the mill of Iris Young's counterposition: that Fraser fails to show that the two kinds of injustice are *really* separate in any meaningful sense – see Young, 'Unruly categories: a critique of Nancy Fraser's dual systems theory', *New Left Review*, 222 (1997), 147–60.
184 *AC*, p. 31. For a slightly different, but related, take on Rorty's apparent failure here to avoid recourse to ontological or metaphysical claims, see Deane-Peter Baker, '"Don't kick the habit": a Taylorian critique of Rorty's *Achieving our Country*', *Theoria*, 101 (2003), 68–93.
185 *FR*, p. 73.

## 4 • Applications: History and Moral Practice

1 Walter Benjamin, *Illuminations* (London: Fontana Press, 1973), p. 257.
2 Theodor Adorno, cited in Andrew Bowie, *Aesthetics and Subjectivity* (Manchester: Manchester University Press, 1993), p. 67.
3 *CIS*, pp. 96, 97.
4 In what follows I use 'positivism' in a rather loose sense, defined by a rigid split between fact and value. I'm aware that this rather thin account will not do justice to the particularity of different orientations – Comte's, Ranke's, or A. J. Ayer's – which have laid claim to the term. Still, it features here as a sort of caricature of certain assumptions from which pragmatists and postmodernists would want to distance themselves, in order to show

that, in some respects, the distance is nott all that great. The prima facie mistaken claim that fact-obsessed positivists deny that we can misdescribe will be explained as we go on.
5. Bryan D. Palmer, 'Old positions/new necessities', in Ellen Meiskins Wood and John Bellamy Foster (eds), *In Defense of History* (New York: Monthly Review Press, 1997), p. 67.
6. Fredric Jameson, *Postmodernism, or, The Cultural Logic of Late Capitalism* (London: Verso, 1991), pp. 6, 21, 25.
7. Peter Novick, *The Holocaust and Collective Memory* (London: Bloomsbury, 2000), p. 4.
8. Alex Callinicos describes this scenario as one in which, 'History seems sometimes to become the raw material for a myriad of theme parks, fuel for the leisure industry . . . [in] which even the artefacts of genocide become so many consumables.' Callinicos, *Theories and Narratives* (Cambridge: Polity Press, 1995), p. 11. In the process, it gets flattened down to digestible, bite-sized items and filleted of complexity, ambiguity, contestation and indeed truth.
9. *CIS*, p. 7.
10. See *CP*, p. xliii.
11. *TP*, pp. 272–3, 270.
12. E. H. Carr, *What is History?* (Harmondsworth: Penguin, 1961), p. 22.
13. Keith Jenkins, *Why History? Ethics and Postmodernity* (London: Routledge, 1999), p. 3.
14. Roland Barthes, 'The discourse of history', in Keith Jenkins (ed.), *The Postmodern History Reader* (London: Routledge, 1997), p. 122.
15. Jenkins, *Why History?*, p. 109.
16. Jenkins, 'Why bother with the past?', *Rethinking History*, 1 (1997), 61.
17. Jenkins, *Why History?*, p. 15.
18. Ibid., back cover.
19. Ibid., p. 9.
20. Ibid., p. 15. Whether Jenkins can, without slipping into an inconsistency which would seem to unravel his entire case, claim to know that the past 'did occur, and in exactly the way it did' is a crucial point which I shall nonetheless leave dangling for now.
21. Cited in Ernst Breisach, *Historiography: Ancient, Medieval and Modern*, 2nd edn (Chicago: University of Chicago Press, 1994), p. 233.
22. A 'French historian' cited in Peter Novick, *That Noble Dream: The 'Objectivity Question' and the American Historical Profession* (Cambridge: Cambridge University Press, 1988), p. 26.
23. Jenkins, 'Introduction', in his (ed.), *The Postmodern History Reader* (London: Routledge, 1997), p. 17.
24. Michael Roth, 'Thin description: Richard Rorty's use of history', in his *The Ironist's Cage* (New York: Columbia University Press, 1995).

25. E. P. Thompson, *The Poverty of Theory*, cited in Perry Anderson, *Arguments within English Marxism* (London: Verso, 1980), p. 6.
26. This does, to be sure, suggest a more Rortian view of the subject – as creative redescriber and meaning creator – than a strictly post-structuralist one, in which the speaking subject is not, in any sure sense, mistress of the language she utilizes.
27. See Christopher Norris, 'Postmodernising history: right-wing revisionism and the uses of theory', *Southern Review* 21 (July 1988), 128–9. Norris separates the valuable lessons that theorists like Hayden White, Foucault and indeed Barthes can teach historians about the need for contextual sensitivity, for careful and critically aware reading, from, on the other hand, the tendency to 'go the whole sceptical hog' *vis-á-vis* the possibility of historiography and so render those lessons pretty much pointless.
28. This is one point at which the distinction between forms of positivism (see n. 4, p. 206) will apply. For while nineteenth-century postivist historians like Ranke were happy to talk of, and to prize, historical 'facts' as radically separate from cultural values, logical positivists such as Ayer were (with good reason, by their own lights) pretty sceptical about the 'reality' of the past for reasons parallel to the postmodernist case – that is to say, the absence of a readily available sense of 'verification' by which we might prove the past's reality.
29. James Conant, 'Freedom, cruelty and truth: Rorty versus Orwell', in *RC*, p. 308. Conant is rightly perplexed by Rorty's own, strangely skewed, take on the Winston Smith/O'Brien encounter in *CIS*, in which O'Brien is presented as speaking, for Orwell, on the malleability of truth, while Winston's torture is taken as a prime example of the humiliation to which we are all, as human beings, potentially subject.
30. George Orwell, *Nineteen Eighty-Four* (Harmondsworth: Penguin, 1989), p. 260.
31. Conant, 'Freedom, cruelty and truth', p. 308.
32. In January 2000 the historian David Irving brought a libel action in London against the American academic Deborah Lipstadt and Penguin Books, author and publisher respectively of *Denying the Holocaust: The Growing Assault on Truth and Memory*, a book which described Irving as an ideologically motivated Hitler apologist set on misrepresentation of data and documents, and as 'one of the most dangerous Holocaust deniers'. On 11 April, the High Court judge, Mr Justice Gray, found in favour of the defendants. He declared Irving – in the course of over 30 years as a Hitler scholar – to have 'portrayed Hitler in an unwarrantedly favourable light, principally in relation to his attitude towards and responsibility for the treatment of Jews', and to be 'an active Holocaust denier' (Glasgow *Herald*, 12 April 2000, p. 3).
33. Robert Faurisson, cited in Jean-François Lyotard, *The Differend: Phrases in Dispute*, trans. Georges van den Abbeele (Manchester: Manchester University Press, 1988), p. 3.

34 Ibid., p. 4.
35 The difference between them being that in Faurisson's, and the 'book publisher' example, there could not conceivably be proof, whereas the question whether Hitler issued a particular order is potentially answerable, whatever the current state of evidence on the matter. But as I say here, the form of evidence demanded is what links all three.
36 Anyone who, for instance, will not allow that the Nazi hierarchy might (aware enough of the significance of their actions) have deliberately avoided putting every last order in writing, will have problems relating any events not in directly observable causal relation.
37 Chris Lorenz, 'Historical knowledge and historical reality: a plea for "internal realism"'. In Brian Fay, Phillip Pomper and Richard T. Vann (eds), *History and Theory* (Oxford: Blackwell, 1998), pp. 366–7.
38 Berel Lang, 'Is it possible to misrepresent the Holocaust?', *History and Theory* 34 (1995), 84.
39 See Martin Heidegger, *Being and Time*, trans. Joan Stambaugh (Albany: State University of New York Press, 1996).
40 Judith Butler, *Bodies that Matter* (New York: Routledge, 1993), p. 2.
41 Jane Flax, *Thinking Fragments* (Berkeley: University of California Press, 1990), p. 213.
42 Iris Marion Young, *Justice and the Politics of Difference* (Princeton: Princeton University Press, 1990), p. 256.
43 Young, 'Together in difference', in Judith Squires (ed.), *Principled Positions* (London: Lawrence & Wishart, 1993), p. 142. The description of liberalism given here is, admittedly, more mine than hers.
44 Ibid., pp. 123–4.
45 This arises from Young's adherence to the standard post-structuralist picture, mentioned above, in which identities are to be characterized in terms of their differences one from another, rather than by anything essential or internal.
46 Cf. Rorty's own overcoming (as I see it) of some aspects of the liberal–communitarian debate, discussed in 3.1.
47 See, for instance, Peter Winch's *The Idea of a Social Science and its Relation to Philosophy* (London: Routledge, 1958) for an influential articulation of this extreme relativist position.
48 As we saw in 3.3, Nancy Fraser has argued, against Young, for an analytical distinction between the spheres of redistribution and recognition – see, for example, Fraser, 'From redistribution to recognition?', *New Left Review*, 212 (1995), 68–93.
49 *ORT*, p. 176.
50 David Miller, *On Nationality*, cited in Phillip Cole, *Philosophies of Exclusion* (Edinburgh: Edinburgh University Press, 2000), pp. 90–1.
51 Cole, *Philosophies of Exclusion*, p. 92.

[52] *CIS*, p. 190.
[53] John Gray, *Endgames: Questions in Late Modern Political Thought* (Cambridge: Polity Press, 1997), p. 91.
[54] Eagleton, *The Illusions of Postmodernism* (Oxford: Blackwell, 1996), pp. 114–15.
[55] This is not to argue, with Hume, that one cannot generate an 'ought' from an 'is'. Rather, it is to insist that moral commitment will entail the possibility of systematic critique of what 'is' in purely empirical terms, in the light of alternative conceptions of what 'ought' to be brought about in the way of intersubjective relations.
[56] Paraphrasing, here, Keith Graham, 'Being some body: choice and identity in a liberal pluralist world', in Bob Brecher, Jo Halliday and Klára Kolinská (eds), *Nationalism and Racism in the Liberal Order* (Aldershot: Ashgate, 1998), p. 187.
[57] Seyla Benhabib, *Situating the Self* (Cambridge: Polity Press, 1992), p. 8.
[58] Karl Marx and Friedrich Engels, *The Communist Manifesto* (Harmondsworth: Penguin, 1967), p. 105.
[59] René Descartes, *Discourse on Method and the Meditations* (Harmondsworth: Penguin, 1968), p. 110; Merleau-Ponty, *Primacy of Perception* (Evanston, IL: Northwestern University Press, 1964), p. 116.
[60] Merleau-Ponty, *The Primacy of Perception*, p. 99. This account bears similarities to George Herbert Mead's description of communicative understanding as dependent upon the subject's capacity to place themselves in the position of their interlocutor – see Mead, 'Social consciousness and the consciousness of meaning', in H. S. Thayer (ed.), *Pragmatism: The Classic Writings* (Indianapolis: Hackett, 1982), pp. 341–50. It is noticeable that Mead, alone among the first generation of pragmatist philosophers, receives virtually no coverage in Rorty's extensive references to the tradition.
[61] Edmund Husserl, *Cartesian Meditations* (Dordrecht: Kluwer, 1995), p. 91.
[62] *TP*, p. 289.

## Conclusions

[1] Rorty, Review of Ernst Tugendhat, *Traditional and Analytical Philosophy: Lectures on the Philosophy of Language*, *Journal of Philosophy* 82 (1985), 721.
[2] In *CP*, p. xiv, Rorty cites with approval Sellars's suggestion that we see philosophy as 'an attempt to see how things, in the broadest sense of the term, hang together, in the broadest possible sense of the term'.
[3] 'Philosophy-envy', in Andreas Vieth (ed.), *Richard Rorty: His Philosophy under Discussion* (Frankfurt: Ontos Verlag, 2005), p. 35.
[4] Example taken from 'Comments and responses', ibid., p. 146.

5 *AC*, pp. 106–7.
6 'Recent Metaphilosophy', *Review of Metaphysics*, 15 (1962), 300.
7 The 'critical realism' referred to has been developed through the work of Margaret Archer, Roy Bhaskar, Andrew Collier, Andrew Sayer and others. The works by these authors referred to in the bibliography will give a flavour.
8 Cited in Andrew Bowie, *Aesthetics and Subjectivity* (Manchester: Manchester University Press, 1993), p. 67.
9 Richard J. Bernstein, 'Rorty's inspirational liberalism', in Charles Guignon and David R. Hiley (eds), *Richard Rorty* (Cambridge: Cambridge University Press, 2003), p. 137.
10 For a discussion of New Labour's ideological mission to dissolve dualisms, see Alan Finlayson, *Making Sense of New Labour* (London: Lawrence & Wishart, 2003).

# References

## Books by Richard Rorty (including edited volumes to which Rorty is a major contributor)

LT    (ed.), *The Linguistic Turn: Essays in Philosophical Method*, 2nd edn (Chicago: University of Chicago Press, 1992; orig. 1967).

PMN   *Philosophy and the Mirror of Nature* (Oxford: Blackwell, 1980; orig. 1979).

CP    *Consequences of Pragmatism* (Minneapolis: University of Minnesota Press, 1982).

PH    (co-ed. with Jerome B. Schneewind and Quentin Skinner), *Philosophy in History* (Cambridge: Cambridge University Press, 1985).

CIS   *Contingency, Irony, and Solidarity* (Cambridge: Cambridge University Press, 1989).

ORT   *Objectivity, Relativism, and Truth: Philosophical Papers*, vol. 1 (Cambridge: Cambridge University Press, 1991).

EHO   *Essays on Heidegger and Others: Philosophical Papers*, vol. 2 (Cambridge: Cambridge University Press, 1991).

HE   *Hoffnung statt Erkentniss: Eine Einfürung in die Pragmatische Philosophie* (Vienna: Passagen Verlag, 1994). Typescript (of the English original) in my possession.

RP   *Rorty and Pragmatism: The Philosopher Replies to his Critics* (exchanges between Rorty and seven others), ed. Herman J. Saatkamp, Jr. (Nashville, TN: Vanderbilt University Press, 1995).

DP   (with Simon Critchley, Jacques Derrida, Ernesto Laclau and Chantal Mouffe) *Deconstruction and Pragmatism* (London: Routledge, 1996).

AC   *Achieving our Country: Leftist Thought in Twentieth-Century America* (Cambridge, MA: Harvard University Press, 1998).

TP   *Truth and Progress: Philosophical Papers*, vol. 3 (Cambridge: Cambridge University Press, 1998).

AB   (with Derek Nystrom and Kent Puckett) *Against Bosses, Against Oligarchies: A Conversation with Richard Rorty* (Charlottesville, VA: Prickly Pear Pamphlets, 1998).

PSH   *Philosophy and Social Hope* (Harmondsworth: Penguin, 1999).

RC   *Rorty and his Critics* (replies to twelve others plus an article, 'Universality and Truth'), ed. Robert B. Brandom (Oxford: Blackwell, 2000).

FR   (with Gianni Vattimo) *The Future of Religion*, ed. Santiago Zambala (New York: Columbia University Press, 2005).

## Articles by Richard Rorty

'Pragmatism, categories and language', *Philosophical Review*, 70 (1961), 197–223.
'Recent metaphilosophy', *Review of Metaphysics*, 15 (1961), 299–318.
Review of *American Pragmatism: Peirce, James and Dewey* by Edward C. Moore, *International Journal of Ethics*, 72 (1962), 146–7.
'Realism, categories, and the "linguistic turn"', *International Philosophical Quarterly*, 2 (1962), 307–22.
Review of *Science and Metaphysics: Variations on Kantian Themes* by Wilfrid Sellars, *Philosophy*, 45 (1970), 66–70.
Review of *The Origins of Pragmatism* by A. J. Ayer, *Philosophical Review*, 80 (1971), 96–100.
'Realism and reference', *The Monist*, 59 (1976), 321–40.
Review of *On Human Conduct* by Michael Oakeshott, and *Knowledge and Politics* by Roberto Mangabiera Unger, *Social Theory and Practice*, 4 (1976), 107–16.
'Derrida on language, being and abnormal philosophy', *Journal of Philosophy*, 74 (1977), 673–81.
'Reply to Dreyfus and Taylor', *Review of Metaphysics*, 34 (1980), 39–46.
'Beyond Nietzsche and Marx', review of *Power/Knowledge* by Michel Foucault, edited by Colin Gordon, *Michel Foucault* by Alan Sheridan, and *Herculine Barbin* by Oscar Panizza, *London Review of Books* (19 February 1981), 5–6.
'From philosophy to post-philosophy', interview with Wayne Hudson and Wim van Reijen, *Radical Philosophy*, 32 (1982), 1–7.
'Against belatedness', review of *The Legitimacy of the Modern Age* by Hans Blumenberg, *London Review of Books* (16 June 1983), 3–5.
'A reply to six critics', *Analyse und Kritik*, 6 (1984), 78–98.
'Philosophy without principles', *Critical Inquiry*, 11 (1985), 459–65.
'Foucault and epistemology', in David Couzens Hoy (ed.), *Foucault: A Critical Reader* (Oxford: Blackwell, 1986), 41–8.
'The higher nominalism in a nutshell: a reply to Henry Staten', *Critical Inquiry*, 12 (1986), 462–6.
'Thugs and theorists', *Political Theory*, 15 (1987), 564–80.
'Philosophy as a literary tradition', review of *Derrida* by Christopher Norris, *New Leader* (3 October 1988), 20–1.
'Truth and freedom: a reply to Thomas McCarthy', *Critical Inquiry*, 16 (1990), 633–43.
'Just one more species doing its best', review of four books about John Dewey, *London Review of Books* (25 July 1991), 3–7.
'Feminism and pragmatism', *Radical Philosophy*, 59 (1991), 3–14.
'Intellectuals in politics: too far in? Too far out?', *Dissent* (Fall 1991), 483–90.

'Putnam on truth', *Philosophy and Phenomenological Research*, 52 (1992), 415–18.

'Trotsky and the wild orchids', *Common Knowledge*, 1 (1992), 140–53.

'Taylor on truth', in James Tully (ed.), *Philosophy in an Age of Pluralism: The Philosophy of Charles Taylor in Question* (Cambridge: Cambridge University Press, 1994), pp. 20–36.

'Taylor on self-celebration and gratitude', *Philosophy and Phenomenological Research*, 54 (1994), 197–201.

'Is Derrida a *quasi*-transcendental philosopher?', *Contemporary Literature*, 36 (1995), 173–200.

'Habermas, Derrida, and the functions of philosophy', *Revue Internationale de Philosophie*, 49 (1995), 437–60.

'Deconstruction', typescript in my possession. Later published as the entry on 'Deconstruction' in *The Cambridge History of Literary Criticism,* vol. 8, ed. Raman Selden (Cambridge: Cambridge University Press, 1995), pp. 166–96.

'Moral universalism and economic triage', *Diogenes*, 173 (1996), 3–15.

'Something to steer by', review of *John Dewey and the High Tide of American Liberalism* by Alan Ryan, *London Review of Books* (20 June, 1996), 7–9.

'Does academic freedom have philosophical presuppositions?', in Louis Menaud (ed.), *The Future of Academic Freedom* (Chicago: University of Chicago Press, 1997).

'Is "postmodernism" relevant to politics?', typescript of lecture given at Cardiff University, 2 May 1997.

Interview with Sean Sayers, London, 18 May 1997. Cassette recording in my possession.

'Religious faith, intellectual responsibility, and romance', in Ruth Anna Putnam (ed.), *The Cambridge Companion to William James* (Cambridge: Cambridge University Press, 1997), pp. 84–102.

'First projects, then principles', *The Nation* (22 December 1997), 18–21.

'Realism, antirealism and pragmatism: comments on Alston, Chisholm, Davidson, Harman and Searle', in Christopher Kulp (ed.), *Realism/Antirealism and Epistemology* (London: Rowman & Littlefield, 1997), pp. 149–71.

'What do you do when they call you a "relativist"?', *Philosophy and Phenomenological Research*, 57 (1997), 173–7.

'Pragmatism', typescript in my possession. Later published as the entry on 'Pragmatism' in *Routledge International Encyclopedia of Philosophy,* vol. 7 (London: Routledge, 1998), pp. 632–40.

'The truth isn't out there', Glasgow *Herald* (2 May 1998), 30.

'Pragmatism and law: a response to David Luban', in Morris Dickstein (ed.), *The Revival of Pragmatism: New Essays on Social Thought, Law and Culture* (Durham, NC and London: Duke University Press, 1998), pp. 304–11.

'Being that can be understood is language', *London Review of Books* (16 March 2000), 23–5.

'Universality and Truth', in Robert B. Brandom (ed.), *Rorty and his Critics* (Oxford: Blackwell, 2000), pp. 1–30.

'Response to Simon Thompson', in Matthew Festenstein and Simon Thompson (eds), *Richard Rorty: Critical Dialogues* (Cambridge: Polity Press, 2001).

## Other Sources

## Books

Adorno, Theodor W., *Negative Dialectics*, trans. E. B. Ashton (London: Routledge, 1973; orig. 1966).

—— and Max Horkheimer, *Dialectic of Enlightenment*, trans. John Cumming (London: Verso, 1979; orig. 1947).

Anderson, Perry, *Arguments within English Marxism* (London: Verso, 1980).

Archer, Margaret S., *Being Human: The Problem of Agency* (Cambridge: Cambridge University Press, 2000).

Arcilla, René Vincente, *For the Love of Perfection: Richard Rorty and Liberal Education* (New York: Routledge, 1995).

Aristotle, *Poetics*, trans. S. H. Butcher (Mineola, NY: Dover, 1997; orig. c.330 BC).

Austin, J. L., *How to Do Things with Words*, 2nd edn (Oxford: Oxford University Press, 1975; orig. 1961).

Balibar, Étienne, *The Philosophy of Marx*, trans. Chris Turner (London: Verso, 1995; orig. 1993).

Balslev, Anindita Niyogi, *Cultural Otherness: Correspondence with Richard Rorty* (Shimla: Indian Institute of Advanced Study, 1991).

Baudrillard, Jean, *Selected Writings*, ed. Mark Poster (Cambridge: Polity Press, 1988).

Bauman, Kenneth, James Bohman and Thomas McCarthy (eds), *After Philosophy: End or Transformation?* (Cambridge, MA: MIT Press, 1987).

Bauman, Zygmunt, *Postmodern Ethics* (Oxford: Blackwell, 1993).

Beiner, Ronald, *Philosophy in a Time of Lost Spirit: Essays on Contemporary Theory* (Toronto:University of Toronto Press, 1997).

Benhabib, Seyla, *Situating the Self* (Cambridge: Polity Press, 1992).

Benjamin, Andrew (ed.), *Judging Lyotard* (London: Routledge, 1992).

Benjamin, Walter, *Illuminations*, trans. Hannah Arendt (London: Fontana Press, 1973).

Berkeley, George, *The Principles of Human Knowledge and Other Writings*, ed. G. J. Warnock (Glasgow: Fontana, 1962; orig. 1710, 1713).

Berlin, Isaiah, *The Proper Study of Mankind* (London: Chatto & Windus, 1997).

Bernstein, Richard J., *Beyond Objectivism and Relativism: Science, Hermeneutics and Praxis* (Oxford: Blackwell, 1983).

——*The New Constellation: The Ethical-Political Horizons of Modernity/Postmodernity* (Cambridge, MA.: MIT Press, 1992).

Bhaskar, Roy, *A Realist Theory of Science* (London: Verso, 1997; orig. 1975).
—— *Philosophy and the Idea of Freedom* (Oxford: Blackwell, 1991).
—— *Dialectic: The Pulse of Freedom* (London: Verso, 1993).
Bloom, Harold, *The Anxiety of Influence* (Oxford: Oxford University Press, 1973).
Borradori, Giovanna, *The American Philosopher* (Chicago: University of Chicago Press, 1994).
Boswell, James, *The Life of Samuel Johnson* (Ware: Wordsworth, 1999; orig. 1791).
Bourdieu, Pierre, *Pascalian Meditations*, trans. Richard Nice (Cambridge: Polity Press, 2000; orig. 1997).
Bowie, Andrew, *Aesthetics and Subjectivity* (Manchester: Manchester University Press, 1990).
Breisach, Ernst, *Historiography, Ancient, Medieval and Modern*, 2nd edn (Chicago: University of Chicago Press, 1994).
Bronner, Stephen Eric, *Of Critical Theory and its Theorists* (Oxford: Blackwell, 1994).
Brunkhorst, Hauke, *Adorno and Critical Theory* (Cardiff: University of Wales Press, 1999).
Butler, Judith, *Gender Trouble: Feminism and the Subversion of Identity* (New York: Routledge, 1990).
—— *Bodies that Matter: On the Discursive Limits of 'Sex'* (New York: Routledge, 1993).
—— *Excitable Speech: A Politics of the Performative* (New York: Routledge, 1997).
—— Ernesto Laclau and Slavoj Žižek, *Contingency, Hegemony, Universality Contemporary Dialogues on the Left* (London: Verso, 2000).
Cadava, Eduardo, *Who Comes After the Subject?* (New York: Routledge, 1991).
—— *Rorty* (London: Weidenfeld & Nicolson, 2003).
Calder, Gideon, Edward Garrett and Jess Shannon (eds), *Liberalism and Social Justice: International Perspectives* (Aldershot: Ashgate, 2000).
Callinicos, Alex, *Making History: Agency, Structure and Change in Social Theory* (Ithaca, NY: Cornell University Press, 1988).
—— *Against Postmodernism: A Marxist Critique* (Cambridge: Polity Press, 1989).
—— *Theories and Narratives: Reflections on the Philosophy of History* Cambridge: Polity Press, 1995).
Cole, Phillip, *Philosophies of Exclusion: Liberal Political Theory and Immigration* (Edinburgh: Edinburgh University Press, 2000).
Collier, Andrew, *Critical Realism* (London: Verso, 1994).
Cooper, David E., *Metaphor* (Oxford: Blackwell, 1986).
Dasenbrock, Reed Way (ed.), *Redrawing the Lines: Analytic Philosophy, Deconstruction, and Literary Theory* (Minneapolis: University of Minnesota Press, 1989).

Davidson, Donald, *Inquiries into Truth and Interpretation* (Oxford: Clarendon Press, 1984).
Deleuze, Gilles, *Foucault*, ed. and trans. Sean Hand (Minneapolis: University of Minnesota Press, 1986).
Dennett, Daniel, *Consciousness Explained* (Boston: Little, Brown, 1991).
d'Entrèves, Maurizio Passerin and Seyla Benhabib, *Habermas and the Unfinished Project of Modernity* (Cambridge: Polity Press, 1996).
Derrida, Jacques, *Margins of Philosophy*, trans. Alan Bass (Hemel Hempstead: Harvester Wheatsheaf, 1982).
Descartes, René, *Discourse on Method and the Meditations*, trans. F. E. Sutcliffe (Harmondsworth: Penguin Books, 1968; orig. 1641).
Devitt, Michael, *Realism and Truth*, 2nd edn (Princeton: Princeton University Press, 1997).
Dewey, John, *Experience and Nature* (New York: Dover, 1958).
—— *The Later Works, 1925–1953* (Carbondale, IL: Southern Illinois University Press, 1984), vol. 4.
Dews, Peter, *Logics of Disintegration: Post-Structuralist Thought and the Claims of Critical Theory* (London: Verso, 1987).
—— *The Limits of Disenchantment: Essays on Contemporary European Philosophy* (London: Verso, 1995).
Dillon, M. C. (ed.), *Merleau-Ponty Vivant* (Albany: State University of New York Press, 1991).
Eagleton, Terry, *The Ideology of the Aesthetic* (Oxford: Blackwell, 1990).
—— *Ideology* (London: Verso, 1991).
—— *The Illusions of Postmodernism* (Oxford: Blackwell, 1996).
—— *The Idea of Culture* (Oxford: Blackwell, 2000).
Empson, William, *Seven Types of Ambiguity*, 3rd edn (Harmondsworth: Penguin, 1961; orig. 1930).
Farrell, Frank B., *Subjectivity, Realism and Postmodernism: The Recovery of the World in Recent Philosophy* (Cambridge: Cambridge University Press, 1994).
Featherstone, Mike, Scott Lash and Roland Robertson (eds), *Global Modernities* (London: Sage, 1995).
—— *Pragmatism and Political Theory* (Cambridge: Polity Press, 1997).
Festenstein, Matthew and Simon Thompson (eds), *Richard Rorty: Critical Dialogues* (Cambridge: Polity Press, 2001).
Finlayson, Alan, *Making Sense of New Labour* (London: Lawrence & Wishart, 2003).
Flax, Jane, *Thinking Fragments: Psychoanalysis, Feminism and Postmodernism in the Contemporary West* (Berkeley: University of California Press, 1990).
Fodor, Jerry, and Ernest Lepore, *Holism: A Shopper's Guide* (Oxford: Blackwell, 1992).
Foucault, Michel, *The Order of Things*, trans. various (New York: Vintage, 1973; orig. 1966).

—— *Discipline and Punish: The Birth of the Prison*, trans. Alan Sheridan (Harmondsworth: Penguin, 1979) [orig. 1975].
—— *The History of Sexuality, Volume 1: An Introduction*, trans. Robert Hurley (Harmondsworth: Penguin, 1979) [orig. 1976].
Foucault, Michel, *Power/Knowledge: Selected Interviews and Other Writings*, ed. Colin Gordon (Brighton: Harvester, 1980).
Fowler, H. W., *Fowler's Modern English Usage*, 2nd edn, ed. Ernest Gowers (Oxford: Oxford University Press, 1983).
Fraser, Nancy, *Justice Interruptus: Reflections on the 'Postsocialist' Condition* (New York: Routledge, 1997).
—— and Axel Honneth, *Redistribution or Recognition? A Political-Philosophical Exchange* (London: Verso, 2003).
Furrow, Dwight, *Against Theory: Continental and Analytic Challenges in Moral Philosophy* (New York: Routledge, 1995).
Gander, Eric M., *The Last Conceptual Revolution: A Critique of Richard Rorty's Political Philosophy* (Albany: State University of New York Press, 1989).
Geras, Norman, *Discourses of Extremity: Radical Ethics and Post-Marxist Extravagances* (London: Verso, 1990).
—— *Solidarity in the Conversation of Humankind: The Ungroundable Liberalism of Richard Rorty* (London: Verso, 1995).
—— *The Contract of Mutual Indifference: Political Philosophy After the Holocaust* (London: Verso, 1998).
Gray, John, *Endgames: Questions in Late Modern Political Thought* (Cambridge: Polity Press, 1997).
Griffiths, Morwenna, *Feminisms and the Self* (London: Routledge, 1995).
Grosz, Elizabeth, *Volatile Bodies: Toward a Corporeal Feminism* (Bloomington: Indiana University Press, 1994).
Guignon, Charles, and David R. Hiley, *Richard Rorty* (Cambridge: Cambridge University Press, 2003).
Gutting, Gary, *Pragmatic Liberalism and the Critique of Modernity* (Cambridge: Cambridge University Press, 1999).
Habermas, Jürgen, *Communication and the Evolution of Society*, trans. Thomas McCarthy (Cambridge: Polity Press, 1984; orig. 1976).
—— *The Philosophical Discourse of Modernity*, trans. Frederick Lawrence (Cambridge: Polity, 1987; orig. 1985).
—— *Autonomy and Solidarity*, ed. Peter Dews, rev. edn (London: Verso, 1992).
Harvey, David, *The Condition of Postmodernity* (Oxford: Blackwell, 1990).
—— *Spaces of Hope* (Edinburgh: Edinburgh University Press, 2000).
Hawkes, Terence, *Metaphor* (London: Methuen, 1972).
Heidegger, Martin, *Being and Time*, trans. Joan Stambaugh (Albany: State University of New York Press, 1996; orig. 1927).
—— *Basic Writings*, rev. edn, ed. David Farrell Krell (London: Routledge, 1993).
Hobbes, Thomas, *Leviathan* (Harmondsworth: Penguin, 1969; orig. 1651).

Hollinger, Robert, and David Depew (eds), *Pragmatism: From Progressivism to Postmodernism* (Westport, CT: Prager, 1995).
Horkheimer, Max, *Eclipse of Reason* (New York: Continuum, 1992; orig. 1947).
—— *Between Philosophy and Social Science: Selected Early Writings*, trans. G. Frederick Hunter, Matthew S. Kramer and John Torpey (Cambridge, MA: MIT Press, 1993).
Hoy, David Couzens (ed.), *Foucault: A Critical Reader* (Oxford: Blackwell, 1985).
Hume, David, *A Treatise of Human Nature, Book 1*, ed. D. G. C. Macnabb (London: Fontana, 1962).
Husserl, Edmund, *Cartesian Meditations*, trans. Dorion Cairns (Dordrecht: Kluwer, 1995; orig. 1929/1933).
James, C. L. R., *Beyond a Boundary* (London: Serpent's Tail, 1999; orig. 1963).
James, William, *Pragmatism* (New York: Dover, 1995; orig. 1907).
Jameson, Fredric, *The Prison-House of Language* (Princeton: Princeton University Press, 1972).
—— *Postmodernism, or, The Cultural Logic of Late Capitalism* (London: Verso, 1991)
Jay, Martin, *Marxism and Totality: The Adventures of a Concept from Lukács to Habermas* (Berkeley: University of California Press, 1984).
Jenkins, Keith, *Why History? Ethics and Postmodernity* (London: Routledge, 1999).
Jessop, Bob, *State Theory: Putting the Capitalist State in its Place* (Cambridge: Polity Press, 1990).
Kant, Immanuel, 'Groundwork of the Metaphysic of Morals', in H. J. Paton, *The Moral Law* (London: Hutchinson, 1948; orig. 1785).
Kirk, Robert, *Relativism and Reality* (London: Routledge, 1999).
Kolenda, Konstantin, *Rorty's Humanistic Pragmatism* (Tampa, FL: University of South Florida Press, 1990).
Kuhn, Thomas, *The Structure of Scientific Revolutions*, 2nd edn (Chicago: University of Chicago Press, 1970).
Kulp, Christopher B., *Realism/Antirealism and Epistemology* (Lanham, MD: Rowman & Littlefield, 1997).
Kymlicka, Will, *Liberalism, Community and Culture* (Oxford: Clarendon Press, 1989).
Laclau, Ernesto, *Emancipation(s)* (London: Verso, 1996).
Lang, Berel, *The Anatomy of Philosophical Style* (Oxford: Blackwell, 1990).
Langsdorf, Lenore, and Andrew R. Smith (eds), *Recovering Pragmatism's Voice: The Classical Tradition, Rorty, and the Philosophy of Communication* (Albany, NY: State University of New York Press, 1995).
Lazarus, Neil, Steven Evans, Anthony Arnove and Anne Menke, 'The necessity of universalism', *Differences*, 7 (1995), 75–145.
Le Doeuff, Michèle, *Hipparchia's Choice: An Essay Concerning Women, Philosophy, Etc.*, trans. Trista Selous (Oxford: Blackwell, 1991; orig. 1989).

Locke, John, *An Essay Concerning Human Understanding*, ed. A. D. Woozley (Glasgow: Fontana, 1964; orig. 1689).
—— *Two Treatises of Government*, ed. Peter Laslett (Cambridge: Cambridge University Press, 1960; orig. 1690).
Lyotard, Jean-François, *The Postmodern Condition: A Report on Knowledge*, trans. Geoff Bennington and Brian Massumi (Manchester: Manchester University Press, 1984; orig. 1979).
—— *Tombeau de l'intellectuel* (Paris: Éditions Galilée, 1984).
—— *The Differend: Phrases in Dispute*, trans. Georges Van Den Abbeele (Manchester: Manchester University Press, 1988; orig. 1984).
—— *Political Writings*, ed. Bill Readings (London: UCL Press, 1993).
—— and Jean-Loup Thébaud, *Just Gaming*, trans. Wlad Godzich (Manchester: Manchester University Press, 1985; orig. 1977).
McCarthy, George E. (ed.), *Marx and Aristotle: Nineteenth Century German Social Theory and Classical Antiquity* (Savage, MD: Rowman & Littlefield, 1992).
McCormick, Peter J., *Starmaking: Realism, Anti-Realism, and Irrealism* (Cambridge, MA: MIT Press, 1996).
McLellan, David, and Sean Sayers (eds), *Socialism and Morality* (Basingstoke: Macmillan, 1990).
MacPherson, C. B., *The Political Theory of Possessive Individualism: Hobbes to Locke* (Oxford: Oxford University Press, 1960).
Malachowski, Alan R. (ed.), *Reading Rorty* (Oxford: Blackwell, 1990).
Margolis, Joseph, *Pragmatism without Foundations* (Oxford: Blackwell, 1986).
Marković, Mihailo, and Robert S. Cohen, *The Rise and Fall of Socialist Humanism: A History of the Praxis Group* (Nottingham: Spokesman Books, 1975).
Martin, Bill, *Humanism and its Aftermath: The Shared Fate of Deconstruction and Politics* (New Jersey: Humanities Press, 1985).
Marx, Karl, *The Communist Manifesto*, trans. Samuel Moore (Harmondsworth: Penguin, 1967; orig. 1948).
—— *The German Ideology*, ed. C. J. Arthur (New York: International Publishers, 1970; orig.1846).
—— *Selected Writings*, ed. David McLellan (Oxford: Oxford University Press, 1977).
—— *Economic and Philosophical Manuscripts*, trans. Martin Milligan (New York: Prometheus Books, 1988; orig. 1844).
Merleau-Ponty, Maurice, *The Phenomenology of Perception*, trans. Colin Smith (London: Routledge, 1962; orig. 1945).
—— *The Primacy of Perception* (Evanston, IL: Northwestern University Press, 1964)
Mill, John Stuart, *On Liberty* (Harmondsworth: Penguin, 1974; orig. 1859).
Miller, James, *History and Human Existence: From Marx to Merleau-Ponty* (Berkeley: University of California Press, 1979).

Moi, Toril, *What is a Woman? And Other Essays* (Oxford: Oxford University Press, 1999).

Mounce, H. O., *The Two Pragmatisms: From Peirce to Rorty* (London: Routledge, 1997).

Mulhall, Stephen, and Adam Swift, *Liberals and Communitarians* (Oxford: Blackwell, 1992).

Nietzsche, Friedrich, *The Viking Portable Nietzsche*, ed. Walter Kaufmann (New York: Viking Press, 1954).

—— *Twilight of the Idols/The Antichrist*, trans. R. J. Hollingdale (Harmondsworth: Penguin, 1968; orig. 1889, 1895).

Niznik, Jósef, and John T. Sanders (eds), *Debating the State of Philosophy: Habermas, Rorty, and Kolakowski* (Westport, CT: Praeger, 1996).

Norris, Christopher, *Reclaiming Truth: Contribution to a Critique of Cultural Relativism* (London: Lawrence & Wishart, 1996).

—— *New Idols of the Cave: On the Limits of Anti-Realism* (Manchester: Manchester University Press, 1997).

—— *Deconstruction and the 'Unfinished Project of Modernity'* (New York: Routledge, 2000).

—— *Minding the Gap: Epistemology and Philosophy of Science in the Two Traditions* (Amherst: University of Massachusetts Press, 2000).

Novick, Peter, *The Noble Dream: The 'Objectivity Question' and the American Historical Profession* (Cambridge: Cambridge University Press, 1988).

—— *The Holocaust and Collective Memory* (London: Bloomsbury, 2000).

Ortony, Andrew (ed.), *Metaphor and Thought* (Cambridge: Cambridge University Press, 1979).

Orwell, George, *Nineteen Eighty-Four* (Harmondsworth: Penguin, 1989; orig. 1949).

Peirce, Charles Sanders, *Philosophical Writings*, ed. J. Buchler (New York: Dover, 1955).

Pettegrew, John (ed.), *A Pragmatist's Progress? Richard Rorty and American Intellectual History* (Lanham, MD: Rowman & Littlefield, 2000).

Plato, *The Republic*, trans. Desmond Lee (Harmondsworth: Penguin Books, 1955; orig. *c.*375 BC].

Popper, Karl, *The Open Society and its Enemies*, vol. 2: *Hegel and Marx* (London: Routledge & Kegan Paul, 1945).

Putnam, Hilary, *Reason, Truth and History* (Cambridge: Cambridge University Press, 1981).

—— *Realism with a Human Face* (Cambridge: Cambridge University Press, 1990).

—— *Pragmatism: An Open Question* (Oxford: Blackwell, 1995).

Quine, W. V. O., *From a Logical Point of View*, 2nd edn. (Cambridge, MA: Harvard University Press, 1961).

—— *Ontological Relativity and Other Essays* (New York: Columbia University Press, 1969).

—— *Theories and Things* (Cambridge, MA: Harvard University Press, 1981).
Rabinow, Paul (ed.), *The Foucault Reader* (Harmondsworth: Penguin, 1984).
Rasmussen, David (ed.), *Universalism vs. Communitarianism: Contemporary Debates in Ethics* (Cambridge, MA: MIT Press, 1990).
Rawls, John, *A Theory of Justice* (Oxford: Oxford University Press, 1971).
Rengger, Nick, *Political Theory, Modernity and Postmodernity* (Oxford: Blackwell, 1995)
Rockmore, Tom, *Habermas on Historical Materialism* (Bloomington and Indianapolis: Indiana University Press, 1989).
Rose, Gillian, *Mourning Becomes the Law: Philsophy and Representation* (Cambridge: Cambridge University Press, 1996).
Ross, Andrew (ed.), *Universal Abandon: The Politics of Postmodernism* (Minneapolis: University of Minnesota Press, 1988).
Roth, Michael S., *The Ironist's Cage: Memory, Trauma and the Construction of History* (New York: Columbia University Press, 1995).
Russell, Bertrand, *History of Western Philosophy*, 2nd edn (London: Unwin, 1979).
Sandel, Michael, *Liberalism and the Limits of Justice* (Cambridge: Cambridge University Press, 1982).
Sartre, Jean-Paul, *Being and Nothingness*, trans. Hazel Barnes (London: Routledge, 1956; orig. 1943).
—— *Nausea*, trans. Robert Baldick (Harmondsworth: Penguin, 1965; orig. 1938).
Saussure, Ferdinand de, *Course in General Linguistics*, ed. Charles Bally and Albert Sechehaye, trans. Wade Baskin (New York: McGraw-Hill, 1966; orig. 1913).
Sayer, Andrew, *Realism and Social Science* (London: Sage, 2000).
Schrag, Calvin O., *The Self After Postmodernity* (New Haven, CT: Yale University Press, 1997).
Shusterman, Richard, *Pragmatist Aesthetics: Living Beauty, Rethinking Art* (Oxford: Blackwell, 1992).
Soper, Kate, *Humanism and Anti-Humanism* (London: Hutchison, 1986).
—— *Troubled Pleasures* (London: Verso, 1990).
Taylor, Charles, *Philosophy and the Human Sciences: Philosophical Papers*, vol. 2 (Cambridge: Cambridge University Press, 1985).
—— *Sources of the Self: The Making of the Modern Identity* (Cambridge: Cambridge University Press, 1989).
Thayer, H. S. (ed.), *Pragmatism: The Classic Writings* (Indianapolis: Hackett, 1982).
Trotsky, Leon, John Dewey and George Novack, *Their Morals and Ours: Marxist vs. Liberal Views on Morality* (New York: Pathfinder Press, 1973).
Vieth, Andreas (ed.), *Richard Rorty: His Philosophy under Discussion* (Frankfurt: Ontos Verlag, 2005).
Voltaire, *Candide, Zadig and Selected Stories*, trans. Donald M. Frame (New York: New American Library, 1961; *Candide* orig. 1759).

Walzer, Michael, *Spheres of Justice* (Oxford: Blackwell, 1983).
Wellmer, Albrecht, *Endgames: The Irreconcilable Nature of Modernity* (Cambridge, MA: MIT Press, 1998).
Winch, Peter, *The Idea of a Social Science and its Relation to Philosophy* (London: Routledge, 1958).
Wittgenstein, Ludwig, *Tractatus Logico-Philosophicus*, trans. C. K. Ogden and B. F. McGuinness (London: Routledge, 1922).
—— *Philosophical Investigations*, trans. G. E. M. Anscombe (Oxford: Blackwell, 1974; orig. 1953).
Wolin, Richard, *The Terms of Cultural Criticism: The Frankfurt School, Existentialism, Poststructuralism* (New York: Columbia University Press, 1992).
Wood, Ellen Meiskins, and John Bellamy Foster, *In Defense of History: Marxism and the Postmodern Agenda* (New York: Monthly Review Press, 1997).
Young, Iris Marion, *Justice and the Politics of Difference* (Princeton: Princeton University Press, 1990).
—— *Throwing Like a Girl And Other Essays in Feminist Philosophy and Social Theory* (Indianapolis: Indiana University Press, 1990).
Žižek, Slavoj, *Looking Awry* (Cambridge, MA: MIT Press, 1991).
—— *The Ticklish Subject: The Absent Centre of Political Ontology* (London: Verso, 1999).

## Articles

Alexander, Jeffrey, 'General theory in the postpositivist mode: the "epistemological dilemma" and the search for present reason', in Steven Seidman and David G. Wagner (eds), *Postmodernism and Social Theory* (Oxford: Blackwell, 1992), pp. 322–68.
Allen, Jonathan, 'The situated critic or the loyal critic? Rorty and Walzer on social criticism', *Philosophy and Social Criticism*, 24/6 (1998), 25–46.
Baghramian, Maria, 'Rorty, Davidson and Truth', *Ratio* (new series), 3 (1990), 101–16.
Baker, Deane-Peter, '"Don't kick the habit": a Taylorian critique of Rorty's *Achieving Our Country*', *Theoria*, 101 (2003), 68–93.
Barthes, Roland, 'The discourse of history', in Keith Jenkins (ed.), *The Postmodern History Reader* (London: Routledge, 1997), pp. 115–26.
Bauman, Zygmunt, 'On communitarians and human freedom, or, how to square the circle', *Theory, Culture and Society*, 13 (1996), 79–90.
Benhabib, Seyla, 'Epistemologies of postmodernism: a rejoinder to Jean-François Lyotard', *New German Critique*, 33 (1984), 103–24.
—— 'In defense of universalism – yet again! A response to critics of *Situating the Self*', *New German Critique*, 62 (1994), 173–89.
Bickford, Susan, 'Why we listen to lunatics: antifoundational theories and feminist politics', *Hypatia*, 8 (1993), 104–23.

Black, Max, 'More about metaphor', in Andrew Ortony (ed.), *Metaphor and Thought* (Cambridge: Cambridge University Press, 1984).

Bordo, Susan, 'Bringing body to theory', in Donn Welton (ed.), *Body and Flesh: A Philosophical Reader* (Oxford: Blackwell, 1998), p. 92.

Brunkhorst, Hauke, 'Rorty, Putnam and the Frankfurt School', *Philosophy and Social Criticism*, 22/5 (1996), 1–16.

Burns, Tony, 'Materialism in ancient Greek philosophy and in the writings of the young Marx', *Historical Materialism*, 7 (2000), 3–40.

Butler, Judith, 'Contingent foundations', in Judith Butler and Joan W. Scott (eds), *Feminists Theorize the Political* (New York: Routledge, 1992), pp. 3–21.

—— 'Gender as performance', interview with Peter Osborne and Lynne Segal, in Peter Osborne (ed.), *A Critical Sense: Interviews with Intellectuals* (London: Routledge, 1996), pp. 109–25.

—— 'Merely cultural', *New Left Review*, 227 (1998), 33–44.

Cazeaux, Clive, Review of Rorty's *Philosophical Papers, Volumes 1 and 2*, *Textual Practice*, 6 (1992), 519–32.

Cole, Steven E., 'Evading the subject: the poverty of contingency theory', in Herbert W. Simons and Michael Billig (eds), *After Postmodernism: Reconstructing Ideology Critique* (London: Sage, 1994), pp. 38–57.

Collier, Andrew, 'Language, practice and realism', in Ian Parker (ed.), *Social Constructionism, Discourse and Realism* (London: Sage, 1998), pp. 48–58.

Cruickshank, Justin, 'Ethnocentrism, social contract liberalism and positivistic-conservatism: Rorty's three theses on politics', *ResPublica*, 6/1 (2000), 1–23.

Cruickshank, Justin, 'Rorty on pragmatism, liberalism and the self', in José López and Garry Potter (eds), *After Postmodernism: An Introduction to Critical Realism* (London: Athlone Press, 2001), pp. 217–24.

Culler, Jonathan, 'Philosophy and literature: the fortunes of the performative', *Poetics Today*, 21 (2000), 503–19.

Davidson, Donald, 'The structure and content of truth', *Journal of Philosophy*, 87 (1990): 279–328.

Derrida, Jacques, 'The *retrait* of metaphor', *Enclytic*, 2/2 (Fall 1978), 11–21.

Festenstein, Matthew, 'Politics and acquiescence in Rorty's pragmatism', *Theoria*, 101 (2003), 1–24.

Fraser, Nancy, 'From redistribution to recognition? Dilemmas of justice in a "post-socialist" age', *New Left Review*, 212 (1995), 68–93.

—— 'Rethinking Recognition', *New Left Review* (2nd series) 3 (2000), 107–20.

Gardiner, Michael, '"The incomparable monster of solipsism": Bakhtin and Merleau-Ponty', in Michael Mayerfeld Bell and Michael Gardiner (eds), *Bakhtin and the Human Sciences* (London: Sage, 1998), pp. 128–44.

Graham, Keith, 'Being some body: choice and identity in a liberal puralist world', in Bob Brecher, Jo Halliday and Klára Kolinská (eds), *Nationalism and Racism in the Liberal Order* (Aldershot: Ashgate, 1998), pp. 176–92.

# REFERENCES

Green, David D., 'Literature without presence: Beckett, Rorty, Derrida', *Paragraph*, 19 (1996), 83–97.
Haack, Susan, 'Surprising noises: Rorty and Hesse on metaphor', *Proceedings of the Aristotelian Society*, 88 (1987–8), 179–87.
Habermas, Jürgen, 'Questions and counterquestions', in Richard J. Bernstein (ed.), *Habermas and Modernity* (Cambridge: Polity Press, 1985).
Hacking, Ian, 'Two kinds of new historicism for philosophers', in Ralph Cohen and Michael S. Roth (eds), *History and . . . : Histories within the Human Sciences* (Charlottesville, VA: University Press of Virginia, 1995), pp. 225–41.
Honneth, Axel, 'The other of justice', in Stephen K. White (ed.), *The Cambridge Companion to Habermas* (Cambridge: Cambridge University Press, 1995), pp. 289–323.
Hull, Carrie, 'The need in thinking: materiality in Theodor W. Adorno and Judith Butler', *Radical Philosophy*, 84 (1997), 22–35.
Jenkins, Keith, 'Why bother with the past? Engaging with some issues raised by the possible "end of history as we have known it"', *Rethinking History*, 1 (1997), 58–71.
Kim, Jaegwon, 'Is the end in sight for epistemology?', *Journal of Philosophy*, 77 (1980), 579–97.
Koczanowicz, Leszek, 'The choice of tradition and the tradition of choice: Habermas's and Rorty's interpretation of pragmatism', *Philosophy and Social Criticism*, 25/1 (1999), 55–70.
Laclau, Ernesto, and Chantal Mouffe, 'Post-Marxism without apologies', *New Left Review*, 166 (November/December 1987), 79–106.
Landry, Lorraine Y., 'Beyond the French fries and the Frankfurter: an agenda for critical theory', *Philosophy and Social Criticism*, 26/2 (2000), 99–129.
Lang, Berel, 'Is it possible to misrepresent the holocaust?', *History and Theory*, 34 (1995), 84–9.
Lom, Petr, 'East meets West: Jan Patocka and Richard Rorty on Freedom', *Political Theory*, 27/4 (1999), 447–59.
Lorenz, Chris, 'Historical knowledge and historical reality: a plea for "internal realism"', in Brian Fay, Phillip Pomper and Richard T. Vann (eds), *History and Theory* (Oxford: Blackwell, 1998), pp. 342–76.
Lyotard, Jean-François, and Richard Rorty, 'Discussion entre Jean-François Lyotard et Richard Rorty', *Critique*, 41 (May 1985), 581–4.
Lysaker, John T., 'The shape of selves to come: Rorty and self-creation', *Philosophy and Social Criticism*, 22/3 (1996), 39–74.
McCarthy, Thomas, 'Private irony and public decency: Rorty's new pragmatism', *Critical Inquiry*, 16 (1990), 356–69.
McCumber, John, 'Reconnecting Rorty: the situation of discourse in Richard Rorty's *Contingency, Irony, and Solidarity*', *Diacritics*, 20 (1990), 2–19.

Mead, George Herbert, 'Social consciousness and the consciousness of meaning', in H. S. Thayer (ed.), *Pragmatism: The Classic Writings* (Indianapolis: Hackett, 1982), pp. 341–50.

Midgeley, Mary, 'Some reductions, good, bad and extraordinary', paper delivered at Cardiff University, 1995.

Moussa, Mario, 'Misunderstanding the democratic "we": Richard Rorty's liberalism and the radical urge for a philosophical foundation', *Philosophy and Social Criticism* 17/4 (1991), 297–312.

Norris, Christopher, 'Postmodernising history: right-wing revisionism and the uses of theory', *Southern Review*, 21 (July 1988), 123–40.

—— 'Metaphor, ontology, and the new antirealism', *Common Knowledge*, 6 (1997), 69–97.

Putnam, Hilary, 'A comparison of something with something else', *New Literary History*, 87 (1985), 61–79.

Quine, W. V. O., 'Carnap and logical truth', in P. A. Schilpp (ed.), *Carnap and Logical Truth* (La Salle, IL: Open Court, 1963), pp. 398–412.

Rawls, John, 'Kantian constructivism in moral theory', *Journal of Philosophy* 77 (1980), 51–72.

—— 'Justice as fairness: political not metaphysical', *Philosophy and Public Affairs*, 14 (1985), 223–51.

Rée, Jonathan, 'Timely meditations', *Radical Philosophy*, 55 (1990), 31–9.

—— 'Strenuous unbelief', review of two books by Rorty *London Review of Books* (15 October 1998), 7–11.

Roderick, Rick, 'Reading Derrida politically (contra Rorty)', *Praxis International*, 6 (1987), 442–5.

Sacks, Mark, 'The subject, normative structure, and externalism', in Anat Biletzki and Anat Matar (eds), *The Story of Analytic Philosophy* (London: Routledge, 1998), pp. 88–107.

Saunders, Ian, 'Richard Rorty and *Star Wars*: on the nature of pragmatism's narrative', *Textual Practice* 8 (1994), 435–48.

Sayer, Andrew, 'Restoring the moral dimension in social scientific accounts', in Margaret S. Archer and William Outhwaite (eds), *Defending Objectivity: Essays in Honour of Andrew Collier* (London: Routledge, 2004), pp. 93–113.

Schmitt, Frederick F., 'Realism, antirealism and epistemic truth', *Social Epistemology*, 12 (1998), 267–88.

Sivanandan, A., 'All that melts into air is solid: the hokum of new times', *Race and Class*, 31 (1990), 1–30.

Tanesini, Alessandra, 'The "spider's web" and the "tool": Nietzsche *vis-à-vis* Rorty on metaphor', in Peter R. Sedgwick (ed.), *Nietzsche: A Critical Reader* (Oxford: Blackwell, 1995), pp. 276–93.

Verges, Frank G., 'Rorty and the new hermeneutics', *Philosophy*, 62 (1987), 307–24.

# REFERENCES

Visker, Rudi, "Hold the being: how to split Rorty between irony and finitude", *Philosophy and Social Criticism*, 25 (1999), pp. 27–45.

Waismann, F., 'How I see philosophy', in H. D. Lewis (ed.), *Contemporary British Philosophy* (London: George Allen and Unwin, 1956), pp. 445–90.

Wolfe, Cary, 'Making contingency safe for liberalism: the pragmatics of epistemology in Rorty and Luhmann', *New German Critique*, 61 (1994): 101–27.

Wood, Ellen Meiskins, 'Intellectuals and universalism', *Imprints*, 1 (1996), 65–71.

Young, Iris Marion, 'Together in difference', in Judith Squires (ed.), *Principled Positions: Postmodernism and the Rediscovery of Value* (London: Lawrence & Wishart, 1993), pp. 121–50.

—— 'Unruly categories: a critique of Nancy Fraser's dual systems theory', *New Left Review*, 222 (1997), 147–60.

# Index

'A reply to six critics' (Rorty) 197
'abnormal' discourse
    see 'normal'/'abnormal' discourse
*Achieving our Country* (Rorty) x, 9, 104, 143–7, 205, 206, 207, 210
Adorno, Theodor W. 8, 24, 27, 49–51, 149, 181, 188, 206, 211
*Against Bosses, Against Oligarchies* (Rorty) 190, 206
agency 8, 66, 85, 90, 94, 135, 170, 177
ahistorical moral standards, possibility of 55–6, 58, 59, 81
Althusser, Louis 157
anti-foundationalism 1, 7, 104
anti-humanism 46, 111, 112
appearance–reality distinction 5, 25, 26, 27, 29, 31, 37, 45, 46, 48, 51, 52, 62, 176
Archer, Margaret S. 91, 94, 139, 198, 205
Aristotle 26, 27, 69, 188, 194
Arnove, Anthony 205
atomism 36, 131–33, 138, 139, 141, 143, 166, 170, 172
Auschwitz 161
Austin, J. L. 70, 73, 195
autonomy 131, 171
Ayer, A. J. 206

Baker, Deane-Peter 206
Balslev, Anindita Niyogi 201
Barthes, Roland 152, 207
Bauman, Zygmunt 108, 113
'Being that can be understood is language' (Rorty) 184, 193
Benhabib, Seyla 170, 201, 210
Benjamin, Walter 151, 206
Berkeley, George 41–4, 48, 49, 158, 187, 190, 191
Berlin, Isaiah 131, 203
Bernstein, Richard J. 182, 204, 211
Bhaskar, Roy 92, 139, 192, 198

Bickford, Susan 203
Black, Max 195
Bloom, Harold 87, 197
Bourdieu, Pierre 124, 143, 205
'bourgeois liberalism' 105, 107
Bowie, Andrew 211
Brunkhorst, Hauke 123, 202
Burns, Tony 188
Burrows, Jo 200
Butler, Judith 66, 97–9, 100, 164, 167, 191, 198, 209

Callinicos, Alex 142–3, 146, 205, 206, 207
capitalism 130, 132, 139, 144–5, 182
Carr, E. H. 152, 158, 207
Cartesian dualism 5, 7, 10, 15, 18, 20, 26, 27, 30, 32, 38, 48, 62, 84, 85, 90, 94–102, 138, 170, 186
    see also Descartes
causal relations 41, 43, 46, 47, 48, 60, 151
Cazeaux, Clive 71, 195
civil society 132
class 81, 134, 144–5, 146
Cohen, Robert S. 206
Cole, Phillip 168, 209
'Comments and responses' (Rorty) 210
communitarianism 9, 95, 120–1, 128, 165, 170, 171
community 108, 118, 120, 122, 123, 128, 132, 134, 135, 138, 165, 166, 167
Conant, James 159, 208
conceptual schemes 36–7, 38, 117
    see also scheme–content distinction
consciousness 13–16, 23, 26, 49, 88, 100, 138
consensus 109, 117, 122, 141, 167
*Consequences of Pragmatism* (Rorty) x, 53, 59, 184, 185, 189, 190, 191, 192, 193, 194, 203, 207, 210

conservatism 8, 129, 133, 135, 144–5
constative statements (Austin) 70
consumerism 150
contingency 8, 16, 29, 37, 105, 123, 135, 153, 170
*Contingency, Irony, and Solidarity* (Rorty) x, 8, 86, 102, 103–43, 149, 159, 189, 191, 192, 193, 194, 195, 196, 197, 198, 199, 202, 203, 206, 207
conversation 7, 38–9, 47, 56, 61, 62, 77, 114, 128, 129, 160, 176
Cooper, David E. 80, 196
cosmopolitanism 7, 117, 135
Critchley, Simon 126, 203
critical realism 10, 180, 211
cruelty 105, 124, 126, 172
Culler, Jonathan 71, 195
'cultural Left' 144–5, 147
culture
 and selfhood 100–1, 138
 and moral/political practice 120, 121, 123, 129, 146, 167, 169, 171

Darwin, Charles; Darwinism 8, 67, 77, 84, 85, 87
Davidson, Donald 6, 22, 36–8, 57, 69, 70–2, 73, 77, 79, 117, 187, 189, 195
*Deconstruction and Pragmatism* (Rorty) 197, 204, 205
democracy 147, 165
Democritus 26, 188
Derrida, Jacques 6, 46, 74, 82–3, 184, 190, 195, 209
Descartes, René 7, 11, 13, 14, 21, 25, 87, 100, 172, 173, 175, 186, 210
 *see also* Cartesian dualism
description
 *see* redescription
Dewey, John 1, 7, 8, 11, 18, 19, 21, 27, 29, 38, 103, 144, 186, 188, 206
Dickens, Charles 106
'differend' (Lyotard) 110–11, 113, 114
Diggins, John Patrick 188
discourse 6, 35, 45, 47, 48, 62, 64, 97, 109, 140–1, 147, 149, 152, 181

'disenchantment of the world' (Horkheimer and Adorno) 27–8, 62, 115
Dreyfus, Hubert 189
dualism, in Rorty's work 45–8, 62, 95, 100
Dworkin, Ronald 131, 203

Eagleton, Terry 61, 125, 168–9, 193, 203, 209
edification 64, 86, 107
emancipatory critique 6, 113, 118, 130, 142, 182
embodiment 98, 101, 138, 141, 164, 169, 173
empiricism 15, 16, 131, 156
'empty realism' 32–3, 43, 55, 151
Engels, Friedrich 172, 210
Enlightenment philosophy 5, 27, 105, 106, 115, 130, 135, 140, 141
Epicurus 188
epistemology 11–33, 43, 44, 48, 69, 114, 152, 162, 179, 181
equality, and equal rights 113, 130, 132, 133, 137, 140, 141, 142, 171
*Essays on Heidegger and Others* (Rorty) 185, 191, 194, 195, 197, 198
essentialism 99, 125, 165
ethics 6, 9, 112, 116, 128, 140, 148, 154, 157, 158, 164, 167, 168, 170
ethnocentrism 7, 12, 31, 32, 57, 58, 122, 123, 124, 135
Evans, Steven 205
existential gap 46–7
existentialism 94

fact–value distinction 156
facts 22, 117, 156, 157, 179
fallibilism 57, 59
Farrell, Frank B. 52, 162, 192, 193, 196
fascism 56, 60, 151, 159
Faurisson, Robert 111–12, 161, 208, 209
'Feminism and Pragmatism' (Rorty) 192, 193, 196, 199, 203
Festenstein, Matthew 119

# INDEX

final vocabulary 105, 125, 126
Finlayson, Alan 211
Flax, Jane 97, 164, 198, 209
Forms (Plato) 25–6
'Foucault and epistemology' (Rorty) 190
Foucault, Michel 46, 130, 147, 190, 203
foundationalism 13, 124, 126
Frankfurt School 8, 22, 27
Fraser, Nancy 146, 147, 199, 203, 206, 209
freedom 103, 104, 132, 140
Frege, Gottlob 157
Freud, Sigmund 93
'From philosophy to post-philosophy' (Rorty) 199
*Future of Religion, The* (Rorty and Vattimo) 206

Gander, Eric M. 127, 203
gender 95, 98, 144, 146, 164
Geras, Norman 90–1, 123, 197, 202
'God's eye view' 61, 67, 118, 155
Goodman Nelson 44, 191
Graham, Keith 210
Gray, John 168, 209
Grosz, Elizabeth 85, 197

Haack, Susan 195
'Habermas, Derrida, and the functions of philosophy' (Rorty) 194
Habermas, Jürgen 5, 6, 11, 83, 140–1, 185, 197, 205
Hacking, Ian 2, 184
harm 126
Harvey, David 130, 203
Hegel, G. W. F., and Hegelianism 35, 64, 65, 93, 187
Heidegger, Martin 6, 80, 112, 115, 164, 201, 209
heterogeneity 109–14, 116, 132, 165
'Higher nominalism in a nutshell: a reply to Henry Staten, The' (Rorty) 197
historicism 19, 20, 39, 52, 104, 121, 124, 129, 134, 137, 149, 167

historicity 10, 148, 149, 150, 153, 163, 164, 181
historiography 9, 149, 150, 152–8
history 1, 36, 141, 148–64
Hitler, Adolf 160, 161, 162
Hobbes, Thomas 26, 132, 139
holism 17, 38, 39
Holocaust 111–12, 160–2
Honneth, Axel 112, 201, 106
horizontal–vertical distinction 3, 7, 33–4, 38, 39, 44, 49–51, 55, 60, 89, 106, 115, 137, 140, 146, 147, 149, 154, 165, 166–7
Horkheimer, Max 8, 24, 25, 26, 27, 49, 187
Hull, Carrie L. 50, 192
human being
  *see* human nature
human nature 7, 9, 86, 89–92, 124, 125, 129, 132, 137, 139, 142, 159, 165, 169, 171, 176
humanism 141–2, 146
Hume, David 89, 92, 197, 210
humiliation 124–5, 126, 127, 172
Husserl, Edmund 11, 173, 210

'idea' idea (Quine) 14, 40, 44
idealism 26, 32, 41–4, 49, 50, 157–75
identity 134–6, 137, 138, 145, 150, 164, 165, 166–7, 170, 171, 172
'identity-thinking' (Adorno) 48–52
incommensurability 37, 60, 109, 114–17, 118, 123, 131
individualism 95, 107, 132, 165
intersubjectivity 58–62, 141, 170, 171, 173
Irving, David 160–3, 208
'Is Derrida a *quasi*-transcendental philosopher?' (Rorty) 184, 190
iterability 74

James, C. L. R. 198
James, William 1, 19, 22–3, 27, 29, 39, 53, 184, 186, 187, 188, 199, 206
Jameson, Fredric 150, 155, 162, 191
Jay, Martin 188

Jenkins, Keith 152–8, 207
Jessop, Bob 32, 43, 191
justice 110, 112, 114, 120, 124, 134–6, 151
'Justice as a larger loyalty' (Rorty) 202, 204
justification 31, 38, 53–60, 174

Kant, Immanuel, and Kantianism 11, 13, 15, 17, 18, 21, 25, 27, 30, 89, 92, 131, 180, 184, 203
Kirk, Robert 193
knowledge 13–15, 21, 36, 38, 53
Kripke, Saul 186
Kuhn, Thomas 63–5, 67, 194
Kymlicka, Will 122, 202

Laclau, Ernesto 133–4, 135, 136, 138, 203
Laclos, Choderlos de 106
Lang, Berel 163, 209
language 6, 13, 16–18, 32, 34–48, 49, 63–84, 109–17, 138, 140–1, 152, 176
language games 109, 110, 116, 117, 133, 134
Lazarus, Neil 205
Le Doeuff, Michèle 104, 124, 137, 143, 172
Levinas, Emmanuel 164
liberal democracy 103, 105, 106, 121, 174
liberal ironism 1, 7, 103–43, 177
liberalism 7, 8, 9, 10, 95, 103, 104, 105, 113, 120, 121, 126, 131–2, 134, 170, 182
linguistic historicism 20, 35
linguistic idealism 8, 40–8, 95, 97, 152, 181
'linguistic turn' 33, 41, 94, 140
*Linguistic Turn, The* (Rorty) 190
Lipstadt, Deborah 208
Locke, John 7, 13, 14, 15, 120, 131, 132, 185, 203
locutionary acts (Austin) 71
logical positivism 16–18, 22, 23, 36
  *see also* positivism

Lorenz, Chris 163, 209
loyalty 103, 134, 170, 171, 177
Lyotard, Jean-François 6, 9, 104, 108–14, 115, 116, 117, 118, 124, 128, 130, 131, 132, 138, 140, 143, 158, 159, 160–1, 168, 200, 201, 208
Lysaker, John T. 106, 198

MacPherson, C. B. 132, 139, 203, 205
Markovic, Mihailo 206
Marx, Karl 26, 27, 132, 133, 138, 139, 141, 147, 170, 172, 188, 203, 205, 210
Marxism 5, 145, 157, 206
materialism 26, 29
McCormick, Peter J. 191
Mead, George Herbert 210
Menke, Anne 205
Merleau-Ponty, Maurice 10, 170, 173, 210
metaphor 8, 13, 65, 67–84, 95, 96, 99, 101
metaphysics 3, 12, 16–18, 21, 22, 23, 25, 44, 61, 96, 106, 107, 115, 128, 136, 149, 159, 163
methodological individualism 95, 102, 120, 138
Mill, John Stuart 103, 126, 127, 131, 199
Miller, David 167–8, 169, 209
mind
  *see* consciousness
'mirror' metaphor 13–15, 61
misdescription 148–64
modernity 108
Moi, Toril 99, 198
moral judgement 110, 121, 122, 123, 128
'Moral universalism and economic triage' (Rorty) 203
Mulhall, Stephen 202
'myth of the given' (Sellars) 16, 142

Nabokov, Vladimir 80, 106
nationality 145, 146, 168

# INDEX

naturalism 17, 19, 20, 39, 85–6, 138
nature 43, 48, 99, 140, 152, 164
necessity 16, 29, 37, 38, 115, 123
New Labour 182–3
Nietzsche, Friedrich 6, 8, 77, 80, 82, 83, 93, 95, 189, 196, 199
nominalism 6, 96, 105
non-reductive physicalism 8, 66, 87
'normal'/'abnormal' discourse 63–5, 102, 107, 116
Norris, Christopher 114, 141, 196, 201, 205, 208
Novick, Peter 150, 153, 162, 163, 207
Nozick, Robert 131, 203

objectivity 4, 6, 7, 18, 41, 50, 52–62, 153, 172
*Objectivity, Relativism, and Truth* (Rorty) 102, 185, 189, 190, 191, 192, 193, 195, 196, 197, 198, 199, 201, 202, 209
ocularcentrism 30–1
'On obligation, truth and common sense' (Rorty) 204, 205
ontology 3, 9, 16, 19, 23, 32, 36, 43, 45, 48, 86, 98, 126, 138, 142, 147, 155, 162, 164, 176, 179, 181, 182
otherness 115, 126, 144, 159, 164, 177
Orwell, George 106, 159–60

Palmer, Bryan 149, 207
particularism 112, 113, 118, 134, 170, 171, 173, 179
Peirce, Charles Sanders 20–1, 51, 67, 186, 187, 188
performativity 66, 70–1, 97–9
perlocutionary acts (Austin) 71, 75
personal identity 88, 92
  *see also* identity
phenomenology 5, 10, 185
'Philosophy-envy' (Rorty) 210
*Philosophy and the Mirror of Nature* (Rorty) 13–20, 33, 42, 53, 63, 65, 84, 86, 90, 107, 116, 185, 186, 189, 190, 192, 194, 197, 199, 201

*Philosophy and Social Hope* (Rorty) 184, 188, 189, 202
'Philosophy'/philosophy distinction ix, 1, 5, 28, 39, 40 148
physicalism 22, 86
  *see also* non-reductive physicalism
Plato, and Platonism viii, 2, 5, 13, 25–6, 27, 29, 30, 36, 59, 124, 188, 191
pluralism 131, 136, 137
poetry 65, 93
  *see also* 'strong poet'
Popper, Karl 131
positivism 16, 20, 22–3, 30, 49, 50, 52, 60, 148, 149, 155–9, 162, 175, 177
  *see also* logical positivism
postmodernism 1, 9, 10, 15, 97, 101, 104, 108, 113, 115, 129, 138, 140, 146, 147, 148, 149, 154–6, 159, 163, 164, 177
post-structuralism 9, 35, 98, 115, 133, 147, 152, 154, 158, 159, 164, 185
practice 6, 27, 38, 61, 62, 96, 99, 101, 119, 138, 139, 141, 146, 147, 169, 173, 180–1
pragmatism viii, ix, 1, 4, 7, 9, 12, 22–5, 27–33, 46, 48, 54, 55–6, 83, 98, 100, 107, 115, 137, 138, 148, 154, 158, 174, 176, 181, 182, 206
'Pragmatism and law: a response to David Luban' (Rorty) 190
'Pragmatism, categories and language' (Rorty) 189, 194
'principle of charity' (Davidson) 37, 117
progress, intellectual/scientific 8, 63–84, 101, 177
progress, moral 106, 117, 179
'pseudo-problems' 11, 12, 178
public–private distinction 8, 105, 106, 107, 124, 125, 126, 127–8
Putnam, Hilary 6, 60–1, 189, 191, 193

Quine, W. V. O. 6, 14, 16, 17, 19, 33, 36, 38, 50, 185, 186, 190

race 95, 119, 134, 144, 146, 166
Ranke, Leopold von 156, 206

rationality 15, 38, 63, 103, 129, 130, 135, 140, 174
Rawls, John 9, 95, 120, 121, 131, 202
Readings, Bill 108, 200
realism 22, 26, 27, 28, 36, 37, 44, 46, 48, 49, 50, 51, 53, 61, 99, 101, 129, 137, 139, 147, 165, 179, 191
'Realism and reference' (Rorty) 186
reason
 *see* rationality
'Recent metaphilosophy' (Rorty) 211
recognition 146
redescription viii, 1, 3, 7, 32, 33, 39, 48, 51, 60, 63–84, 103, 107, 124–7, 138, 142, 169, 172, 174, 175–6
reductionism 86, 136
Rée, Jonathan 101, 198
Reichenbach, Hans 186
relationality 137–43, 148, 167, 170, 171, 173, 177
relativism 31, 36, 53, 59, 60, 61, 114, 129, 138, 148, 164, 165, 168, 169, 171, 173, 177
'Reply to Dreyfus and Taylor' (Rorty) 190
representationalism 13–15, 23, 26, 49, 88, 100, 138
respect 134, 135, 137, 138, 141, 172
Roderick, Rick 201
Romanticism 8, 28, 64, 87, 107, 145, 149, 157
Rose, Gillian 203
Roth, Michael 207
Rousseau, Jean-Jacques 120, 147
Russell, Bertrand 187

Sacks, Mark 186
Sandel, Michael J. 120, 198
Sartre, Jean-Paul 46, 48, 49, 56, 87, 95, 157, 159, 191, 193
Saussure, Ferdinand de 34–5, 36, 189
'scheme–content distinction' (Davidson) 36–7, 40, 48, 51, 60, 62, 69
Schrag, Calvin O. 108, 200

science 8, 16, 21, 109, 136
self 6, 32, 85–6, 88–102, 170, 172, 173, 176, 177
self-creation 8, 10, 89–102, 103, 124
self-redescription 8, 84–102, 124, 177
Sellars, Wilfrid 16, 18, 38, 104, 105, 119, 122
sense-experience 14, 16
sex 98, 164
Shusterman, Richard 90, 197
slavery 55–6, 58, 59, 60, 81, 135
social constructionism 98, 139, 164
social contract 95, 120
solidarity 8, 9, 55, 58, 103, 105, 106, 108, 118, 122, 124, 126, 165, 177
Soper, Kate 102, 198, 205
'spectator theory of knowledge' (Dewey) 19
'spectatorial Left' 145, 146
state neutrality 131
'strong poet' 86–7, 89, 93
structuralism 34, 185
structure 95, 102, 138
subject–object relation 18–19, 32–3, 45, 49–50, 90, 139, 141, 153
subjectivity 6, 7, 10, 62, 115, 139, 142
 *see also* self
Swift, Adam 202

Tanesini, Alessandra 196
Tarski, Alfred 55
Taylor, Charles 84, 85, 100, 131, 189, 191, 197, 203
'Taylor on self-celebration and gratitude' (Rorty) 197
'Taylor on truth' (Rorty) 197
textualism 46
Thébaud, Jean-Loup 200
Thompson, E. P. 157, 208
Thompson, Simon 56–9, 193
'Thugs and theorists' (Rorty) 203
toleration 106
tradition 121, 122, 136, 170
truth 4, 7, 21–5, 28–30, 31, 35, 40, 49, 53–60, 67, 83, 103, 114, 129, 151, 157, 174

# INDEX

*Truth and Progress* (Rorty) 190, 192, 193, 197, 198, 199, 202, 204, 207, 210
'unencumbered' self 95, 120
universalism 6, 7, 9, 10, 60, 104, 110, 113, 114, 115, 118, 120, 123, 124, 125, 128, 131–43, 167, 168, 170, 171, 177, 179, 180
'Universality and truth' (Rorty) 202
utilitarianism 103, 199
utopia 107, 136, 179

Vattimo, Gianni 147
vertical–horizontal distinction
  *see* horizontal–vertical distinction
vocabularies 35, 40, 43, 45, 52, 60, 62, 64–6, 67, 70, 76, 84, 95, 101
Voltaire 194
voluntarism 96, 164, 165

Waismann, Friedrich 30, 189
Walzer, Michael 118, 123, 202
'we-intentions' 104, 105, 117–18, 122, 123, 126, 133, 136
Wheeler, Samuel C. 80, 196
Whitman, Walt 93, 144
Winch, Peter 209
Wittgenstein, Ludwig 11, 12, 28, 30, 51, 114, 117, 185, 186, 187
Wolin, Richard 141, 205
Wood, Ellen Meiskins 130, 203

Yeats, W. B. 65
Young, Iris Marion 14, 15, 135, 137, 146, 165–7, 168, 171, 185, 204, 206, 209

Žižek, Slavoj 84, 197